Hoodwinked

Hoodwinked

How Intellectual Hucksters Have Hijacked American Culture

JACK CASHILL

NELSON CURRENT

A Division of Thomas Nelson, Inc.

Published in Nashville, Tennessee, by Nelson Current, a division of a wholly-owned subsidiary (Nelson Communications, Inc.) of Thomas Nelson, Inc.

Nelson Current books may be purchased in bulk for educational, business, fundraising, or sales promotional use. For information, please e-mail SpecialMarkets@ThomasNelson.com.

Library of Congress Cataloging-in-Publication Data

Cashill, Jack.
   Hoodwinked : how intellectual hucksters have hijacked American culture / Jack Cashill.
      p. cm.

ISBN 1-5955-5011-9

   1. Popular culture—United States.   2. United States—Intellectual life.   3. Political culture—United States.   4. New Left—United States.   5. Liberalism—United States.   6. Radicalism—United States.   7. United States—Politics and government.   8. United States—Social conditions.   9. Multiculturalism—United States.   I. Title.

E169.1.C2966   2005
306.2'0973—dc22   2005006138

Printed in the United States of America
05 06 07 08 09 QWK 5 4 3 2 1

To my wife,

Joan,

a sane and supportive voice

from within the academy.

Contents

1
The Poster Boys

Churchill, Mumia, and Moore

In the early morning hours of December 9, 1981, twenty-five-year-old police officer Danny Faulkner pulled his patrol car behind a light blue Volkswagen Beetle in the heart of Philadelphia's red light district. Alarmed by the circumstances, he radioed for a wagon to help with an arrest.

A police car arrived two minutes later. To his unending horror, the arriving patrolman found Faulkner face up on the sidewalk, a bullet in his back and another right between his eyes—"complete instantaneous disability and death."

Sitting dazed nearby, with Faulkner's bullet in his chest, was a cabdriver named Mumia Abu-Jamal. Next to Mumia was his gun, all five bullets spent, two of them in Faulkner. Four eyewitnesses at the scene, two of them black, immediately identified the dreadlocked Mumia as the shooter.

Although his attorneys would later serve up the classically lame TODDI defense—"the other dude did it"—Mumia never offered an alternative story, nor did his brother, William Cook, the driver of the Volkswagen and the man Faulkner tried to arrest before Mumia intervened. Cook's only words of explanation were the honest ones he muttered at the scene, "I ain't got nothing to do with it."

Mumia was, as our Southern friends say, guilty as a goose. By comparison, the cases against Scott Peterson or O.J. Simpson were strained and circumstantial. The prosecutor claimed often and publicly that "he never had a stronger murder case" in his long and successful career, and he was not exaggerating. To no one's surprise, a mixed-race jury convicted Mumia of murder and sentenced him to death.

One would think at this point that the man's career options were not terribly attractive, ranging as they did between gas and electric. But to think thusly is to underestimate the creative mischief of the American cultural community. Truth be told, Mumia's career was just about ready to shift into high gear.

Mumia, you see, was not your average prisoner on death row. The one-time journalist was well spoken, well versed in Marxist claptrap, and, above all, cute. That last item was critical. He emerged as the human equivalent of a baby seal, big-eyed and vulnerable.

Daniel Williams, a leftist activist and Mumia's defense lawyer during the appeals process, provides a valuable inside account of the evolution of Mumia into a leftwing "rock star," one whose first name, like Elvis or Madonna, has enough marquee value to stand alone.

In his book, *Executing Justice,* Williams traces the origins of the Mumia mania to the "Trotskyist" Partisan Defense Committee (PDC), which first started making noise on Mumia's behalf. The slightly more mainstream Quixote Center, a cohort of "liberation theology Catholics," soon added to the PDC din.

National Public Radio served up "the defining moment" of the increasing clamor by signing Mumia to do a series of commentaries on prison life for *All Things Considered.* Addison-Wesley published a book of Mumia's ramblings called *Live from Death Row.* The students at

Evergreen State College in Olympia, Washington, heard from the man himself via tape. They had made him—parents, are you listening?—their commencement speaker.

The noise soon reached the sensitive ears of the international left, culminating in a visit to Mumia's remote Pennsylvania prison cell by one Danielle Mitterand, the former first lady of the dependably gullible France. Indeed, in a defining moment of international tomfoolery, the city of Paris officially named Mumia "Citizen of Honor," the first such honoree since artist Pablo Picasso thirty years prior.

In December 1997, representatives from France and eight other countries—as well as a few local street gangs—were among the twelve hundred enlightened souls who attended the "The People's International Tribunal for Justice" in Mumia's native Philadelphia. After a spirited performance by Swarthmore's "Mumia Abu-Jamal Singers," the attendees got down to business. They had less interest in debating Mumia's guilt or innocence—that was a foregone conclusion—than in indicting the system that imprisoned him.

Of those present, none served up a more forceful indictment than a "Keetowah Cherokee" writer by the name of Ward Churchill. The University of Colorado professor was not at all shy in his accusations. He boldly charged that the U.S. government targeted "key agitators" like Mumia based not on their guilt or innocence but on their ability "to communicate ideas." Although little known outside of radical circles, Churchill showed a feel for the stage that would one day make him even more of a household name than Mumia.

Churchill and his fellow partisans ruled the day. After six hours of hearing evidence and an hour of weighing it, the forum's judges brought back their verdict: "The authorities are guilty of the crimes as charged in the indictment." Those crimes included violating Mumia's constitutional and human rights, convicting him unjustly, incarcerating him unlawfully, and sentencing him to death illegally.

Despite Mumia's seeming innocence, NPR eventually "capitulated to intense rightwing pressures" and dropped Mumia from its lineup. The capitulation, however, only burnished Mumia's star. Mumia wrote still another book, this time about the NPR experience and adroitly titled *All Things Censored*. The title, as Williams would later ruefully admit, "bespeaks a distaste for suppressing speech." By this time, Williams himself had learned how fully situational was the hard-left's affection for the first amendment, but more on that later.

The left's attraction to the obviously false is nothing new. For well nigh a century, in fact, America's intellectual elite has been crafting and enabling fraud on a wide range of critical subjects, among them history, anthropology, political science, science, sexology, health, and criminal justice. The culture that this fraud has produced is a veritable house of cards, one vulnerable to the first unprotected zephyr of truth.

And "fraud" here does not mean bias, revisionism, or an unorthodox interpretation—although there is plenty of all that. Nor does it refer to the kinds of omissions and misstatements that routinely occur in the production of daily or weekly news. Fraud here means outright fabrication: inventing, plagiarizing, suppressing obvious facts, and spinning "nonfiction" out of whole cloth.

Specific cases range on a continuum from unwitting self-deception to conscious manipulation of data, from the merely false to the purely fraudulent. Journalist Christopher Hitchens provides a useful working baseline definition of fraud in his withering critique of popular author and filmmaker Michael Moore's, *Fahrenheit 911*:

> So I know, thanks, before you tell me, that a documentary must have a "POV" or point of view and that it must also impose a narrative line. But if you leave out absolutely everything that might give your "narrative" a problem and throw in any old rubbish that might support it, and you don't even care that one bit of rubbish flatly contradicts the next bit, and you give no chance to those who might differ, than you have betrayed your craft. (298)

Ward Churchill meanwhile has built a career on a purely fraudulent identity. All of his adult life he passed himself off as an American Indian and pulled his moral force from that identity. Unfortunately for Churchill, reporters from the *Rocky Mountain News* traced his lineage back multiple generations and could not find a drop of Indian blood. This single fact undermines everything he has ever written, particularly books with titles like *From a Native Son,* and renders his entire body of work suspect.

It is unlikely that Churchill will ever own up to this mischief. Intellectual hucksters almost never do. Thus, motives are difficult to discern. For fairness's sake, this book will focus on the higher end of that continuum and on long forms of cultural expression, books and movies in particular, whose formats allow ample time and space to tell something like the truth if the author or producer so chooses.

A book is not a solitary adventure. A successful one requires an author, an agent, a publisher, an editor, any number of obliging reviewers, and, in some cases, willing allies in the film and broadcast industries. Movies and TV shows are, if anything, even more of a community adventure. In addition to a director and producer, actors and crew, they require a good deal of up-front money and thus approval from people of influence throughout the production and distribution chain. To succeed, they generally rely on support from the critical community, both in the print and broadcast media.

The individuals who man the New York-Hollywood axis and the university outposts in between might justifiably be called America's cultural establishment. One obvious reason that cases like Mumia's and Moore's and Churchill's are so common is that those perpetrating a given fraud almost inevitably are advancing causes that this establishment wants to see advanced. Although there are obvious exceptions, the people who guard the cultural gates tend to be liberal on sexual and social issues, socialist on economic ones, internationalist in their worldview, and Democratic in their voting preferences.

The one rubric that perhaps best unifies them at the present, and one that many of them prefer, is the curiously nostalgic "progressive." In the mid-twentieth century, "progressive" distinguished the Stalinist left from the anti-Stalinist left. Indeed, in the 1930s and 40s, America's intellectual community came alive only when debating which brand of Marxism was best for America. Today, with the phrase "liberal" in disfavor and Stalin long dead, "progressive" seems to apply broadly and comfortably across the board. Writer David Horowitz, who grew up in an Old Left household and helped create the New Left, defines and italicizes the progressive mission as follows, *"The world is cursed by ignorance, and the task of progressives like us is to set everybody right."*

In the introduction to Margaret Sanger's 1922 book, *The Pivot of Civilization*, H.G. Wells affirms the self-congratulatory spirit of this movement, a spirit that has scarcely changed a whit in the eighty years since:

> Contrasted with the ancient civilization, with the Traditional disposition, which accepts institutions and moral values as though they were a part of nature, we have what I may call—with an evident bias in its favour—the civilization of enquiry, of experimental knowledge, Creative and Progressive Civilization.

As shall be seen, there are many currents within the larger progressive movement. Some even seem to be operating at crosscurrents to one another. What has unified them over time is a shared distaste for that "Traditional disposition," a disposition that Wells assigned—and is assigned today—to the defenders of Judeo-Christian culture.

Not unnaturally, people of influence in the cultural establishment are inclined to promote, praise, and protect those creative individuals who think as they do. As a case in point, they have published no fewer than five sympathetic books about Mumia and another five by Mumia himself. The foreign press has contributed more still.

Many of those not in the loop on a given book have contributed their moral support through petitions, rallies, newspaper ads, and the like. One can understand the shallow sympathies of film stars like Alec Baldwin and Tim Robbins, who will endorse just about anything provocative and dumb. Harder to explain is the sustained adulation from presumed literary greats like Maya Angelou, Noam Chomsky, E. L. Doctorow, Norman Mailer, Joyce Carol Oates, William Styron, and even Salman Rushdie, all of whom publicly declared their support for Mumia.

In their own defense, of course, the more prudent among his supporters will argue only that Mumia deserves a fair trial. And indeed, a careful observer can find flaws in any trial, especially one whose witnesses were recruited on an inner city street corner at 4:00 AM. But if truly interested in American justice, these cultural icons could have found a thousand worthier causes in which to invest their moral energy. Instead, they squandered it on an unrepentant cop killer as transparently guilty as any man on death row anywhere.

Control of the cultural establishment is just one reason why fraud plagues the political left. The less obvious but more fundamental reason is that progressive authors and their cultural support groups live in a world where God, if not fully dead, is irrelevant. By default, progressives tend to ground their morality in the shaky materialist philosophy introduced by the Greek philosopher Epicurus and popularized by Darwin and Marx.

A progressive herself, birth control advocate Margaret Sanger caught the gist of the radical restructuring of the universe just a few years after the Russian Revolution.

The heaven of the traditional theology had been shattered by Darwinian science, and here, dressed up in all the authority of the new science, appeared a new theology, the promise of a new heaven, an earthly paradise, with an impressive scale of rewards for the faithful and ignominious punishments for the capitalists.

Obviously, not all progressives identified with the Russian Revolution. To repentant Soviet agent Whittaker Chambers, that didn't much matter. As he saw it, the difference between the "communist" on the one hand and "those miscellaneous socialists, liberals, fellow travelers, unclassified progressives, and men of good will" on the other was one of commitment, not one of vision. The vision of a man-centered world they all shared.

"If there is no God," concluded Jean Paul Sartre in his famous paraphrase of Dostoevsky's Ivan Karamazov, "everything is permitted." Given this grounding, the less scrupulous among progressive activists judge sentiments not by their veracity but by their utility. As Nikolai Lenin once coldly noted, "A lie told often enough becomes the truth." With good reason, the more honest in the progressive community fear the less scrupulous.

Author Williams learned this lesson the hard way. If *Executing Justice* is essentially a dishonest book—Williams, for instance, cleanses from the record all evidence of the emotional collapse that turned the "intelligent, passionate, overtly life affirming" journalist Mumia into an angry cabdriver—it is occasionally insightful. He does at least lay out the case against Mumia, including the inconvenient fact that the bullets found in Faulkner's back and head did indeed come from Mumia's literally smoking gun.

Despite Williams's eager endorsement of Mumia's innocence, Mumia shocked Williams by suing to block the publication of his book. Mumia's supporters added to Williams's misery by harassing him and charging that he had "blood on his hands" for citing the evidence against Mumia. "The whiplash of the [case's] sharp left turn," as Williams described the reaction, left him smarting and dispirited.

Williams should have seen this coming. Although at pains to accommodate his radical allies throughout the trial, he rightfully described their view on the Mumia case as "extreme." As they saw it, the police knew Mumia was innocent and framed him anyhow. According to them, the police were less interested in getting the bad guy who killed their fellow officer than in retaliating against MOVE, a radical black group with which Mumia was affiliated. To the hard-left, said Williams prophetically and with routinely misapplied religious imagery, "It was sacrilegious to believe otherwise."

Popular author and filmmaker Michael Moore also misjudged the power of Mumia's appeal. Although a shameless trafficker in fraud himself, Moore has his occasional honest moment. In his best-selling book, *Dude, Where's My Country*, Moore dared to say of the revered Mumia, "He probably killed that guy. There, I said it."

In a world without God, false gods reign. By dint of his race, radicalism, and easy sex appeal, Mumia had enshrined himself in the progressive pantheon. Without fully understanding the consequences, Moore had blasphemed. "Michael Moore is a fraud," said leftist author Ewuare Osayande, angrily denouncing Moore at a public forum in Philadelphia before adding an insider dig, "There, I said it."

Caught in an unexpected truth and savaged on his *Dude* tour by Mumia's acolytes for uttering it, Moore tried to pacify dissenters by claiming that his Mumia remark was "satire" and they just didn't get the joke. In so doing, Moore too showed less commitment to the "truth," as that concept is known in the Judeo-Christian tradition, than to the imperatives of power, progress, and even popularity. In the naturalist tradition, truth is what works, and this is now, to a scary degree, the unvoiced creed of the cultural left.

Although cultural fraud has any number of variations, one can discern a general pattern: The hard left attracts the intellectual left with its almost Rousseauvian purity and rawness. The intellectual left in turn intimidates the soft center left that so dominates America's news production into silence and/or compliance. The news producers educate the open-minded center and the less informed liberals in their audience.

On issues of race, this general pattern long predated the Mumia incident and pre-conditioned the media. Thus, from the beginning of

Mumia's ordeal, the *Philadelphia Inquirer* was describing Mumia in sub-headlines "as an eloquent activist not afraid to raise his voice." Although Williams criticizes the local press for its biases, he seems unaware just how few accused murderers garner such favorable headlines. Abortion protestors, even the nonviolent ones, are never "eloquent." Lacking such media cover, and with a faith-based commitment to truth, the right has never had a Mumia.

The left has a history of Mumias, nearly a century's worth, often with lethal consequences. The specific Mumia fable follows a shockingly consistent pattern, one sensationally fashioned in a murder sixty years prior. What Nicola Sacco and Bartolomeo Vanzetti had in common with Mumia—beyond their good looks, radical posturings, and claims of ethnic victimization—were that they too were as guilty as sin. To their friends in the progressive literary community, however, the truth simply did not matter. The friends were the ones to inject politics into the proceedings and to make it an international *cause célèbre,* the truth be damned.

In the ongoing culture war, politicized trials are frequently used to breach enemy defenses, but these spearheads are inevitably part of a larger front. This book identifies four such fronts: radical naturalism, sexual hedonism, Marxism, and multiculturalism. All share an enemy in traditional Western culture, an antagonism to a Judeo-Christian God, an indifference to truth, and common ancestors in Charles Darwin and Karl Marx.

Until now, no one person has fully documented the sweep of this assault. But for years, an unconnected and largely apolitical squad of literary detectives, biographers, anthropologists, scientists, historians, classicists, and cultural critics has been picking off the frauds and their enablers one by one. Taken together, the work of these critics is devastating. This book will synthesize their dogged research and reveal the depth and breadth of the rot at the very foundation of progressive culture.

The corruption goes deep. In the conspicuous absurdity of their careers, Mumia and Churchill and even Michael Moore make excellent poster boys for the prevalence of falsehood and fraud in the culture, but they are a mere symptom. So too are less successful flim-flammers like the *New Republic's* Stephen Glass and the *New York Times* Jayson Blair, both publicly undone by their recklessness and their larger irrelevance.

"In the end-justifies-the-means environment I worked in," writes Blair, "I had grown accustomed to lying." So had many others. In his self-indulgent memoir, *Burning Down My Masters' House,* Blair does make one compelling point. How is it, he asks, that his mischief is considered "a low point" in the paper's history when truly destructive *Times* luminaries like Walter Duranty and Herbert Matthews have gone unpunished? As Blair understands—and this book confirms—the real danger to the culture comes not from devious cub reporters like Blair but from those writers and intellectuals of influence whose misrepresentations have helped redefine America and reshape the world.

2
The Sounds of Silence

"The death of one man is a tragedy, a million deaths is a statistic."

—JOSEPH STALIN

THE INNOCENTS' CLUBS

Martin Amis calls it the "chief lacuna" of the twentieth century. By "lacuna" he means gap or hole, specifically that great rat hole into which the cultural establishment has shoved the memory of the most sustained experiment ever in human misery. That experiment has been described by a variety of adjectives—"Marxist," "Marxist-Leninist," "communist," "soviet," or even the euphemistic "socialist." Whatever the name, at the end of the day, the contribution of this experiment to world culture is almost inevitably measured in body count.

Amis is arguably the leading literary light of contemporary Britain. Early in this new century, he took it upon himself to unearth the sins of the century past. Specifically, he wanted to know how it was that his father, equally renowned author Kingsley Amis, came to join the Communist Party in 1941 and remained a member for the next fifteen years. What intrigued Amis about his father's story was its very banality. His father did what everyone seemed to be doing. "The world was offered a choice between two realities," he writes in his book *Koba the Dread,* "and the young Kingsley, in common with the overwhelming majority of intellectuals everywhere, chose the wrong reality."

What distinguished Kingsley Amis from most of his contemporaries, what made his story worth sharing, was that he publicly atoned for his participation in this transparent madness. In "Why Lucky Jim Turned Right," an essay excerpted in *Koba the Dread,* Kingsley Amis describes the attraction of that madness:

> We are dealing with a conflict of feeling and intelligence, a form of willful self-deception whereby a part of the mind knows full well that its overall belief is false or wicked, but the emotional need to believe is so strong that knowledge remains, as it were, encysted, isolated, powerless to influence word or deed.

There was much in the way of "knowledge" that the Soviets were pleased to isolate. There was that awkward knowledge of the Volga famine of 1921, of the Ukrainian terror-famine of 1932–1933, of the "Great Terror" and the Moscow Show Trials of 1936–1938, of the Nazi-Soviet Pact of 1939, and of the subsequent dismembering of Poland, of the subversion of the Spanish Republic, of the invasion of Finland, of the forced annexation of the Baltic states, and of the assassination in Mexico of party co-founder Leon Trotsky. All of this happened *before* Kingsley Amis joined the party. He at least half knew about all of it. None of it dissuaded him.

After the war, despite efforts to contain it, the knowledge base kept expanding as did the vocabulary to explain it. The Soviet Union gave the world the "gulag." China offered its own equivalent, the "lao gai," as well as the murderous nonsense of the "Great Leap Forward" and the "Cultural Revolution." In Cuba, Castro popularized the Spanish phrase "parédon," meaning "to the wall." Vietnam gave sinister new meaning to the words "reeducation camp" and "boat people," and the Khmer Rouge made "ruralization" an expression of pure horror.

At century's end, a group of French intellectuals, all of them former communists or sympathizers, assembled this almost forgotten knowledge into the epic and authoritative *Black Book of Communism*. They translated the language of international communism into cold statistics: 25 million dead in the Soviet Union, 65 million in China, 1.7 million in Cambodia, and on and on.

"The dictatorship of the proletariat was a lie," writes Martin Amis. "Union was a lie, and Soviet was a lie, and Socialist was a lie, and Republic was a lie. *Comrade* was a lie. The Revolution was a lie."

And yet, from the very beginning until the present, the Marxists and their heirs have done a masterful job of sustaining the lie, of perpetuating the fraud, of keeping virtually all memory of this undeniable evil out of the public consciousness. It is true, as critic Hilton Kramer has argued, that Aleksandr Solzhenitsyn's *Gulag Archipelago* in the early 1970s "reduced this whole tradition of political falsehood to ideological rubble." But Solzhenitsyn's truth did not really penetrate beyond limited intellectual circles, most of those in Europe.

Nor has *Gulag* stopped the world's vestigial Marxists from playing their ultimate shell game: conceal the Marxist evil and expose a Western one, even if imaginary. "Marxism's greatest success," notes British historian Robert Conquest, "has been the demonizing of capitalism." This success did not happen by accident. It was all part of a strategic plan, one that could never have succeeded without the enthusiastic participation of the British and especially the American cultural establishment, and it continues to this day.

The fraud began with Karl Marx himself. As British historian Paul Johnson shrewdly observes of Marx, "He was not interested in finding the truth but in proclaiming it." This book is not the appropriate venue to examine Marx in depth. But as the chief theorist for socialism and communism, Marx had a powerful responsibility to the truth, a responsibility he all but ignored.

A nineteenth century contemporary of Charles Darwin, Marx coauthored the *Communist Manifesto* with Friedrich Engels in 1848 and published the first of several volumes of his masterwork, *Das Kapital,* twenty years later. At the core of his work, like that of just about every author considered in this book, is a hostility towards tradition, especially traditional religion, Judaism and Christianity most specifically. Indeed, the one person most responsible for banishing God from the twentieth century was Marx. His reach was greater than Darwin's, and his ambitions keener. "Religion is only the illusory sun around which man revolves," claimed Marx, "until he began to revolve around himself."

The self-revolving Marx lived his life without reference to a higher authority, and it showed even in his literary efforts. In the mid-1880s two Cambridge scholars noticed that in *Das Kapital* Marx consciously distorted the quotes he was using from various authorities. Although the scholars decided not to pursue a case of "deliberate falsification," they charged him with an "almost criminal recklessness in the use of authorities." Marx couldn't have cared less. Like so many of those who followed him, he used facts strategically, as weapons in a larger war. "From start to finish," writes Johnson, "not just *Kapital* but all his work reflects a disregard for truth which at times amounts to contempt."

The early Soviets absorbed not just Marx's economics but also his amorality. In their pursuit of the larger truth—*Pravda*—they scorned any petty factual truth—*istina*—that stood in its way. The man who brought this new system of power, the so-called "lying for the truth," to the West was an unlikely German communist named Willi Munzenberg. A sort of roughneck publisher, Munzenberg had an instinctive feel for the power of the media and persuaded Lenin to let him apply it.

As British author Stephen Koch details in his masterful book, *Double Lives,* Munzenberg pioneered two new lines of secret service work: the propaganda front controlled covertly from afar and the "fellow traveler," a friend of the revolution who voiced the dogma *du jour* as artlessly as if it were his own. The messages being voiced varied wildly over time, but they remained consistent in their intent, namely that "any opinion that happened to serve the foreign policy of the Soviet Union was derived from the most essential elements of human decency."

Munzenberg worked his wonders in all manner of subjects in all media, both in Europe and in America, and among a wide range of opinion makers. He had a good base in his own network of leftwing publications and willing accomplices in a wider network of progressive media outlets. His essential challenge was to sculpt their opinions to his own designs and then to conceal his own handiwork in the sculpting. He proved very good at both.

Lenin had made Munzenberg's task a good deal easier when he launched the Communist International—or Comintern—in the early days of the revolution. This was the network through which Lenin exercised the political control, and Munzenberg the cultural control, over the worldwide left.

Always the cynic, Munzenberg described the idealists who unwittingly hewed to the party line as "innocents." The fronts to which he guided them he called "Innocents' Clubs." In fact, Munzenberg may be the person most responsible for a phenomenon that plagues us to this day, the political radicalization of the cultural elite.

The marriage of modernism and socialism may have stripped this elite of almost all traditional faith, but not of the need for the same. Munzenberg filled the void, directing aspiring radicals to any number of causes that offered, as Koch notes, "a substitute for religious belief." For the first twenty years after the Russian Revolution, Munzenberg would identify the causes worthy of the elite's moral attention. As it happened, these causes were inevitably linked to some seeming injustice, not in the East of course, but in the West.

A COUPLE OF WOPS IN A JAM

On May 5, 1920, police from several small Massachusetts towns set a trap for a man named Michael Boda, a suspect in an aborted Bridgewater payroll robbery five months prior. Stumbling into the trap were Nichola Sacco, a shoemaker, and Bartolomeo Vanzetti, a fish peddler. They had taken a streetcar to Boda's house to retrieve his car and were promptly apprehended.

Three weeks before their arrest, there had been a second payroll robbery in South Braintree, Massachusetts—this one successful and lethal. When arrested, Sacco had in his pocket six obsolete bullets, which matched the bullet found in the body of Alessandro Berardelli, a security guard killed in the South Braintree robbery. Stuffed in Sacco's waistband was the gun through which the fatal bullet had been fired. As to Vanzetti, he carried Berardelli's revolver in his pocket as well as four shotgun shells of the sort used in the attempted Bridgewater robbery. The police found both men to be nervous and evasive.

The day after the arrest, District Attorney Frederick Katzmann questioned both defendants through an interpreter in the presence of a stenographer and, by all accounts, in a gentlemanly way. When asked where he was on the day of the murders three weeks earlier, Sacco said he was at work. As was later proved beyond doubt, and as Sacco finally admitted, he was elsewhere. If anything, Vanzetti's alibis were even more dubious.

Vanzetti was convicted for his role in the attempted Bridgewater robbery in July 1920 and sentenced to twelve to fifteen years. No fuss was made about the trial at the time. Vanzetti headed quietly to state prison, and no one accused judge or prosecutor of wrongdoing. Nor was there any mention of radicalism. As to the jurors, they were almost all industrial workers themselves. Case seemingly closed.

On September 14, 1920, Sacco and Vanzetti were both indicted for the South Braintree murder. At their request, the trial was delayed until May 1921. At first, Sacco and Vanzetti held little appeal for anyone. A socialist newsman sent up to review the case quickly lost interest. "There's no story in it," he reported back to his editor, "Just a couple of wops in a jam."

A local Italian anarchist cell did come to the pair's aid before the murder trial and formed a Defense Committee. The committee enlisted the help of the fledgling ACLU among other sponsors and the aid of maverick western attorney Fred Moore. An eccentric leftist in the Clarence Darrow tradition and a cocaine addict, Moore quickly came to the opinion that there was no hope for the pair unless he could politicize the trial. As he projected the case, Sacco and Vanzetti were no longer just a pair of thugs on trial for murder. They were powerless immigrants persecuted for their unpopular political belief and ethnic origins.

In fact, the two Italian immigrants had met when they both fled to Mexico in 1917 to avoid the draft. Upon their return, disillusioned with their adopted country, they got involved in the then popular anarchist movement. This movement occasionally turned deadly. An anarchist had assassinated President McKinley twenty years prior. On September 16, 1920, two days after Sacco and Vanzetti were indicted for murder, Italian anarchists blew up the Morgan Bank in lower Manhattan, killing thirty and injuring three hundred more. This Wall Street institution was as iconic in its day as the World Trade Center was in ours, and the iconoclasts were just as deadly and determined.

Despite the risks, there was a method to attorney Fred Moore's madness. The pair had to come up with some rationale as to why they had been looking for Boda's car, why they were nervous around the police, and why they lied to the prosecutor. Their unpopular political beliefs made as good an excuse as any. Upon advice of counsel, and against the advice of the judge, they told the jury about their radicalism and their draft dodging. They spun the story that they were seeking Boda's car as a place to stash their anarchist literature. The jurors didn't buy the story. They convicted the pair of murder.

"The so-called radicalism of the defendants played no part in the verdict," wrote Edward Simmons who interviewed the seven living jurors for the New Bedford *Standard-Times* in 1950. "In fact, the jury is astounded still at the charge to the contrary, and amazed the trial ever became a *cause célèbre*."

With the verdict rendered and an appeal in process, Moore and his allies went to work on public opinion. If they were to paint Sacco and Vanzetti as innocent victims, they had to identify a guilty party, and for this role they settled upon the Massachusetts legal establishment, now the evil instrument of the pair's "judicial murder." Even before Munzenberg got involved, Moore pursued this strategy vigorously and without conscience. Before the century was out, his spiritual heirs would use the same strategy for a score of more celebrated radicals, Mumia among them.

In 1923, however, Sacco fired Moore. It seems that Moore lost confidence in the pair's innocence, and Sacco, in the midst of a paranoid episode, lost confidence in Moore. With Moore gone, the case lost its luster. As it dragged through the appeals process, Sacco and Vanzetti morphed back into shoemaker and fish peddler, their Cinderella moment seemingly over.

In 1924, fate intervened when Lenin died and Stalin replaced him. Always the realist, Stalin had no illusions that the Comintern or the fledgling Communist Party in America could inspire an American revolution. He focused his American efforts instead, notes Koch, "on discrediting American politics and culture and assisting the growth of Soviet power elsewhere."

With Stalin's blessing, Munzenberg and his colleagues set out to find a case that would undermine the idea of America, which at the time held great sway throughout the world. America was widely perceived as the land of opportunity, the ever beckoning home of the free and the brave. "Give us your tired, your poor" indeed! For the Soviet experiment to prevail, the American experiment had to yield. The world had to see America through fresh, unblinking eyes, not as the great melting pot but as a simmering stew of xenophobic injustice.

In 1925, the Comintern came looking for Sacco and Vanzetti, glass slipper in hand. "It was Munzenberg's idea," his widow Babette Gross would casually tell Stephen Koch, not realizing the full implications of her remark. Working with the Comintern, Munzenberg had set up an organization in Chicago called the International Labor Defense and gave it, as a first assignment, the creation of a worldwide myth around the fate of Sacco and Vanzetti. Almost immediately, "spontaneous" protests sprung up throughout the world. Europe's great squares filled with sobbing, shouting protestors, declaiming the innocence of the immigrant martyrs and denouncing the vile injustice of their persecutors. These protestors, many of them poor and most of them sincere, donated hundreds of thousands dollars to the cause, almost none of which found its way to the real Defense Committee.

Only rarely did Munzenberg and the Comintern attempt to dictate literary response to a given event. When they did so, it was usually in Europe and often with writers whose sympathies they could count on, like the influential French intellectuals Andre Malraux and Andre Gide or the Russian Maxim Gorky. In America, they preferred to create theater and allow the actors to find their way to the parts.

The casting call for the Sacco and Vanzetti protests attracted a who's who of literary leading lights. Prominent American authors Upton Sinclair, Katherine Ann Porter, John Dos Passos, and Edna St. Vincent Millay not only protested the seeming injustice but also created literary works around it. Scores more picketed, protested, or signed petitions. International luminaries joined in as well. George Bernard Shaw and Albert Einstein wrote letters on behalf of the anarchists. French Nobel Prize winner Romain Rolland sent a telegram to the Massachusetts governor.

The Crime Library lists a total of twenty-five books written about the case, a dozen of which are still in print. The tone of most are best reflected in titles like *Justice Crucified* by Roberta Strauss Feuerlicht in 1977 and *The Passion of Sacco and Vanzetti* by Howard Fast. This latter book was published in 1953, the same year, coincidentally, that Fast, an American communist, was awarded the oxymoronic Stalin Peace Prize.

The modes of expression differed. Edna St. Vincent Millay, for instance, unleashed her outrage in a poem, "Justice Denied in

Massachusetts." Upton Sinclair, the author of *The Jungle,* expressed his in a two-volume, 750-page novel called *Boston.* Their politics differed as well, ranging from an innocent liberalism to an actively subversive communism. What bound these intellectuals together was a shared progressive contempt for democratic capitalism and the ordinary Americans who made the system work. Dos Passos captures this spirit well in his 1930 book, *Big Money,* the third volume of his *USA* trilogy. The lack of punctuation and capitalization reflects Dos Passos's democratic style:

all right we are two nations
America our nation has been beaten by strangers who have bought the laws and fenced off the meadows and cut down the woods for pulp and turned our pleasant cities into slums and sweated the wealth out of our people and when they want to they hire the executioner to throw the switch

This gloomy Manichean divide has devolved downward over time to become a standard Democratic stump speech. "Today, under George W. Bush, there are two Americas, not one," echoed John Edwards in the 2004 presidential campaign. "One America that does the work, another America that reaps the reward. One America that pays the taxes, another America that gets the tax breaks."

Despite protestations to the contrary, progressives worldwide have historically shown little faith in the wisdom of their fellow citizens. When America reelected Bush president, this collective disdain was perhaps best captured by the British *Daily Mirror* headline, "How can 59,054,087 Americans be so dumb?"

Given this bias, each of the progressive authors who wrote about the Sacco and Vanzetti case began his or her work with the *a priori* assumption that the pair was innocent. They could do so in good conscience because, in their view, the jury that had reviewed the evidence and found Sacco and Vanzetti guilty was not to be taken seriously. As they saw it, these twelve ordinary Massachusetts citizens, like most ordinary Americans, were easily inflamed and incapable of reason. In reality, however, the jurors were neither.

"The only thing we considered in the jury room was whether the defendants were guilty as charged," juror John Dever would recount some years later, a sentiment shared by every juror interviewed. "I can repeat it over and over again. That talk of radicalism is absurd. Radicalism had nothing whatsoever to do with it."

The intellectuals in question, however, had a studied indifference to the sentiments of the jurors or the facts that had persuaded them. Liberal historian Arthur Schelsinger Jr. provides a classic illustration of elite *hauteur* in his much acclaimed 1957 work, *The Age of Roosevelt*. Writes Schlesinger of the pair's arrest:

> In May 1920, following the murder of a paymaster in South Braintree, Massachusetts, Brockton police picked up two Italians in an automobile filled with innocent and febrile literature of anarchistic propaganda.

When Robert Montgomery, a corporate attorney in Massachusetts, read Schlesinger's account, he was appalled. He had followed the case from the beginning. He knew many of the principals involved. For him, this was one gratuitous insult too many. So he wrote to Schlesinger and engaged him in an extended correspondence. As Montgomery pointed out, Sacco and Vanzetti were not arrested in a car but in a streetcar. They had no literature—that was a later concoction to justify their hunt for the car. What they did have, however, were guns, bullets, and shotgun shells that would match those used in the two crimes. Budging but barely, Schlesinger revised this account for his next edition:

> In May 1920, following the murder of a paymaster in South Braintree, Massachusetts, Brockton police picked up two Italians

who had been seeking an automobile in order to dispose of a bundle of anarchistic propaganda.

The fact that Schlesinger refused to reevaluate the pair's culpability thirty years after the execution reflects the enduring power of the Munzenberg narrative. Note, too, that Schlesinger had presumed the imagined anarchist literature to be "innocent"—this despite the fact that Sacco and Vanzetti were arrested just four months prior to the massive Wall Street bombing.

Although Munzenberg directed the spectacle from Berlin, his lieutenants worked up close. One of the innocents they manipulated was the "comically useable" Gardner Jackson, a leading liberal on the Defense Committee. Under Comintern prodding, Jackson went to work on Marion Frankfurter, the emotionally unstable wife of Felix Frankfurter, the prominent Harvard law professor who would later become a Supreme Court justice. Jackson courted Marion shamelessly. He even allowed her to co-edit with him the letters of Sacco and Vanzetti. His goal all along was to lure Felix to the case, and in this he succeeded.

After the convicted pair's last appeal was denied, Frankfurter wrote and published a searing attack on the justice system in the March 1927 *Atlantic Monthly*. Given Frankfurter's writing skills and his reputation, this polemic shook the world in a way that no previous publication had. An extended version of the article was published in book form soon afterwards as *The Case of Sacco and Vanzetti*.

In his own authoritative way, Frankfurter launched a new literary genre, the politically myopic true crime book, a genre that would culminate in the preposterous Mumia mini-library. Without exactly lying about the trial itself, Frankfurter marshals his details to confuse the innocent and sway the susceptible. In his retelling, the police charge Sacco and Vanzetti with their respective crimes for no apparent reason other than their inability to account for their whereabouts on the critical dates. Vanzetti, lacking alibis for both days, gets charged with both crimes.

Frankfurter mentions the guns later in the text only to dismiss their relevance. "The extensive carrying of guns by people who are not 'gunmen' is common knowledge," he sniffs. As to the ballistic evidence, that is all dubious and subject to interpretation.

Although the Supreme Judicial Court of Massachusetts had found "no error" in any of the judge's rulings in the trial, Frankfurter, of course, finds plenty. He also identifies a pervasive ethnic and political hostility on the part of the judge and prosecutor reflective of the judicial "lawlessness and hysteria" afoot in the land, particularly in Boston.

In his account of the trial, Frankfurter remains safely within the realm of mere bias. He crosses the frontier into the false and fraudulent when he explores the "new proof" that the defense has allegedly dug up. As it happens—as so often happens—a jailmate of Sacco's, a Portuguese immigrant convicted of murder, "confesses" to the South Braintree killings. According to Frankfurter, this confession and other bogus TODDI ("The other dude did it") evidence prove "not only that Sacco and Vanzetti did *not* commit the murders, but also, positively, that a well-known gang of professional criminals *did* commit them."

Unfortunately, the gang members with whom Sacco's jailmate allegedly planned the South Braintree robbery never told him their names. He could describe them only as a "gang of Italians," a scapegoat as convenient as O.J.'s "Columbian drug dealers." Still, this was enough for the fair-minded Frankfurter to "positively" identify the bunch as the dreaded Morelli gang. Without so much as a shred of real evidence or a day in court, Frankfurter seems willing to send this less ideologically charmed group of Italian Americans to the chair.

As the August 1927 execution date approached, Munzenberg went to work. His Berlin office arranged for the Frankfurter material to be reprinted and distributed throughout the world. In London, H.G. Wells disseminated an inflammatory summary of Frankfurter's writing that quickly became accepted British wisdom. Protest movements swelled in major American cities and European capitals. On the night before the execution, five thousand militants roamed the streets of Geneva savaging everything from cars to movies that smelled of America.

On the night of the execution, August 22, an outpouring of rage and grief swept the world and left common sense buried in its wake. The French communist daily *Humanité* published an extra edition with one word on the front cover, *Assassinés.* Reacting to the news that the pair had, yes, been "assassinated," crowds swarmed through the streets of Paris on the way to the American embassy, ripping out lampposts and smashing windows. Only the tanks that ringed the embassy stopped them. In London, masses of people surged around Buckingham Palace, shouting and singing "The Red Flag." Germany meanwhile witnessed a series of demonstrations and torchlight parades more intense than any the volatile Weimar Republic had yet seen. A half dozen German demonstrators were killed during the course of them.

Munzenberger had pulled all the right strings in this international puppet show. True, Sacco and Vanzetti were executed, but it had never been his job to save them. In her memoir, *The Never-Ending Wrong,* published on the fiftieth anniversary of the pair's execution, Pulitzer Prize–winning author Katherine Ann Porter relates how she first came to understand this. As the final hours ticked down, Porter had been standing vigil with other artists and writers in Boston. Ever the innocent liberal, Porter approached her group leader, a "fanatical little woman" and a dogmatic communist, and expressed her hope that Sacco and Vanzetti could still be saved. The response of this female comrade is noteworthy largely for its candor:

> "Saved," she said, ringing a change on her favorite answer to political illiteracy, "who wants them saved? What earthly good would they do us alive?"

"The whole point," argues Koch, "was that 'justice' in the world's leading liberal democracy was a murderous lie. The men *had* to die." In the process, the Comintern revealed the seeming injustice of the system that had condemned the men as well as the impotence of the liberals and anarchists who had failed to save them. In the Spanish Civil War, ten years in the future, the Comintern attack on liberals and anarchists would turn lethal.

If the Frankfurter article and book could not save the lives of the accused, it surely helped sustain their legend. It passed into history as the definitive account of the case, at least among the cultural elite. Few among that elite, however, ever questioned whether the account was true. The indefatigable Robert Montgomery most certainly did. In 1958, he began a correspondence with Frankfurter, then on the Supreme Court. Montgomery's appeal focused on the case's Achilles heel, a single Frankfurter footnote. In it, Frankfurter argued that Vanzetti did not take the stand in his own defense in the non-capital Bridgewater payroll robbery trial because his attorneys did not allow him to. According to Frankfurter, they feared "that his radical opinions would be brought out and tell against him disastrously."

As a Massachusetts attorney, Montgomery could not buy this argument. He knew that, given the evidence presented by the prosecution, Vanzetti's own testimony was about the only thing that could possibly have saved him. If Vanzetti were innocent, Montgomery would have advised him to take the stand in his own defense. There was no reason not to. Massachusetts law clearly established that Vanzetti's radical ideas could not have been introduced unless Vanzetti introduced them himself.

In his first letter to Frankfurter, Montgomery asked Frankfurter only to identify the source for his claim that Vanzetti's counsel had urged his silence. In a wearily patronizing response, Frankfurter ignored the specific question. He relied instead on Harvard president Abbott Lawrence Lowell's earlier assertion that he, the esteemed Frankfurter, was reliably "accurate" and that only a "fool" would "enter into controversy" with him. Lawrence's opinion mattered because he had served on the governor's three-person advisory committee in the months leading up to the execution.

Not satisfied, Montgomery reviewed the public record to see what, in fact, Lowell did have to say about his Harvard colleague. He found the answer in a letter written by Lowell to William Howard Taft, then chief justice of the Supreme Court:

> We [the Governor's Advisory Committee] certainly started with no prejudice against Sacco and Vanzetti. Indeed, all I had read was Frankfurter's article in the *Atlantic* which, though partisan argument, I supposed stated the facts correctly; and that naturally left the impression that something was wrong with the trial; but on reading all the facts, none of us had the least question about the men's guilt. The proof seemed to be conclusive.

Where Lowell did find "gross misstatement" was in the "propaganda in [Sacco and Vanzetti's] favor." Seeking more evidence, Montgomery corresponded with James Graham, who represented Sacco and who participated in Vanzetti's trial for the aborted Bridgewater holdup. By his own admission, Graham was only one of three people other than the accused who knew why Vanzetti did not take the stand. Unlike Frankfurter, he sent Montgomery a long, thoughtful, and credible response. As Graham affirmed, counsel preferred that Vanzetti take the stand, but Vanzetti chose not to, possibly on the advice of Sacco. "Incidentally," added Graham, "there was no fear that his radical opinions, if he had any, might be brought out during the trial."

Armed with this information, Montgomery wrote back to Frankfurter asking if he would consent to a correction of the historical record that he had more or less established. Frankfurter was not about to oblige. He had taken "great pains" to verify the statement in question in 1927, and "of course, I cannot say that I was in error." Besides, as he repeated, President Lowell had "attested to my accuracy in the strongest language."

If Vanzetti was clearly involved in the attempted Bridgewater robbery, his involvement in the South Braintree murder is less certain. Best evidence shows that it was Sacco—"beyond all reasonable doubt" according to Koch—who murdered the one guard, a fellow Italian American, after he had fallen to his knees and begged for his life. If so, Vanzetti remained silent in brave solidarity with his less honorable compatriot. "Vanzetti laid down his life on the bloody altar not of justice but of propaganda," writes Koch. "He died lying for the truth."

THE FAMINE IS MOSTLY BUNK

The most thrilling month of Walter Duranty's professional life, bar none, was November 1933. The one-legged, British-born, American citizen had just arrived in Washington D.C. from Moscow. He had come these many miles to witness President Roosevelt officially recognize the Soviet Union. Duranty glowed throughout the ceremony. He knew, and everyone else knew, that were it not for his reporting the president would never have pushed for recognition. After the event, FDR sought out this now famed *New York Times* correspondent and asked him, "Don't you think it's a good job?" Duranty did indeed.

A little more than a year later, Simon & Schuster published Duranty's take on the Soviet experiment. The title of the book was the scarily appropriate, *I Write As I Please.* In this classic of willful blindness, the presumably objective journalist sheds his usual cynicism only to show his affection for Comrade Stalin.

As Duranty relates, he "felt as pleased as punch" when Stalin had announced the Five-Year Plan in the fall of 1928. Stalin, after all, was the world's "greatest living statesman," the one man capable of pulling off this extraordinary task. As part of the plan, Stalin was prepared "to socialize, virtually overnight, a hundred million of the stubbornest and most ignorant peasants in the world." More astonishingly still, Stalin and his apparatchiks would make this happen despite an antiquated transportation system, a dwindling food supply, and an unceasing pressure to maintain existing production levels. "When all these factors are considered," writes Duranty, "it is a little short of a miracle that the plan was carried through."

Yes, the plan was carried through. With the fall of the Berlin Wall, and the opening of the Soviet archives, scholars have been able to school themselves beyond serious debate as to what really did happen during the years of the plan, 1928-1933, the years that netted Duranty his Pulitzer Prize. The story that Duranty missed—or, more accurately, concealed— is no longer a matter of speculation. It is a matter of fact. And the fact is that no single Western journalist has so profoundly misreported a story as Walter Duranty of the *New York Times*. "The influence of his false reporting was enormous and long-lasting," affirms Robert Conquest.

As the *Black Book of Communism* notes, "Recent research in the newly accessible archives has confirmed that the forced collectivization of the countryside was in effect a war declared by the Soviet state on a nation of smallholders." Although the war had actually begun in 1928 with the conception of the Five-Year Plan, Stalin specifically named the enemy in December 1929 when he demanded "the eradication of all kulak tendencies and the elimination of all kulaks as a class."

By definition, a kulak was a wealthy land-owning peasant, "wealthy" meaning anyone who produced more than his family consumed. In time, the Soviets defined the term down to just about anyone who resisted collectivization, these being the hundred million stubborn and ignorant peasants of Duranty's glib retelling. Besides, by 1930, the ever-increasing taxes had impoverished even those who once were wealthy.

Early in that same year, as the Soviets attempted to appropriate kulak property and force them into collectives, the kulaks and other peasants resisted. In March 1930 alone, there were more than 6,500 mass demonstrations centering on the Ukraine and expanding outwards. Roughly 1,500 civil servants were killed or wounded in the 800 of those demonstrations that turned violent. In all of 1930, some 2.5 million peasants participated in the 14,000 revolts or riots that engulfed the countryside. During a six-week period including March 1930, the Ukrainian GPU, the justice arm of the Soviet state, sentenced more than 20,000 people to death through its courts for resisting collectivization. Many others were executed without judicial niceties. Somehow, this all seems to have escaped the attention of Moscow correspondent Walter Duranty. Much worse would escape him in the years ahead.

In 1930, the GPU got serious about deporting the kulaks and other "socially dangerous elements" like priests, nuns, shopkeepers, and rural artisans. By the end of 1930, 700,000 people had been shipped to the nether regions of the Soviet Union. By the end of 1931, that number had swollen to 1.8 million. The coordination of this effort was chaotic at best. A report sent to Stalin in 1933 details an all too common "abandonment in deportation," this one involving 6,000 lost souls exiled to the uninhabited island of Nazino:

> There were no tools, no grain, and no food. That is how their new life began. The day after the arrival of the first convoy, on 19 May, snow began to fall again, and the wind picked up. Starving, emaciated from months of insufficient food, without shelter, and without tools, . . . they were trapped. They weren't even able to light fires to ward off the cold.

By stripping the countryside of its more productive citizens and reducing the rest to penury, Stalin had set the stage for the horror show that was to follow. He and his cohorts began by shaking down those left on the land for a bigger slice of the action. In 1932, for instance, the government take was to be 32 percent higher than the year before. By that year, the peasantry was faced with a grim choice: resist the collection or starve to death. They resisted. Stalin sent in his shock troops. They had come to enforce the infamous 1932 "ear law," so dubbed because an individual could and would be arrested for withholding any "socialist property" right down to an ear of corn. By the end of 1933, authorities had arrested more than 125,000 people under the law and sentenced more than 5,000 to death. In areas of widespread resistance, the authorities would deport whole towns.

If Walter Duranty chose not to report on what was transpiring, others did. One was the Italian consul in Novorossiik, who sent a communiqué back to his own government on Stalin's pitiless, if futile, war against his own people:

> The Soviet state is powerful, and armed to the teeth, but it cannot fight this sort of battle. There is no enemy against which to take up a battle formation on the steppes. The enemy is everywhere and must be fought on innumerable fronts in tiny operations: here a field needs hoeing, there a few hundredweight of corn are stashed; a tractor is broken here, another sabotaged there; a third has gone astray.

To defeat an enemy this insidious, there could be only one recourse. Notes the *Black Book,* "He would have to be starved out."

During this period, it should be noted, the Soviet Union was exporting wheat. That was as it had to be, all part of the "plan." By late summer 1932, when even hard-liners began to plea for some relief for these peasants, Moscow turned them down cold. "We Bolsheviks cannot afford to put the needs of the state—needs that have been carefully defined by Party resolutions—in second place, let alone discount them as priorities at all," wrote Stalin's minister, Vyacheslav Molotov. This hard-heartedness gave birth to the adage, "Moscow does not believe in tears."

Harassed and starving, with no hope for the future, millions fled these rich agricultural lands for the cities. At this point, Stalin got serious. In December 1932, in order to "liquidate social parasitism," he mandated the equivalent of passports for all internal migration. In January 1933, Molotov and Stalin instructed local authorities and the GPU to stop the peasants from leaving their farms "by all means necessary." These "means" included mass execution. In February 1933 alone, the secret police reported that it had stopped more than 219,000 desperate peasants in their tracks.

In April 1933, after touring this ravaged countryside, the writer Mikhail Shokolov wrote a plaintive letter to Stalin. He detailed the tortures used by local communist officials to meet their quotas. In the "cold" method, whole brigades of collective workers were forced to stand naked in the frigid night until they revealed hidden grain stashes. In the "hot" method, officials would set fire to the bottom of women's skirts and refuse to douse them until they too gave up their family's food. In a combination of hot and cold, officials would splay peasants on a hot stove and then make them nurse their burns naked in the cold. "These are not abuses of the system," wrote Shokolov. "This is the system for collecting grain."

The recounting of these "minor inconveniences" did not move Stalin. "These people deliberately tried to undermine the Soviet state," he wrote back. "It is a fight to the death, Comrade Shokolov."

The net result of what Duranty calls Stalin's "curt vigor" in pursuing the plan and establishing order was the seemingly bountiful harvest of 1933. Duranty describes it as "the greatest Russia had ever known." In fact, the Soviet Union did manage to ship eighteen million hundred-weight of grain abroad in 1933, a fitting conclusion, as Duranty would have it, to "a heroic chapter in the life of Humanity."

The capital "H" is Duranty's touch. If large "H" humanity advanced, small "h" humanity fell by the wayside, and Duranty knew it. He had told fellow reporter Eugene Lyons and others that he estimated the victims of the terror-famine at around seven million. "According to Mr. Duranty the population of the North Caucasus and the Lower Volga had decreased in the last year by three million, and the population of the Ukraine by four to five million," wrote the British *chargé d'affaires* in Moscow just a month before Duranty was to head back to America to witness the Soviet Union's official recognition. The British official knew this was no accident. "The Ukraine had been bled white," he added.

Two questions need to be asked here. One is how an Anglo-American like Duranty could countenance such evil. The second is how he could get away with concealing it. The answers are becoming depressingly familiar. Debt is owed here both to S.J. "Sally" Taylor, whose painstaking research into Duranty's life resulted in the insightful 1990 book, *Stalin's Apologist,* and to British historian Robert Conquest, whose ground-breaking work on the terror-famine lent Taylor's work historical relevance.

For the sake of context, Walter Duranty was born in 1884, five years after Stalin, and five years before Hitler, on the twenty-fifth anniversary of Darwin's *On the Origin of Species.* Although he was born into a comfortable middle-class family in Liverpool and attended all the right schools, Duranty would grow estranged from his past and his family and write both out of his lives. In his autobiography, *Search for a Key,* he orphans himself at age ten by killing his parents off in a railway accident. In fact, his mother would live for another twenty years and his father another forty years after their imagined deaths.

In the real world, Duranty absorbed the progressive Anglo-American currents flowing around him like a sponge. Nineteen thirteen found the ambitious, if unfocused, Duranty in Paris. He was making useful connections in the city's Anglophone community by serving as something of a deacon in an ongoing series of black masses known as "the Paris workings." The mantra of this unholy affair, *"sanguis et semen"* (blood and semen), nicely captures its over-the-edge, homoerotic flavor. In his later life, Duranty would not say much about these "workings," or about his religious inclinations, "only that he no longer believed in anything." That same year, 1913, Duranty finessed his connections to secure a job with the *New York Times* in Paris.

Duranty's timing proved, for him at least, fortuitous. The following year, fighting broke out in Europe, and Duranty was there to cover it.

"The war in France had taught me a measure of indifference to blood and squalor, and fear and pity," writes the already thick-skinned Duranty. The war had taught him one other life lesson as well. The "truth" was what the *New York Times* reported it to be.

Allegedly under duress from his superiors, Duranty concocted a morale-boosting story about how the arriving American expeditionary force had bravely fought off an attack by German U-boats. So guilty did Duranty feel about writing an article that he knew to be "bunk and hokum" that he composed something of an epic poem "in the e.e. cummings manner" to explain himself:

I sat and wondered whether the End justified the Means (sic)
As many another reporter has wondered before me
And whether that meant any end justified any means
I decided it didn't
Or whether a noble end justified any means
I wasn't so sure about that
And finally whether a noble end justified somewhat doubtful means
At this point I fancied it might

It was only in the Soviet Union that Duranty would find the "noble end" that justified his "somewhat doubtful means." Yet, Duranty was never quite the dewy-eyed idealist. Cynical and self-indulgent, he showed more interest in the perks of the revolution than in its impact on humanity. He did not so much buy into the Soviet state as he was bought off by it. His point of greatest vulnerability remained his fondness for kinky sex. In this regards, his hosts kept him well entertained. Conquest believes, however, that they supplied the sex to blackmail him, a practice of theirs that has since been well documented.

By the time of the terror-famine, Duranty had been in the Soviet Union for more than ten years. He knew the terrain and the people as well as anyone but proved as indifferent to humanity as he was to the truth. His callousness rivaled Stalin's own. "Russians may be hungry and short of clothes and comfort," he wrote in the *New York Times* in 1932. "But you can't make an omelet without breaking eggs."

Not everyone was so callous. In that same year, Canadian economist Andrew Cairns toured the collectivized areas to write a report for the Empire Marketing Board. Not surprisingly, he was horrified by what he found. Cairns, however, did not go public with the truth. As reason why, he would later cite the extreme pressure, even the threats, he received from the British cultural establishment.

Malcolm Muggeridge's experience with that establishment tends to confirm Cairns's. A reporter and an idealistic young communist, Muggeridge ventured in to the afflicted area un-chaperoned and with eyes wide open. What he saw changed his life and would lead him in time to convert to Christianity. He described the terror-famine as "one of the most monstrous crimes in history, so terrible that people in the future will scarcely be able to believe it ever happened." In trying to tell the story, however, he ran into the same left-leaning wall that Cairns had. As a seeming traitor to the progressive cause, he was vilified and slandered and unable to find work. Although he would later emerge as one of Britain's great twentieth century literary figures, in the 1930s no one wanted to hear what he had learned.

Duranty had his own reasons for suppressing the truth. As the British Foreign Office openly discussed, he was angling for U.S. recognition of the Soviet Union. One dispatch bluntly noted that such recognition "would greatly enhance his reputation in the Soviet Union and give him a cheap triumph in the United States." And cheap triumph is exactly what he got.

"The 'famine' is mostly bunk," Duranty wrote to a friend in June 1933. He used his and the *Times'* authority to feed the story to a progressive establishment that had developed a taste for just such bunk. The Pulitzer Committee awarded him its top prize for news correspondence in 1932. The Committee cited the "scholarship, profundity, impartiality, sound judgment, and exceptional clarity" of his reporting on the Five-Year Plan in the Soviet Union. The *Nation*, the quintessential progressive journal, cited the *Times* and Duranty on its annual "honor roll," describing his as "the most enlightening, dispassionate, and readable dispatches from a great nation in the making which appeared in any newspaper in the world."

Then, of course, came America's formal recognition of the Soviet Union in November 1933. For Duranty, though, the "cheap triumph" was just starting. A few days later, fifteen hundred worthies surged to their feet at a Waldorf-Astoria dinner when the diminutive newsman was introduced as "one of the great foreign correspondents of modern times." If the Soviet Union were indeed a "great nation" then, yes, by the same progressive logic, Duranty surely was a "great correspondent."

Jayson Blair first encountered Walter Duranty when he toured the *New York Times* during an internship sixty-five years later. He found Duranty's gold-framed photo in the *Times*' hallowed hall of Pulitzer winners on the eleventh floor. All that distinguished Duranty from his fellow honorees was an asterisk beneath his picture and a disclaimer: "Other writers in the *Times* and elsewhere have discredited this coverage." The disclaimer was in small type. The headlines would be reserved for Blair.

Curiously, one of the few contemporary progressives to evoke the memory of the Soviet terror-famine is Colorado professor Ward Churchill. In his 1997 book, *A Little Matter of Genocide,* he observes correctly that under Stalin "millions of people were deliberately starved to death as a matter of developmental economic policy." He raises this issue not so much to scold Stalin—later portrayed as an innocent victim of America's Cold War "bellicosity"—as to deny Jews the uniqueness of the Holocaust experience. The progressive mind is a many-turned thing.

SCOUNDREL TIME

On the night of January 24, 1980, Lillian Hellman settled into a comfortable chair in her Park Avenue home and turned on the *The Dick Cavett*

Show. This relatively cerebral talk show was just about the only one on TV a would-be intellectual like Hellman could watch with her self-respect intact.

Had Hellman been in a reflective mood that night she would have had cause to smile on the decade just past. Although seventy-five years of age, her star had never been brighter. In 1976, Little Brown had published the third and most political of her memoirs, *Scoundrel Time,* and, if anything, the praise and the sales exceeded that for her highly popular first two volumes, *An Unfinished Woman,* which won the National Book Award, and *Pentimento.*

"Let it be recorded that she is merely great," observed the legendary Studs Terkel in the *Chicago Daily News.* "She has indeed written a history of her time. Never has it been more necessary." As the esteemed Walter Kerr noted in the *New York Times,* Hellman penned her memoirs "with candor, calm, and a weariness no longer capable of anything but honesty." The cultural establishment had given her its seal of approval for recording history and recording it honestly, and that establishment was just warming up.

In 1977, when presenting an Oscar for best documentary, she told the Academy audience that she "had no regrets" about the period of American history that she had been forced to endure and had lived to expose, the so-called "scoundrel time" of the late 1940s and early 1950s. For those who may have forgotten or those who never knew, her memoir evoked the hour when she alone proved brave enough to defy the House Un-American Activities Committee, the dread HUAC, twenty-five years earlier.

"I cannot and will not cut my conscience to fit this year's fashion," she had famously told the ruthless men on that committee. At this heady moment, now with the entire Academy on its feet, one could forgive Hellman for thinking that her words would resonate in American history alongside those of Patrick Henry and Nathan Hale.

Several of Hellman's more successful plays had already been turned into movies—*The Children's Hour, Little Foxes, Watch on the Rhine, Toys in the Attic.* That same year, 1977, Hollywood released *Julia,* a film about Hellman herself. The movie reminded this new generation that Hellman had once risked her life to aid the resistance movement against Nazi Germany. In a kind of progressive baton-pass, Jane Fonda, then at the peak of her game, played the young and quietly heroic Hellman. The movie proved highly successful, and the New Left found a new heroine. In 1978, an appropriately fawning BBC-produced documentary renewed Hellman's fame around the world.

Indeed, throughout the 1970s, the currents of history seemed to be flowing Hellman's way. The sexual revolution, a movement that she had pioneered, was in full flower pre-AIDS. That "villainous liar" Richard Nixon, the man who made HUAC glamorous in the 1940s, had left the White House in disgrace. The anti-communism that Nixon preached had, at least in Hellman's account, led to the conspicuous failure of Vietnam. If these currents had roiled the nation, they had cleansed Hellman of any communist taint. For that matter, communism itself was in its ascendancy worldwide.

Historian Paul Johnson describes the Hellman of this era as "the most important single power-broker among the progressive intelligentsia and the society people who seethed around them." A colorful personal history had transformed Hellman into a feminist icon as well. Her multiple abortions, her many lovers, her long-term, live-in relationship with radical writer Dashiell Hammett, and her spectacularly successful, godless, childless self-sufficiency found a ready audience in this first post-pill, post-Roe generation of newly liberated women.

And then Mary McCarthy, an almost equally successful writer and critic and a progressive icon in her own right, walked on to the set of *The Dick Cavett Show* and spoiled everything.

Hellman had provoked a few earlier spats with McCarthy, always prettier than the mannish Hellman and seven years her junior. But nothing too serious, nothing that might have foretold what was about to happen live on *The Dick Cavett Show* in those next dreadful minutes. After a little sparring and witty banter, Cavett asked McCarthy to name any contemporary writers who were "overpraised."

"The only one I can think of," said McCarthy with claws out and flashing, "is a holdover like Lillian Hellman, who I think is tremendously overrated, a bad writer, and a dishonest writer, but she really belongs to the past."

When Cavett asked what was dishonest about Hellman, McCarthy scratched right ahead with the most intemperate and ultimately expensive quip of her career. "Everything," McCarthy answered, "I said once in some interview that every word she writes is a lie, including 'and' and 'the.'"

Although McCarthy would argue that the dispute was not political, politics lay at the root of it. "It's not just two old ladies engaged in a cat fight," said *Dissent* editor Irving Howe with some justification. The issue at stake, according to Howe, was their respective attitudes towards communism, "the central political-cultural-intellectual problem of the twentieth century." However catty her remarks, McCarthy had just turned a literary cold war into a hot one, one that had the potential to clear away a half-century of detritus and deceit.

If Hellman's story had been unique in American cultural circles during this period, it would not be worth relating. But, if anything, it was indicative. She differed from many of her peers in the Hollywood-Broadway axis only in her success and her lack of discretion. Munzenberg and his comrades had done a brilliant job infiltrating Hollywood, particularly the trade unions and the talent guilds. The trade unions would cause the studio bosses massive headaches, but it was the talent guilds, particularly the Screen Writers Guild, that were quietly eating away at the movie industry like a cancer. As Lenin had precociously observed, "Communists must always consider that of all the arts the motion picture is the most important," and in this regard at least, he was on the money.

To be sure, McCarthy had overstated the breadth of Hellman's dishonesty. Obviously, not everything Hellman had written was a lie. Just everything important. The most critical of the deceits was that of Hellman's own political affiliations. About this, she would tell many stories. In *An Unfinished Woman* she passes through the world as an unschooled naïf. In *Scoundrel Time*, she denies ever having joined the Communist Party. She admits only to having attended a few meetings with Hammett, who, she was "fairly sure," had joined the Party in 1937 or 1938. "It was true," she blithely lies about her own role, "that Hammett became a committed radical and I didn't."

In 1952, when preparing her testimony before HUAC, she had been a bit more honest. "I joined the Communist Party in 1938 with little thought as to the serious step I was taking," she wrote in an early draft of the statement she would make to the committee. Her attorney, Joe Rauh, was horrified. She had not only admitted to being a communist, but she had also failed to express any regret at having done so. He rewrote her testimony for her. Hellman added the line about cutting her conscience to fashion and followed it with the unconvincing nonsense, "I was not a political person and could have no political place in any political group." Although she pled the fifth, HUAC chose not to cite her for contempt as they had others, largely because she was a woman, a public and feisty one at that.

Despite her disclaimers, Hellman was an entirely political person. Her official status in the Party may never be known. The Comintern often allowed a certain distance for celebrities whose careers might be compromised by recognition, especially flighty ones like Hellman. The surest way to gauge the depth of her attachment is to track her own political shifts alongside those of her ultimate mentor, Joseph Stalin.

It would take a person of great callousness and deviousness to make a good Stalinist, and Hellman had seemingly all the right stuff. Born in 1905 into a Jewish family, a faith she ignored all her life when not mocking it, Hellman grew up comfortably in New Orleans and New

York. An indifferent student at NYU and Columbia University, Hellman married young and strategically and began cheating on her husband almost before the birds could eat the rice.

The defining moment in Hellman's life took place in Hollywood, in 1930, when she met the dashing and highly successful mystery writer, Dashiell Hammett. Hammett's old American stock attracted the self-hating Jew in Hellman, and his drunken abuse satisfied her general self-loathing. As to Hammett's wife and children, they were no more meaningful to Hellman than a vow. "Hammett, obsessed by lying women, took up with a woman who lied to him from the start, a woman who was addicted to lying." So observes his and Hellman's biographer, Joan Mellen. Using the truth selectively, Hellman and Hammett would define Hollywood radical chic for the next thirty years.

By 1930, Hammett had a good head start on the road to radicalism. In his 1929 novel, *Red Harvest*, Hammett had originally called America "Poisonville," a land dominated by corrupt capitalists and their lackey police. This was a theme he would repeat in his other fiction even before the Depression made radicalism fashionable.

Hellman started young as well. She flirted with socialism as early as her high school years, though she wondered even then how she could ever reconcile it with her material ambitions, a dialectic that went unre-solved until the end of her life. In *Pentimento*, however, she traces her political awakening to the rise of Hitler, who "had shaken many of us into radicalism."

"By 1935 or 1936," according to Hellman, accounts from Germany had grown increasingly "horror-tragic," and she, like others, had to respond. The fact that Stalin had countenanced the murder-starvation of some seven million kulaks by this date mattered not at all. Walter Duranty had seen to it that Hellman and Hammett could look the other way if they chose to, which they obviously did. There would be more to ignore in the years ahead, and they would prove steadfastly up to the task.

"Columbus discovered America," Otto Katz used to boast, "and I discovered Hollywood." Katz, a communist of German-Czech origin, served as Willi Munzenberg's right-hand man in the cultural colonization of the movie colony. He did his work well. Later estimates would place the number of communists in the talent guilds alone at more than three hundred.

In 1935, Katz traveled to Tinseltown incognito to strengthen the Party's grip on celebrity Stalinists and to help propagandize Soviet ambitions in the West.

For Koch, the already radicalized Hammett and Hellman had to be an attractive target. Hammett's popular novels of the early 1930s, *The Maltese Falcon, The Glass Key,* and *The Thin Man* had attracted the attention of Hollywood. The 1934 production of Hellman's first play, *The Children's Hour,* which was "virtually written" by Hammett, attracted both Hollywood and Party attention. This provocative story of two schoolteachers accused of lesbianism also proved to be a great commercial success. As Stephen Koch observes, Katz would soon become "Hellman's senior mentor for the cultural politics of Stalinism."

In New York, the role of mentor was being played by the Polish-born Victor Jeremy (V.J.) Jerome, a member of the Central Committee of the Communist Party and the guardian of Party cultural doctrine in the United States. In 1936, Jerome would attend a dinner at Hellman's New York apartment as guest of honor. According to biographer Mellen, this was proof "that Hellman and Hammett were already Party faithful."

The Comintern made new membership easy in 1935 and the next few years. Munzenberg's public relations apparatus was exploiting Western anti-fascist sentiments with a strategy that came to be known as the "Popular Front." By aligning with the hated Western democracies in a campaign allegedly to "stop Hitler," the Comintern empowered its foot soldiers to cooperate with local governments, mouth patriotic platitudes, and sublimate class warfare to long-term strategic goals. In other words, says Koch, the Popular Front was "politically a strategic tactic and morally a fraud."

Fraud or not, the cultural elite of the Western world fell hard. "Party membership swelled," writes Koch, "fellow traveling became *de rigeur*, some sort of revolutionary pose seemed morally—or at least socially— indispensable." For Hellman and Hammett, the timing could not have been better. Now, they could be rich and radical simultaneously. They and other Party loyalists consciously embraced newcomers to their ranks, giving them not only a political philosophy but also a social life. A sobering number of major screenwriters would follow Lil and Dash through Stalin's many twist and turns. "All over town," observed Philip Dunne, a liberal screenwriter dismayed by Hollywood's Soviet swoon, "the industrious communist tail wagged the lazy liberal dog."

To this point in their respective political developments, Hellman and Mary McCarthy were largely in sync. McCarthy traced her own radicalization to her reading of John Dos Passos while a Vassar student in the early 1930s, particularly his writings on the Sacco and Vanzetti trial. In 1936, however, she fell in with popular author James Farrell and his circle. Farrell alerted her to the Moscow Show Trials that were then in process. The following year, McCarthy began a long affair with future *Partisan Review* editor Philip Rahv, another Marxist who also had grown wary of Stalin.

Farrell and Rahv were among the few intellectuals who paid real attention to what was taking place in the Soviet Union. From the beginning, Stalin had used the Popular Front to distract attention from his true enemy—not the Nazis but the unreliable in his own party. While the world's cultural elite were cheering on his seeming fight against inequality at home and fascism abroad, Stalin was quietly liquidating his internal enemies in the millions. In the convenient logic of the Popular Front, to oppose Stalin was to support fascism. In Europe, such a gesture could easily cost one his life. In Hollywood, it cost something almost as dear: one's social life.

Those in the West who chose not to look too hard at the Soviet Union would see only the three spectacular public trials staged in 1936, 1937, and 1938 respectively. If McCarthy was growing increasingly dubious about the Stalinist project, Hellman was not. Hellman supported the verdict of the purge trials in 1938 and even signed a public petition to that effect, "Leading Artists, Educators Support Soviet Trial Verdict." When famed liberal philosopher John Dewey began an independent investigation of the trial evidence, Hammett denounced him as a "fascist agent of Leon Trotsky." Needless to say, Hellman mentions none of this in her memoirs. "I did not even know I was [in Moscow] in the middle of their ugliest purge period," writes Hellman disingenuously in *An Unfinished Woman*, "and I have often asked myself how that could be."

Likewise, Hellman had little to say about the victims of the Great Terror, despite her several trips to the Soviet Union, including one trip of five months in 1944. The *Black Book of Communism* puts the official number of those arrested in the Soviet Union for political crimes at 1,575,000, and this just for the years 1937 and 1938. Of those, 681,692 were executed. Scores of thousands more died of abuse or neglect during the process. Those singled out for execution included Trotskyites and other suspected enemies of the state as well as the surviving kulaks, most of the upper ranks of the Red Army, virtually all the clergy, many teachers and professors, and ironically most of the Soviet Union's cultural elite— writers, publishers, directors, and journalists.

Hellman could not credibly claim ignorance about all of this. For Stalin had taken the Great Terror to Spain. There, in the midst of a civil war, his secret police (NKVD) were spending more energy purging their non-Stalinist "allies" on the left than they were fighting the "enemy" forces of General Franco on the right. Lillian Hellman was there when it happened. John Dos Passos and George Orwell, both leftists, quit the country in disgust and fear. "Lillian Hellman didn't notice," writes biographer Mellen. "Nor did Dash."

"I had up to the late 1940s," writes Hellman in *Scoundrel Time*, "believed that the educated, the intellectual, lived by what they claimed to believe: freedom of thought and speech, the right of each man to his convictions, a more than implied promise of aid to those who might be persecuted." That aid apparently did not extend to the literally millions of victims of Stalin's wrath in the Soviet Unions, nor to the thousands slaughtered in Spain on her own watch.

During this same trip to Europe in 1937, Hellman tells the reader in the "Julia" chapter of *Pentimento,* she took a train to Germany, carrying with her a hatbox full of money. After much highly detailed intrigue, she hands off the hatbox to her brave socialist friend, Julia—the radical actress Vanessa Redgrave in the movie—who tells her that the money will save as many as a thousand Jews and other dissenters. "So believe that you have been better than a good friend to me," says Julia to the young Hellman. "You have done something important."

As it happens, the man who had persuaded Hellman to go to Spain in the first place was none other than Otto Katz, the Christopher Columbus of Hollywood. In *An Unfinished Woman,* Hellman, the self-effacing heroine of her own stories, claims that Katz stayed in Spain until the Franco victory and that she and others raised the bail money to extricate him and send him on to Mexico.

After her return to New York from Spain, with one more abortion and an Ernest Hemingway fling under her belt, Hellman met McCarthy at a dinner party. "I'm not sure I knew at first that she was a Stalinist," remembered McCarthy, "but in the discussion of Spain it became evident and I spoke out, perhaps rather fiercely." So began their feud.

After the McCarthy accusations on *The Dick Cavett Show* years later, the always-litigious Hellman sued McCarthy for more than two million dollars. This vengeful misstep gave McCarthy and her allies an excuse to document the lies that littered Hellman's life. The 1937 trip to Spain and beyond provided plenty to work with. For it seems that the farther Hellman traveled from home, the further she stretched the truth.

In the spring 1981 issue of the *Paris Review,* Hemingway's major flame in Spain and later his wife, Martha Gellhorn, dismembers the time-line of Hellman's 1937 trip to Europe and documents eight major lies Hellman had told about Spain. That was not hard to do. As Stephen Koch comments on her story of rescuing Otto Katz, "It must be said that every clause, if not perhaps every word, in this summary is false." Katz had, in fact, been in New York at the time of his presumed detainment, working with Hellman among others.

It was with the Julia story, however, that Hellman had left herself most vulnerable, especially given her claim that "I trust absolutely what I remember about Julia." When *Pentimento* came out, no one challenged it publicly, but a woman named Muriel Gardner read it and sent a friendly letter to Hellman pointing out the similarities between Julia's story and her own. During the 1930s, Gardner, a young American heiress studying in Vienna, had gotten involved in the anti-Nazi underground. She used the code name "Mary" when smuggling out messages and people. In 1939, after war broke out, she and her husband escaped to New Jersey where they became good friends with Hellman's lawyer among others, and her story got around.

In 1983, Gardner published her own memoirs, *Code Name Mary*. Noting the similarities, reporters began to ask Hellman if perhaps "Mary" was the real "Julia," and if not, who that real Julia was. Cornered, Hellman started spinning wildly that Julia was dead, and her real name could not be revealed lest German reactionaries punish her mother, who was still alive.

In 1984, Boston University professor Samuel McCracken ended the controversy with a devastating *Commentary* article, "Julia and Other Fictions by Lillian Hellman." McCracken checked all the facts that could be verified—train times, boat-sailing schedules, theater programs—and came to the inescapable conclusion that "Julia" was, in fact, pure fiction. As he discovered, Hellman had apparently absorbed the "Mary" story and made it her own with herself as heroine.

"Almost every detail," writes McCracken, "is either improbable to a degree that would disgrace a third-rate thriller, or plainly contradicted by the historical record." He found it "remarkable" that Hellman would claim the most certainty about the part of her past that "when placed against the template of reality, displays the most incongruities."

If the mischief in Spain and the Soviet Union alienated those sunshine Stalinists attracted by the Popular Front, the next shift in Soviet policy would test the commitment of even the hardcore. Rumors of the shift started floating in the summer of 1939. On August 14, Hellman and Hammett joined four hundred other important signatories denouncing the "fantastic falsehood" that Germany and the USSR were essentially alike and were planning on uniting their efforts. After all, what held the various subsets of the Popular Front together was their mutually presumed hatred of Hitler and all that he stood for. Hellman was particularly troubled. She had just completed the first draft of a new play, the classic, anti-fascist agitprop, *Watch on the Rhine*.

On August 23, Stalin rocked the alliance he had pulled together when he signed the Nazi-Soviet pact. This unholy agreement ceded the Baltic States to the Soviet Union and divided Poland between the USSR and Hitler's Germany. To many, it came as a rude wakeup call. Less than a year after the savage Nazi pogrom of Kristallnacht, committed anti-fascists found themselves in bed next to their ancient enemy with no memory even of a courtship. Long in the planning, the pact revealed the Popular Front for the fraud it had always been.

Some quit the Party in disgust, but not Lil and Dash. They discarded their belligerent anti-fascism and now posed as ardent pacifists horrified by the democracies' "imperialist war." They were in good company. Almost overnight, Hellman's mentor, V.J. Jerome, had transformed the Hollywood Anti-Nazi League into the Hollywood League for Democratic Action. Hellman herself helped create the Keep America Out of War Committee for the League of American Writers and drafted anti-war resolutions from the League offices. During the Battle of Britain, when Churchill cried out for American help, the mischievous Hammett helped launch a Yanks-Are-Not-Coming Committee. Never one to sacrifice material comfort for the cause, however, Hellman let *Watch on the Rhine* proceed, even if did alienate her newfound fascist buddies.

The Soviet Union further confused the Hollywood innocents by invading Finland, an act that got it booted from the League of Nations. But Hellman didn't blink. "I don't believe in that fine, lovable little Republic of Finland that everybody gets so weepy about," she told the Hearst press. "I've been there, and it looks like a pro-Nazi republic to me." Of course, she had not been to Finland, but truth had never been an issue either for her personally or for the party to which she gave her allegiance.

Like many of his colleagues, Hollywood's best-paid screenwriter, Dalton Trumbo, hung tough as well. After the pact was signed, he authorized the official Party organ, *The Daily Worker*, to serialize his anti-war novel, *Johnny Got His Gun*. In the spring of 1940, he started a book and screenplay, *The Remarkable Andrew*, in perfect sync with the Party line. In it, the ghost of warrior-president Andrew Jackson lectures the protagonist on—of all unlikely things—the virtues of peace. "I don't think it's pacifism to be against war," the spectral Jackson says with a straight face. "I think it's just being decent." Although Trumbo would not officially join the Party until 1943, he admitted to his friendly biographer, Bruce Cook, "It was literally no change. I might as well have been a communist ten years earlier."

Had the consequences been less tragic, what happened next would appear to future generations as pure burlesque. On June 22, 1941, Hitler surprised Stalin by attacking the Soviet Union. "The Motherland has been invaded," Hellman cried out upon hearing the news. Immediately thereafter, Hellman and Hammett and scores of other writers shed their uneasy pacifism like a cheap suit and took up the battle against fascism as if they had never abandoned it. The pair both signed the League of American Writers' call to arms, urging "full support to Great Britain and the Soviet Union in their struggle for the demolition of fascism."

With the bombing of Pearl Harbor months later, Hellman, Hammett, and their fellow Stalinist screenwriters got to play at patriotism for the next several years. Hellman contributed the screenplay for *Watch on the Rhine*, whose anti-Nazi viewpoint was now acceptable to everyone, as well as *North Star*, a preposterously cheerful take on the Soviet Union.

Trumbo chipped in with patriotic classics like *A Guy Named Joe* and *Thirty Seconds over Tokyo.* Other Soviet sympathizers added one pro-war script after another, many of them featuring hideous caricatures of the Japanese and German enemy. The Party, of course, heartily approved internment camps for Japanese Americans.

Meanwhile, the Party's embedded story analysts and script readers proved even more effective in blocking anti-communist themes. "Every screen writer worth his salt wages the battle in his own way," wrote Trumbo, "a kind of literary guerilla warfare." Kudos goes here to Kenneth Lloyd Billingsley for smoking out the guerillas in his excellent and exhaustive book, *Hollywood Party.*

As Billingsley relates, Party boss Earl Browder instructed his charges not to make obvious and easily avoided propaganda films but rather to sneak "a drop of progressive thought" into ordinary movies. Five minutes of Party line in every script was just about right—so screenwriter and instructor in communism, John Howard Lawson, told his students. During the war, Lawson scripted *Sahara* and *Action in the North Atlantic,* both starring Humphrey Bogart.

The pro-war classic *Casablanca,* coauthored by fellow traveler Howard Koch, offers an example of how a drop might be added. When Captain Renault accuses the Humphrey Bogart character, Rick Blaine, of being a sentimentalist, having run guns to both the Ethiopians and the leftist forces in the Spanish Civil War, Blaine responds, "I was paid well both times." Renault counters, "The winning side would have paid you more." Blaine demurs, "I'm a poor businessman."

No, the audience understands, Blaine is not a poor businessman. He may be a crooked businessman, but in communist-scripted films all businessmen are crooked. Blaine is a man of principle. Never mind the brutal Stalinist purges or the anarchist slaughter of priests and nuns or the wild instability of the whole leftist collective, the "loyalists" were the good guys in the Spanish Civil War. Hollywood would repeat this line until it became accepted wisdom.

This Potemkin patriotism would last until April 1945. With the war in Europe all but over, Stalin sent word through the French journal *Cahier du Communisme* that any thought of post-war cooperation between the Soviets and the Americans was a "notorious revision of Marxism." This article was reprinted in *The Daily Worker* and other communist journals all over the world. America may have been a useful ally during the war, but now she was *glavy vrag,* the main enemy.

American Party boss Browder called the *Cahier* article "the first public declaration of the Cold War." The article had been directed at him, as a champion of post-war cooperation, and he knew it. Although Browder had been popular in Hollywood, he was quickly purged from Party leadership and was lucky to escape with his life. From this moment on, no one who remained in the Party could delude himself into thinking that his marching orders were coming from any place other than Moscow. "It came down to this," said Trumbo, "if Lenin was right, then Browder was wrong—and vice versa. I prefer to believe Lenin was right." Now, only the hardcore Stalinists soldiered on, Hellman and Hammett among them, and Party discipline grew firmer.

Screenwriter Albert Maltz learned this the hard way. One of Hollywood's most successful writers, Maltz had joined the patriotic chorus during the war, penning *Pride of the Marines* and *Destination Tokyo* among others. In February 1946, he wrote a bold article for the Party magazine *New Masses* in which he challenged Party wisdom on using "art as a weapon." In making his case, he cited Hellman's "magnificent play," *Watch on the Rhine,* which had alternately been attacked and praised by the same leftist critics based on the mood of the moment. He also told of the many screenplays or books he had seen revised or abandoned because, as he noted with typical discretion, "the political scene altered."

It is likely that Maltz was allowed to publish in *New Masses* only so that this kind of "deviationism" could be publicly rejected and purged. The Party struck back hard. Writing in *The Daily Worker,* unflinching

Stalinist Michael Gold denounced Maltz as a comrade who had lost his soul in the "phony atmosphere of Hollywood." The timing of Maltz's article was even worse than its content, Gold claimed, as the capitalists were now plotting "to establish an American fascism as a prelude to American conquest of the world."

Party leaders and their trade union muscle summoned Maltz before a series of tribunals brutal beyond anything HUAC or Joe McCarthy would ever attempt. A witness later described one of these sessions as a "hyena attack" in which the participants, including many of his fellow screenwriters, forced the frightened Maltz to "crawl and recant." As to Trumbo, he denied that he had participated in the attack. "Did he say that?" The disbelieving Maltz would respond when later confronted with Trumbo's denial. "I suppose I'll have to let that stand then."

Thoroughly chastened, Maltz wrote a second article for *The Worker* that appeared two months after the initial one. In a swoon of self-debasement, Maltz denounced his previous article as "a one-sided, nondialectical treatment of complex issues." No, he now argued, it was not the left wing that put "artists in uniform." It was the dreadful social conditions in the Western world. George Orwell could not have imagined a more tortured definition of artistic freedom than the one Maltz actually offered:

> The left wing, by its insistence that artists must be free to speak the absolute truth about society, by the intellectual equipment it offers in Marxist scientific thought, is precisely the force that can help the artist strip himself of the many uniforms into which he has been stepping since birth.

A year later, in 1947, HUAC held its first round of Hollywood hearings. The committee had selected forty-five industry people to query, most of whom were friendly but nineteen of whom were not. Of those nineteen, eleven did testify but refused to answer questions, and

Congress cited them for contempt. When playwright Bertolt Brecht fled to East Germany, the group passed into legend as the Hollywood Ten. After two of the group, John Howard Lawson and Dalton Trumbo, were convicted, the others, Albert Maltz included, waived jury trials and were sentenced to up to a year in prison.

The "innocents" of Hollywood—Humphrey Bogart in the lead—were formed into a new "club." This club, the Committee for the First Amendment, seemed fully unaware of who was doing the forming. The Committee rallied to the cause of the Hollywood Ten, thinking them innocent liberals like themselves. When Bogart found out otherwise, he was appalled by his own activism on their behalf, calling it "ill-advised, impetuous, and foolish."

Lillian Hellman entertained no such qualms. She knew that the Ten—and many more—were Party faithful. Still, she wrote a defiantly mendacious editorial in the magazine of the Screen Writers Guild that same year, claiming that "there has never been a single line or word of communism in any American picture at any time." She called the HUAC hearings a "honky tonk show" and a "sickening, sickening, immoral and degraded week."

For all her bluster, however, Hellman had little stomach for self-sacrifice. In July 1951, with the Soviets now in possession of the bomb and a war on in Korea, the atmosphere was colder than it had been in 1947 when one could still grandstand at communism. Still, Dashiell Hammett insisted on taking the Fifth Amendment before a grand jury in a communism-related trial. As a witness, this was a right he did not have, and the judge sentenced him to six months in prison.

When Hammett turned to Hellman for bail money, she lost her celebrated nerve. Not wanting to risk her career for an accused communist, even her lover, she made plans to leave the country. Finally, an anonymous, rich comrade put up the money for Hammett. Years later, in what biographer Mellen calls the "most deplorably dishonest of her emendations," Hellman made up a detailed story of how she tried to pawn her jewelry to raise the bail money, swollen in the recounting to a hundred thousand dollars.

The lies finally didn't matter. Despite Mary McCarthy's accusations and Mellen's powerful biography and the stream of new revelations emanating from the Soviet Union, Hellman and her progressive allies maintained a chokehold on the American cultural narrative. In the year 2000, Little Brown issued a new edition of *Scoundrel Time.* In the freshly drafted Foreword, actress and director Kathy Bates lauded Hellman's "courage" and lamented the "scoundrels" who "deprived fellow Americans of the right to dissent." In the introduction, noted author Gary Wills remembered Hellman's "undefended decency" and her "code of honor."

In the way of postscript, the story did not end so happily for others involved in advancing Hellman's career and her self-created biography. Willi Munzenberg, the man who first thought to colonize American culture, fell afoul of Stalin's Great Terror. After two years of running, he was found dead, hanged at the edge of a French forest with a farmer's baling wire. Otto Katz, the "Christopher Columbus" of Hollywood and Hellman's mentor, "confessed" to being a Zionist traitor during one of Stalin's anti-Semitic purges, and he too was hanged. As to Trotsky, the antichrist of the Stalinist liturgy, an assassin put an ice axe through his skull in Mexico City in 1940.

Hellman had little to say about Katz's death, and Hollywood had nothing to say about any of them. To this day, not one movie has shown even a hint of Soviet brutalities. Nor has any movie celebrated the life of a single Russian or Eastern European dissident who risked everything to "tear down that wall." Hollywood has instead invested its storytelling resources in its own progressive mythology. The power of that myth was on full display in October 1997 when the four major talent guilds staged "Hollywood Remembers the Black List," a multimedia celebration of the Hollywood Ten at the Samuel Goldwyn Theater hosted by Billy Crystal and featuring scores of luminaries.

"It is fitting on this fiftieth anniversary," said the guild presidents in their announcement, "that we pause to remember those who suffered through those horrific times to assure political despotism will never again be allowed to flourish in our nation." As for the despotism to which the Hollywood Ten paid homage, the despotism that starved millions of its own people, executed millions more without reason, found common cause with Nazi Germany, and created "horrific times" like none known before or since, that was best left forgotten.

I Got My Job through the *New York Times*

In his more impish days as young editor of the *National Review,* William Buckley ran a cartoon showing communist dictator Fidel Castro sitting pretty on the island of Cuba and waving a gun. Underneath ran a caption made famous by an ad campaign for the paper's classified section, "I got my job through the *New York Times.*"

New York Times correspondent Herbert Matthews may not have thought the cartoon fair or funny, but he got the joke. As he well understood, he was almost single-handedly responsible for securing Castro his lifetime gig as *el Presidente de la República de Cuba.* "I discovered," writes Matthews in his 1971 book, *A World in Revolution,* "that a journalist can make history."

In February 1957, only two months after landing a small force on Cuba, the beleaguered young rebel leader Fidel Castro had sent for a foreign journalist, any journalist, to counter the rumor that he had been killed upon landing. As the story goes, one almost too fortuitous to be believed, his men stumbled upon Matthews, a veteran *Times* reporter. Castro biographer Georgie Ann Geyer calls Matthews "the right person at the right moment." A hopeless romantic and a committed "liberal"—by his own description—Matthews was looking to rekindle the revolutionary spirit that seemed so much alive in the world of his youth. In Castro, he found that spirit's embodiment. "Taking him, as one would at first, by physique and personality," wrote Matthews in that critical first article, "this was quite a man—a powerful six-footer, olive-skinned, full-faced, with a straggly beard."

Although he would never admit it, Matthews was serving as an audience of one in an absurdist guerilla theater. Castro had fully stage-managed this meeting. He circulated his men throughout the camp and took "reports" from other distant "columns" in Matthews's presence. As a result, Matthews convinced himself that there were at least forty fighters in this camp and many more deep in the mountains—"the most dangerous enemy General Batista has yet faced."

In fact, Castro had no more than twenty fighters in his ragtag band, but not for long. His force would start growing when he made his heroic debut a week later on the front page of the *New York Times.* "Matthews thought he was in a jungle," writes Geyer, "and in truth he was: a jungle of obfuscation and deliberate deceit."

This was not the first such jungle into which the clueless Matthews had stumbled. Just about twenty years earlier, the *New York Times* had assigned Matthews to cover the most deliberately misreported conflict in world history, the Spanish Civil War. Despite the *Times'* historic insistence on objectivity and its reputation as the authoritative "paper of record," Matthews's reporting was openly subjective and stunningly wrongheaded. "I agree that we oversimplified a very complex situation," Matthews would later write, but in fact, oversimplification doesn't do justice to the preposterous botch job that followed.

By way of background, a Popular Front coalition, composed of a variety of socialist and communist parties, had won a narrow victory in Spain's general elections in February 1936. Although the anarchists had a powerful presence in Spain, they did not participate in the election. They did, however, participate in the unrest that followed the election and that led to a state of near anarchy throughout the country. The chaos and the confiscations of property alarmed the Spanish military and the conservative Falange faction that backed it. The war itself began in July 1936 when General Francisco Franco's army in Morocco mutinied against the duly elected Republican government and attempted to restore order.

With war declared, all hell broke loose, almost literally. Under the banner of anarchism or communism or no banner at all, the populist left declared its own war on the Catholic Church, killing 12 bishops, nearly 300 nuns, more than 2,000 monks and 4,000 priests in the first three months. Needless to say, these atrocities horrified the Catholic Church, particularly in America. On the Nationalist side of the line, Franco's side, the purges of the left were ruthless and the violence likely comparable.

Where others saw outrages, Willi Munzenberg saw opportunity. By 1936, at the height of the Popular Front honeymoon, the Comintern enjoyed a near monopoly on world media. With just a little prodding, many of the best and brightest of the international left rushed to Spain as war correspondents. The *New Statesman* sent George Orwell. The North American Newspaper Alliance sent Ernest Hemingway. *Collier's* sent Martha Gellhorn. The *Times of London* sent Kim Philby. The *London News Chronicle* sent Arthur Koestler. *The Nation* sent Louis Fischer.

No sooner had Fischer arrived, than he was briefing the Soviet ambassador on war strategy. He soon went to work as quartermaster for the Communist International Brigades, all the while sending news dispatches to *The Nation, The New Statesman,* and papers throughout Europe. Koestler meanwhile was working undercover for the Comintern. Philby, of course, was a Soviet agent spying on the Nationalists. Gellhorn was a fellow traveler and outspoken supporter of the Republican cause, who still found time to finesse Hemingway away from his wife. Hemingway, when not rutting or reporting, was drilling the International Brigades. And the young Orwell actually joined a Republican—often called "Loyalist"—fighting force. So much for objectivity.

After being captured by the Nationalists and freed three months later in a prisoner exchange, Koestler wrote a powerful book called *The Spanish Testament.* Gruesomely detailed, the book caused worldwide revulsion against Franco and his forces. Years later, however, Koestler would abandon communism and admit that he wrote the book in the Comintern's Paris office under the prodding of Willi Munzenberg.

"Too weak. Too objective," Munzenberg would shout at Koestler after reading his early drafts. "Hit them! Hit them hard! Tell the world how they run over prisoners with tanks, how they pour petrol over them and burn them alive. Make the world gasp with horror."

Meanwhile, Munzenberg's right-hand man, the ubiquitous Otto Katz, outdid even his boss in the mendacity department. In contemplating ways to delay a French arm shipment to the Nationalists, he decided to create an entirely fictitious battle in all its gory detail and then report on it. "In the end," wrote the reporter who conspired with Katz on the article, "it emerged as one of the most factual, inspiring, and at the same time sober pieces of war reporting I ever saw." But than again, the competition for honesty and sobriety was none too stiff. The more astute of media critics dismissed even Hemingway's war correspondence as "abysmally bad."

At the time, few noticed just how banal and unbalanced Hemingway's reporting had become. In the 1930s he stood atop the literary world. His reputation was so luminous that it blinded almost everyone to his flaws. That reputation attracted Munzenberg as well. As Koch notes, "The directors of the Popular Front hoped to transform [Hemingway] into the biggest literary fellow traveler of them all."

The vehicle of transformation was to be a high-class propaganda film called *The Spanish Earth,* fully produced and directed by Munzenberg men. The committee that fronted the film, Lillian Hellman among its worthies, hoped to make Hemingway the unwitting mouthpiece for its message. To heighten the film's fundraising cachet, the committee also invited the participation of John Dos Passos, the most prominent writer on the hard-left before the emergence of Hemingway. Dos Passos agreed to come to Spain as well.

Before Dos Passos arrived, Stalin had decided to exploit the chaos in

Spain for his own purposes. In late 1936, he began to send a small army of agents, including the feared NKVD. As the *Black Book* notes, the goal of the NKVD was "to purge all political opponents among the Republicans." This included Social Democrats, Trotskyites, the anarchists, and the more rebellious of the communists. "To the communist mind," adds the *Black Book,* "political deviation was the equivalent of treason, and everywhere it was met with the same punishment." Best estimates of those so "punished" range from ten to fifteen thousand.

Hemingway chose not to notice. In his history of war correspondence, British author Phillip Knightley, a loyalist sympathizer, chastizes Hemingway for his "total failure to report the communist persecution, imprisonment, and summary execution of 'untrustworthy' elements on the Republican side, when he knew this was happening and when disclosing it might well have prevented further horrors like this."

Dos Passos could not help but notice. When he arrived in Spain in spring 1937, he was unable to find a good friend that he had come to see, José Robles, a major player on the Republican side. Scarier still, no one could or would tell him where Robles was. Not even Robles's wife knew, and she turned desperately to Dos Passos for help. When Dos Passos caught up with Hemingway and the *Spanish Earth* crew and began asking questions about Robles, he merely annoyed the great Hemingway. The notoriously macho author had little use for Dos Passos' unmanly worries. This was war after all.

Soon thereafter, Hemingway was tipped off to Robles's fate. In the midst of a small public gathering, Hemingway had the sadistic pleasure of informing Dos Passos that his buddy had been exposed as a fascist spy and shot. Dos Passos refused to accept the lie. He continued to press for the truth, a dangerous pastime in the would-be Soviet Socialist Republic of Spain. And then he found it: the Soviet NKVD had executed Robles as it had thousands of other Republican leaders. "And so it was," writes Koch, "that Dos Passos left Spain and communism."

Before leaving Spain, Dos Passos was met by a frightened young man in a Barcelona hotel lobby. The man, an aspiring young British writer by the name of Eric Blair, knew of Dos Passos' quest for the truth and clued him in on what he himself had seen on the front lines and in the riotous streets of Barcelona. Blair lacked the clout to get the word out on his own. When he had tried to report the facts about the ruthless Soviet oppression in Spain, the *New Statesman* suddenly had no use for his dispatches.

The fact that Blair had fought for those "untrustworthy" elements made him a marked man. "This was not a round up of criminals," he would write, "it was merely a reign of terror. I was not guilty of any definite act, but I was guilty of Trotskyism." Although wounded on the front lines, Blair was forced into hiding, and when the opportunity presented, he fled the country.

Back in England, Blair attempted to publish his elegantly written and carefully reported account in book form, but the Anglo-American literary establishment had no interest. Finally, a small British press published *Homage to Catalonia* under Blair's pen name, George Orwell. The book sold six hundred copies in his lifetime. No American publisher would touch it until after he died in 1950. If nothing else, Orwell's Spanish adventure provided the nightmare blueprint for his futuristic classic, *1984*. As to Dos Passos, fully disillusioned, he would abandon the left altogether, and when he did, America's literary critics decided that his talent had abandoned him.

It was into this morass of intrigue and deceit that the *New York Times* sent the seemingly innocent Herbert Matthews. Then in his late thirties, Matthews wrote with the wide-eyed wonder of a cub reporter. Although there is no evidence to suggest that he was the "rabid Red partisan" the Catholic Church accused him of being, his dispatches make one wonder. Media critic Knightley, like most observers, sees no more than an "open, honest bias." Still, as Knightley notes, that bias "affected his judgment" and led Matthews to see the war as a "struggle against the forces of evil."

Orwell and Dos Passos arrived in Spain with the same mind frame as Matthews. Reality changed their minds. Reality even got to Hemingway, who was not quite the dupe the Comintern hoped he would be. His novel *For Whom the Bell Tolls,* written soon after the war, showed the treacherous underside of the Soviet's Spanish adventure. But Matthews had little use for reality. He remained as blind in leaving Spain as he did upon arriving.

Matthews's 1971 book, *A World in Revolution,* shows almost no awareness of the story he missed. He does admit that the "disorder in the country got completely out of hand" after the 1936 election, prompting the generals to rebel. As to the horrific attacks on Catholicism, those were the result of its "extremely, almost medievally, orthodox" outlook. Stalin "reluctantly" sent aid to the Republicans in October 1936 only to counter the aid Italy and Germany had sent to Franco. After Stalin "saved" the Loyalists, "The war took on the semblance of democracy against fascism, and it was this aspect, more than anything that caused liberals every-where in the world to champion the Republican cause."

Matthews admits to being one of those "who championed the cause." He has no regrets. After all, as any clear-thinking progressive could see, the Republican cause was one of "justice, legality, morality, decency." Although Matthews acknowledged reading Orwell's *Homage to Catalonia,* he fully ignores its content. He rejects as paranoid Orwell's Catalonian-derived vision "of a world turned into a police state." He revels instead in his righteous and romantic memory of Spain and of the "warm, generous, brave, and always friendly" folks like Hemingway who made that time so memorable.

At the end of the day, of course, the Republicans lost, and this Matthews believes to have been a "tragedy." If they had prevailed, he is confident that victory "would not have led to a communist Spain." In the way of evidence, Matthews claims to have known Premier Juan Negrin and understood "the strength of the Spanish and Russian communists." Just as Franco booted the Italians and Germans at war's end, Matthews is sure that Negrin would have sent Stalin packing.

It is at this point one recalls Martin Amis's "lacuna," that rat hole into which good progressives shove sordid socialist realities. Willful disbelief is a more accurate way of describing the phenomenon than fraud, but the result is the same. Evil submerges to surface another day. In a book entitled *Why the Revolution,* one would expect some accounting of why the Republicans lost. It is not forthcoming. Matthews chooses not to mention how the Soviets liquidated the Republican leadership, bled the Spanish treasury of all its gold, and abandoned the Loyalists to defeat just months before signing the notorious non-aggression pact with Nazi Germany, one that had been years in the planning.

As to Juan Negrrin, the *Black Book* claims that the NKVD installed him as a puppet, one "in thrall" to the Soviets. The Soviets put him there to do the dirty non-work that his predecessor refused to do, namely to turn his head while the NKVD liquidated the indigenous Marxist faction, POUM. More damning, the *Black Book* quotes a letter from Negrin to Matthews himself subtly outlining his intentions to do just that. Koch agrees, calling Negrin "obedient and corrupt," an opportunist whose major claim to fame had been helping the Soviets loot the Spanish treasury. The Soviets named Negrin's faction the "Victory Party" as kind of an Orwellian inside joke. According to Koch, the Soviets had no interest in victory, and if they had, a victorious Spain would have looked very much like a Soviet satellite.

No set of facts could shake Matthews from his wide-eyed progressive wonder. "I still say," he writes in summary, "that the Loyalists wrote a glorious page in Spanish history."

Superficially at least, there seems little out of the ordinary in Matthews's background. He was born in 1900 in New York City, enlisted in World War I but got to France after the fighting was over, and returned to New York to study Romance languages at Columbia University. The fact that he studied at Columbia in the same time frame that Margaret Mead, Lillian Hellman, and Whittaker Chambers also studied there suggests the potential of that time and place for radicalism, but if Matthews indulged, he did so quietly. In his prime, he would admit only to being an "old-fashioned liberal." Indeed, he bristled when in 1968 an assistant secretary of state publicly called him an "extreme leftist."

In Spain, Matthews was just one willfully blind reporter out of many, but he parlayed his experience with things Spanish to become the *Times'* principal authority on Latin America. In fact, he wrote virtually all of the *Times* editorials on Latin America from 1949-1967, a frightening thought. It was this prime position at the world's most influential newspaper that gave his reporting on Castro so much weight.

For Castro, deceiving Matthews about the scope of his ambitions proved even easier than deceiving him about the size and strength of his force. All he had to do was talk. For this more sophisticated second act in the guerilla theater, Matthews provided the perfect audience of one. Had he been a Soviet agent, he could not have been more effective. His February 24, 1957, report in the *Times* was all that Castro could hope for and more.

After much breast beating about how he alone has gotten to see this "flaming symbol" of the revolution, Matthews addresses the critical question of Castro's intentions. He admits that Castro heads "a revolutionary movement that calls itself socialistic," but he cautions the generally conservative 1957 *New York Times* reader not to worry.

"The program is vague and couched in generalities," writes Matthews, "but it amounts to a new deal for Cuba, radical, democratic, and therefore anti-communist." The "new deal" reference reads like so much Popular Front agitprop. In fact, Castro's "new deal" went well beyond anything even Eleanor Roosevelt might have imagined. Besides, Castro nursed a deep hatred for things American.

His claim that Castro was "anti-communist" suggests that, at best, Matthews had been hoaxed. Castro's two closest confidantes, his brother Raul and Ernesto "Che" Guevara, were communists from the beginning. In 1957, the same year as the Matthews interview, Guevara wrote to a friend, "My ideological training means that I am one of those people who believe that the solution to the world's problems is to be found behind the Iron Curtain." There could be no greater proof of Che's love for Lenin than the fact that he named his son "Vladimir."

It is impossible to believe that Raul Castro and Guevara did not influence Fidel in both style and substance. Guevara had been with Castro since 1955. As a commander of a detachment, he gained, as the *Black Book* notes, "a reputation for ruthlessness." On one occasion, he had a child shot to death without trial for stealing a little food. His close comrade, Regis Debray, described Che as "an authoritarian through and through." He was captured and executed during his futile effort to spread the Marxist-Leninist gospel to an unappreciative Bolivia. Matthews missed all of this, and not just in 1957. "Che Guevara," he would write four years after Che's death, "was one of those people who bolster a man's faith in the human race."

As Castro began his two-year march on Havana, the favored Matthews saw no sign of the Marxist revolution to come. "He has strong ideas of liberty, democracy, social justice, the need to restore the Constitution," Matthews wrote of Castro in that pivotal 1957 article. Disarmed by Matthews's authoritative reports, the CIA and the U.S. State Department offered no resistance. In fact, most American diplomats supported Castro enthusiastically. Meanwhile, the American media treated Castro as something of a folk hero, a cross between Robin Hood and George Washington. The romance, however, did not last long. No sooner did Castro take power in January 1959 than he began to renege on every promise he had made to Matthews and the Cuban people.

"There is no question," writes biographer Geyer, "that Fidel had intended a far more radical revolution than he, at first, expounded." She quotes a speech Castro made in December 1961 to this point: "Naturally, if we had said that we were Marxist-Leninists in the heights of Pico Turquino when we were only a handful of men, we never would have arrived in the plains."

When Castro and his men did arrive, they wasted little time disabusing their supporters of any hopes they might have had for a constitutional democracy. The *Black Book* narrates the all too familiar litany of

Marxist abuses. Castro and his comrades summarily executed six hundred Batista supporters within the first five months, often after carnival-like show trials in an open-air stadium. They quickly began removing democrats from the government. They radicalized the agrarian reform program and started seizing estates. They shut down the independent newspapers. They drove protesting priests into exile and infiltrated the church that remained. They forced the judiciary to surrender its independence. They organized an extensive intelligence service with watches in every neighborhood. They savagely oppressed homosexuals. And, of course, they indefinitely cancelled elections—all of this within two years of taking power. By the end of decade, the Castro government had executed between 7,000 and 10,000 political opponents, imprisoned 30,000 more, and driven several hundred thousand into exile, many of whom drowned at sea. Regardless of these abuses, Matthews, writing at the end of that same decade, remained convinced that Castro's "solid virtues and ideals far outweigh the weaknesses."

In his 1964 book, *Cuba,* something of a primer on the island's history, Matthews acknowledges that Castro may have used the "wrong means." He balances that, however, by speaking of Castro's eagerness "to do what is best for Cuba and the Cuban people." Castro has, after all, made life for Cuba's children "more exciting" and the distribution of wealth "more equal." If his government has gone wrong, it is largely a matter of "youthful inexperience and amateurishness." In Matthews's eyes, when all is said and done, Castro stands as "one of the most extraordinary men of our times."

Even Jayson Blair recognized that Matthews had dramatically misreported this story. "I was now in the same category as Herbert Matthews," Blair laments, "the reporter who described Fidel Castro in the *Times'* pages as an 'agrarian reformer' who supported democracy while ignoring evidence that he was torturing and murdering his own people."

To no one's surprise but Matthews's, the *New York Times* eventually yielded to public outrage and "muzzled" its ace Cuba beat reporter. "Cuba was an open book to me," protested Matthews. If so, he fatally misread it.

Ye Shall Be as Gods

In 1937, shortly before moving to Alger Hiss's apartment, Whittaker Chambers marveled at his little girl as she happily sat in her high chair and ate her porridge. "She was the most miraculous thing that ever happened in my life," Chambers recalls in his classic memoir, *Witness*.

As he watched her, he zeroed in "on the delicate convolutions of her ear—those intricate perfect ears." It was at this unlikely moment that he began his break with communism, a faith that he had served zealously for the previous twelve years:

> The thought passed through my mind: "No, those ears were not created by any chance coming together of atoms in nature (the communist view). They could have been created only by immense design. The thought was involuntary and unwanted. I crowded it out of my mind. But I never wholly forgot it or the occasion. I had to crowd it out of my mind. If I had completed it, I should have had to say: Design presupposes God.

As Chambers would come to see, the individual makes but one profound choice in his life: "God or man." For the first many years of his adult life, Chambers had chosen man, "the second oldest faith," the one first preached to humanity under the Tree of the Knowledge of Good and Evil with the beguiling words, "Ye shall be as gods."

For Chambers, communism was simply the boldest manifestation of that faith—"the vision of man's mind displacing God as the creative intelligence of the world." This was, by the way, not man as historically known, the one created in the image of God. Rather this was man as biologically rendered, the chance product of the forces of nature, "the most intelligent of all the animals."

This humanist vision was the tie that bound progressives of all stripes together. What distinguished the committed communist from the rest of the dissident lot was his "moral strength." With the tools of "science and technology" in hand, the "New Communist Man" did not flinch from reorganizing the world according to his highest powers of reason. He had the strength to act, the heart to endure, and the will to prevail—by any means necessary.

"I am not and have never been a member of the Communist Party," Alger Hiss said under oath on August 5, 1948, and calmly refuted Chambers's accusation to the contrary. The House Un-American Activities Committee had subpoenaed Chambers two days before. Then a senior editor at *Time* magazine, Chambers had testified reluctantly.

Hiss, however, was not content to deny his communist ties. "So far as I know," he added, "I have never laid eyes on [Chambers], and I should like the opportunity to do so." The unruffled demeanor of Alger Hiss unnerved the HUAC members, who had trusted Chambers, but it did not surprise Chambers. He knew from experience that Hiss had the strength to be a communist, "that sense of moral superiority which makes communists though caught in crime, berate their opponents with withering self-righteousness." What would have shocked Chambers is if Hiss had yielded and wept and told the truth.

It would take fifty years to satisfy the educable among the cultural establishment that on this memorable August day Hiss was lying through his teeth. The only proof that many on the left would accept, and even then kicking and screaming, came from the hardest of lefts, the people who had supervised both Chambers and Hiss, the Soviets themselves. In the interim, Hiss seduced America's easily-led progressive elite into perhaps the most preposterously enduring multimedia fraud in American history, a fifty-year road show whose fictions were obvious to the disinterested observer from day one.

The story deserves retelling. In January 1980, when Mary McCarthy shattered Lillian Hellman's world, one of the first friends to rush to her side was fellow New Yorker, Alger Hiss. This was not unlike him. Even Chambers spoke of Hiss's "great gentleness" and his "deep considerateness." In addition to their shared contempt for the truth, Hiss and Hellman had much in common, including the year of their respective births, 1904.

Like Hellman, Hiss had all the quietly right opportunities to become a communist. At Johns Hopkins in the perfervid 1920s, he may not have studied Marx or Lenin as his friendly biographer, John Chabot Smith, is at pains to assure the reader. But every influence on Hiss that Smith lists had the potential, if not the outright intent, to separate him from his traditional beliefs: the Fabian socialist George Bernard Shaw, whom Hiss "revered"; Sinclair Lewis, the man who had unmasked America's "Main Street"; the "anti-war" Maxwell Anderson; the self-declared communist Theodore Dreiser; and that hometown "scourge of middle-class values," H.L. Mencken.

At Harvard Law School during the Sacco and Vanzetti years, Hiss fell under the sway of the ubiquitous Felix Frankfurter. In turn, Frankfurter recommended Hiss to the man who "most influenced" Hiss during his formative year, the legendary Supreme Court Judge Oliver Wendell Holmes. Hiss, who worked for Holmes as a private secretary, remembered him fondly as "a skeptic of the first order," one who "denied the existence of God." As Holmes would remind Hiss, "Man's highest good is to do his own work well and enjoy the doing of it."

Once Hiss had left Holmes's employ, wife Priscilla continued his progressive education. Hiss had met the "modern" and politically "advanced" young woman in 1924. But it was not until 1929—one marriage, one child, one affair with a married man, and one abortion later—that Priscilla consented to marry Hiss. In 1930, Priscilla joined a Socialist Party branch in New York and likely encouraged her husband to do the same.

Although the contours have not been fully mapped, Hiss chose a speedy route to communism. Having rejected God, he now saw FDR's 1933 inauguration as a "holy moment." Soon after, Frankfurter urged Hiss to take a post at the new Agricultural Adjustment Administration, and this he did. There, he fell in with other idealistic young men presumably keen on changing the world faster than FDR could or would, and by 1935, Hiss had joined a Soviet spy ring known to history as the Harold Ware Group.

One can only infer why and how Hiss reached the destination he reached. In his own retelling, he never did become a communist. In fact, he bristled when counseled to beg forgiveness for his past as the indiscretions of a radical youth. By his own lights, he had never even been "a parlor pink."

Chambers, of course, leaves a much clearer record. Three years older than Hiss, he endured a childhood that was comparably unsettled. Each of their fathers abandoned them as young boys, Hiss's father by suicide. Each lost a sibling to suicide as well. They both lived lives with middle-class expectations but without middle-class means.

There were obvious differences. More depressive and introspective than Hiss, Chambers sought answers early on to the large questions that seemed to engulf him. He flirted with the Fabian Socialism that Hiss revered but moved on quickly to Lenin. "Only in communism," he writes in *Witness*, "had I found any practical answer at all to the crisis, and the will to make that answer work." One day in 1925, after a deep contemplative moment on a park bench, he stood up, left Columbia University where he was studying, and sought out the Communist Party.

Chambers would meet Hiss ten years later, now as a secret agent of that same party. He had been sent to Washington to organize a new apparatus, and as his first *apparatchik*, he was offered Hiss, a rising star in the Ware Group. Hiss would not disappoint. He left the AAA to serve as counsel for a Senate committee investigating munitions. And from there, he moved on to the State Department. At State, he proved willing and able to funnel documents to Chambers.

Hiss proved the better communist. When Chambers finally broke with the Party in 1938, he stopped by the Hiss home in Georgetown to explain himself. Despite a chilly reception from the couple, who had been tipped off to his defection, Chambers tried to make his case. He recited the "political mistakes and crimes" of the Party: the "deliberate murder by mass starvation" of millions of peasants; the betrayal of the Spanish Republican government; the Great Terror then at its peak; and more. When finally Chambers begged Hiss to quit the Party as well, Hiss flared back in anger, "What you have been saying is just mental masturbation." The two would not meet for another ten years.

When they did meet in 1948, the seeming advantage was all Hiss's. The political gods had been kind to him. Tall and trim, with his academic pedigree and patrician bearing, Hiss had advanced swiftly through the State Department to become director of the Office of Special Political Affairs. In that role, he worked closely with Secretary of State Edward Stettinus.

In February 1945, Hiss had traveled with Stettinus to the Yalta Conference in the Soviet Union. There FDR, Churchill, and Stalin divided the world among them, much to Stalin's satisfaction. At the very least, Hiss helped draft the documents that sealed the deal. After the conference, he was also able to visit Moscow.

In the spring of 1945, Hiss helped Stettinus plan for the new United Nations then housed in San Francisco. On an interim basis, Hiss even served as the U.N.'s first secretary general. Also helping Stettinus, oddly enough, was Hollywood Ten stalwart Dalton Trumbo. "In the two weeks preceding the trip [to the Pacific]," Trumbo wrote casually to a friend, "I went to San Francisco and ghosted Stettinus's Report to the Nation on the Conference." Trumbo would later deny that Hiss "brought" him to San Francisco. But if not Hiss, who did?

After the war, his increasingly wary superiors finessed Hiss out of the State Department, and he accepted a prestigious position as president of the Carnegie Foundation for International Peace. Elegant and quintessentially Anglo-Saxon, Hiss moved in the best of circles. His establishment friends were appropriately appalled when the self-described "short, squat, solitary" Chambers had come out of nowhere to malign Hiss before this committee of know-nothings. When Hiss coldly rebutted

Chambers's charges two days later, his friends cheered. Biographer Smith described Hiss's presentation as a "triumph."

"Most of the press were on his side," adds Smith. Many of the establishment papers weighed in with scathing editorials about the already unpopular HUAC. That next morning, President Truman was reported to have mocked the pursuit of communists in government as a political "red herring." He didn't, but he let the report stand. The committee was in a panic. Most of its members wanted to drop Hiss and move on to some more vulnerable prey. It took a first-term congressman from California to check the retreat. The young Richard Nixon finally convinced his colleagues that they did not have to prove that Hiss was a communist. That would be admittedly difficult. They only had to prove that Hiss was a liar, and this they could do by showing he knew Chambers.

Hiss and Chambers had to meet. Their first public confrontation, this "sad play" in Chambers's words, took place twelve days after the Hiss denial. It bordered on the surreal. At first, Hiss feigned uncertainty as to whether he had ever even seen Chambers before.

"Will you ask him to say something," Hiss said to Nixon. When Chambers began to speak, Hiss looked puzzled. He then said to Chambers, as he might to a small child, "Would you mind opening your mouth wider?" Chambers complied. Preposterous as it seemed to Chambers and Nixon, Hiss wanted to check his dental work.

Still faking ignorance, Hiss asked that Chambers name the dentist who had done the work. Nixon could take no more of this dumb show. As he knew, the two men and their families had been intimates for four years. Chambers had even stayed with the Hisses on several occasions. They all looked much the same as they had just ten years ago.

"Excuse me," Nixon interrupted. "Before we leave the teeth, Mr. Hiss, do you feel that you would have to have the dentist tell you what he did to the teeth before you could tell anything about this man?"

"The comedy had gone far enough," Nixon had concluded and with good reason. A few minutes into this first official encounter, it should have been plain to all who were willing to see that Chambers was telling the truth, and Hiss wasn't even coming close.

Still, the comedy persisted. Hiss pleaded his innocence through multiple hearings and trials before finally being convicted for perjury. In March 1951, after exhausting his appeals, Hiss entered federal prison, a convicted traitor in the eyes of the nation. There, he met Morton Sobell, who had recently been convicted along with Julius and Ethel Rosenberg of passing nuclear secrets to the Soviets. Sobell assured Hiss that "he and the Rosenbergs had been framed." The Rosenbergs would generate their own library of supportive literature, culminating in a haunting cameo come-back for Ethel in the 1990 Pulitzer Prize-winning play, *Angels in America*. As the Soviet archives proved, the Rosenbergs too were as guilty as sin.

In 1952, Chambers published his stunning eight-hundred-page masterwork, *Witness*. Not only was it beautifully written and well argued, but it was also exquisitely detailed. This case seemed to be closed. Hiss knew better. In late 1954, he left prison. A wiser man—or a weaker one—would have heeded his wife's pleas and faded quietly into oblivion. But this was not Hiss. As Chambers understood better than anyone, Hiss had the "moral strength" to persist. He also had a keen understanding of the way the cultural establishment worked. After all, he was its golden boy. His values were its values.

In his insightful book, *Alger Hiss's Looking Glass War*, distinguished law professor G. Edward White traces Hiss's relentless forty-two-year generalship in his battle for vindication. The story is an extraordinary one. Hiss was still in prison when the first literary salvo was fired on his behalf. In 1953, shortly after the publication of *Witness*, William Allen Jowitt, then Lord Chancellor of England and the country's highest legal authority, weighed in with *The Strange Case of Alger Hiss*. In addition to his jabs at American justice, Jowitt raised the question of Chambers's sanity. "I should be profoundly interested," he wrote, "to hear the opinion of distinguished American psychiatrists on all the new circumstances revealed in *Witness*."

While most Americans read *Witness* as the testament of faith it was meant to be, Jowitt and many other Anglo-American progressives saw it as the delusions of a madman. "True wisdom comes from the overcoming of suffering and sin," Chambers had written. But for Jowitt and company, still in thrall of the not yet discredited Freud, sin was a delusion, and suffering was relieved on a psychiatrist's couch.

Jowitt also introduced a theme that would gain momentum over the decades, namely that U.S. agencies, needing to appear zealous in their pursuit of communists, were looking for scapegoats. Fred Cook added imagined detail in a *Nation* article that he lengthened to a 1958 book, *The Unfinished Story of Alger Hiss*. Lacking any new evidence, Cook speculated about Chambers's mental state, his likely hatred of Hiss, and his complicity with "official collaborators" who may have helped him "in the perfection of his story and the completeness of his deed." In 1956, Hiss weighed in with his own brief, *In the Court of Public Opinion*. Although the book proved too dry and legalistic for popular taste, it succeeded in keeping his name and cause alive.

Intrigued by the rush of pro-Hiss books, and particularly by their revelations about Chambers's mental health, psychiatrist Dr. Meyer A. Zeligs took up Hiss's cause as a crusade. Hiss chose to cooperate, and why not? He was confident that Zeligs would ignore any evidence that would hurt him. As a psychiatrist, Zeligs could explore with some authority the themes that had been introduced during Hiss's trials, namely Chambers's alleged homoerotic obsession with Hiss and his pathological lying. As the details of the case faded from public memory, Hiss reasoned, the more attractive personality might very well prevail in the only court that now mattered, that of public opinion.

Chambers, who would not cooperate with Zeligs, died in 1961, two years after Zeligs began his research. Regardless, Zeligs felt he had enough insight on Chambers to render an accurate diagnosis, which he presumed to do in *Friendship and Fratricide*. "As a work of scholarship, which it purported to be," writes G. Edward Wilson, "*Friendship and*

Fratricide was an almost comical failure." Where the book did succeed, however, was in revealing the tragic early history of the Hiss family and thereby reclaiming for Hiss his often-overlooked humanity.

As much as the books and articles helped Hiss's cause, it took a tectonic shift in national mood to reorder reality in his favor. The sixties had arrived. The New Left had no more reverence for "the unholy trinity" that had "fabricated" his case than Hiss did. The young activists were learning to despise Nixon and dread J. Edgar Hoover. As to the third member of Hiss's trinity, Chambers, most did not even know who he was. The cultural establishment had shoved him into that rat hole, Amis's "lacuna." Nor did the young honor or even respect "the theology of anti-communism" that, as Hiss would have it, bound this trinity together. Without even trying hard, Hiss soon found himself as a star on the college lecture circuit.

The Hiss narrative was trickling down and to the center. In 1973, the popular and youthful *Rolling Stone* magazine ran a feature in which Hiss's son, Tony, representing the magazine, interviewed his father. One exchange during this Watergate-heated interview nicely captures the way in which Hiss hitched his star to the progressive supernova:

> Tony: Talk has been going round Washington recently that all the political trials, beginning with the Hiss case, were fixed.
>
> Alger: Yeah, and there's a certain unpleasant similarity about all of them, that they're contrived for political purposes. But the big difference, I think, is the difference in public opinion, so the juries now aren't led by the nose. At the time when my case came up, the Cold War was already well under way, there was a great deal of hysteria.

Hiss positions himself here as just one in a long line of progressives who have fallen victim to the prevailing "hysteria" of the day. This was a tradition forged by Sacco and Vanzetti and friends and trotted out by just about every leftist lawbreaker since. What makes Hiss's use of the strategy particularly tasteless is his exploitation of the natural trust of a son for his father. Without shame or regret, he turns the otherwise innocent Tony into a conduit for his lies.

By the mid 1970s, Hiss had reason to believe that America would absolve him. In 1974, the architect of his downfall, Richard Nixon, left office in disgrace. Watergate had revealed him to be the liar and abuser of power Hiss had long claimed. In 1976, John Chabot Smith released his entirely sympathetic book, *Alger Hiss: The True Story*. And in 1977, Tony Hiss followed up with *Laughing Last*, whose very title made vindication seem like an already done deal.

For a moment, the Smith book gave the illusion of final authority. A respected journalist, Smith had covered the Hiss trials for the *New York Herald Tribune* twenty-five years earlier. He had picked up the biography project from *New York Times* reporter Alden Whitman after Whitman fell ill. From afar, this book had all the appearance of unbiased objectivity. But not up close. Whitman himself had pled the fifth before a congressional committee on the question of his own communist affiliations. Smith acknowledges that he had been accused of being "pro-Hiss" in his reporting during the trials. He also spent six weeks in the Soviet Union in 1935 presumably to research his senior thesis at Princeton. To be sure, he disavows any Soviet sympathies, but he does so to the point of excess, claiming more than once, for instance, that Chambers—or any American who worked for a communist revolution—"had to be some kind of a nut."

Whatever his politics, Smith delivered a classic, front-loaded piece of progressive agitprop. Like those last pre-Copernican astronomers, who struggled to fit each newly discovered planet into the orbit of an earth-centered universe, Smith vainly sought a rationale for each bit of incriminating evidence. In a case where a man is guilty as accused, however, all evidence, old and new, is incriminating.

Smith repeats the old canards about Hiss protecting his wife and his allegedly homosexual son even to the point of refusing a lie detector test.

For all his assumed brilliance, the Hiss of Smith's imagination is constantly digging himself "into deeper trouble" by making one "more damaging mistake" after another, and if he's not, his lawyer is. And finally, it is Chambers who plays the "Other Dude" role in Hiss's TODDI defense. To protect his job at *Time* magazine, which allegedly hung on his anti-communist credentials, Chambers framed Hiss even though he knew he wasn't a communist. If Chambers seemed sincere, it was only because he was such a "psychiatric case" that he had come to believe his own fantasies about spying.

Absurd as it seems, the narrative more or less worked. An April 1976 *Harper's* poll of American intellectuals found them split down the middle on Hiss's innocence. The more progressive of the respondents, Lillian Hellman and Noam Chomsky among them, backed Hiss. If he had not won a clear-cut victory, Hiss had at least achieved a level of respectability, and history seemed to be listing in his favor.

Hiss, however, knew he had one more roadblock to circumvent. In 1971, a little known professor at Smith College, Allen Weinstein, had published an article in the *American Scholar,* "The Alger Hiss Case Revisited." The carefully written article advanced the thesis, fairly typical for its time, that there was not enough evidence to support the charge that Hiss had been a Soviet agent.

A dogged researcher, Weinstein chose to pursue the case more comprehensively. Knowing the mindset of the American intellectual, Hiss chose to cooperate and turned over his defense files to Weinstein. Weinstein also took advantage of the liberalized disclosure laws and gained access to Hiss's FBI files. Perhaps even more importantly, he listened closely to those who had known Chambers at the time he broke with communism.

In March 1976, Weinstein screwed up his nerve to visit Hiss at his New York apartment. Although he had interviewed Hiss on numerous occasions earlier, this visit was going to be different to the point of painful. After some anxious small talk, Weinstein finally let go. "When I began working on this book four years ago," he told Hiss, "I thought that I would be able to demonstrate your innocence, but unfortunately, I have to tell you that I cannot; that my assumption was wrong."

"I'm not surprised," Hiss answered coolly and said no more.

Weinstein stumbled forward to fill the void, telling Hiss, among other things, "Every important question in my mind about Chambers's veracity has been resolved." For some indefinite time, Hiss refused to make eye contact, and when he finally looked up, he said dismissively, "I've always known you were prejudiced against me."

Weinstein's book *Perjury* was released in spring 1978. The first reviews were largely favorable and seemed to derail Hiss's campaign for vindication. Some reviewers went so far as to suggest that the case was closed, but again Hiss knew better. Before its publication, he had gotten hold of page proofs of *Perjury*, made notations, and quite likely circulated them among his allies.

Only a week after *Perjury* was published, *Nation* editor Victor Navasky retaliated with a nine-page essay, "The Case Not Proved against Alger Hiss." He accused Weinstein of being "an embattled partisan, hopelessly mired in the perspective of one side" and made him out to be a sloppy and biased researcher. Of course, he could not refute any of Weinstein's major contentions, but that didn't matter. He had shifted the center of controversy from Hiss to Weinstein. When leftwing journalists discovered that Weinstein had confused two men with the same name and depicted one—wrongly and at some legal expense—as a communist, they mocked Weinstein far and wide. Whether Weinstein had intended to or not, Hiss supporters could see that he had gone over to the enemy, and it was now open season on the unwary professor.

By this time, the left had to protect Hiss. He had wormed his way into the core of progressive mythology. If he were a Soviet agent as accused, then others might have been as well, and "McCarthyism" would lose its symbolic punch. That could not be.

By this time too, the left had one more reason to bury Chambers. In his exhaustively researched book, Weinstein uncovered the truth behind Chambers's rumored homosexuality. As Chambers told the FBI in 1949, he had begun yielding to his homosexual urges soon after he had gone underground as a Soviet agent, but always anonymously and never with Party members. He abandoned this practice at the same time and in the same manner he abandoned communism—"with God's help," after "embracing, for the first time, religion." Chambers would go on to become a dedicated Christian, a dutiful husband and father, and an inspiration to young conservatives like William Buckley Jr. From the perspective of the cultural establishment, his story was pure poison.

In 1980, John Lowenthal renewed the counteroffensive with a film, *The Trials of Alger Hiss.* Despite its documentary nature, the film reinforced the idea of an innocent man caught up in an anti-red hysteria. In 1983, the Public Broadcasting System (PBS) produced *Concealed Enemies,* a four-hour dramatization of the Hiss case. This presentation did much the same, picturing Hiss in the end as a naïve idealist who had underestimated his enemies. In 1988, Hiss continued his own rehabilitation with another memoir, *Recollections of a Life.* If he could not secure public absolution post-Weinstein, he could at least perpetuate the ambiguity.

And then the Berlin Wall fell, and the archives opened, and this willful octogenarian had one last spectacular moment in the sun. Filmmaker John Lowenthal commissioned a Russian official, General Dmitri Volkogonov, to do some research. Volkogonov reviewed the KGB files and presented Lowenthal with a one-page letter, a veritable bill of health. The letter declared that after examining a "great amount of materials," Volkogonov had found not one document to substantiate the allegation that "Mr. A. Hiss collaborated with the intelligence sources of the Soviet Union." Not content to clear Hiss on the Soviet side, the willing Volkogonov ascribed Hiss's conviction to "false information or judicial error." "You can tell Alger Hiss," the Volkogonov letter concluded, "that the heavy weight should be lifted from his heart."

The major media exploded in a collective sigh of relief. All three major networks reported on the Volkogonov memorandum the day it was released, with CBS claiming that Hiss had been "apparently exonerated." The *New York Times* and the *Washington Post* chimed in with comparable claims. The news magazines followed suit, *Newsweek* calling the finding "bittersweet vindication." The *New Yorker* published an essay by Tony Hiss. "Now people everywhere know," wrote Tony, "what my family and my father's devoted friends and well-wishers have always known—that Alger Hiss was not a communist, not a spy, not a traitor."

In the way of meting out justice, God deemed that Alger Hiss should live four more years. They weren't pretty. Weinstein immediately went on the offensive. He pointed out the obvious, namely that Volkogonov had only reviewed KGB files. Chambers had always been clear that he and Hiss had worked for the GPU, Soviet military intelligence, another operation altogether. The embarrassed Volkogonov now admitted that he had, in fact, only spent two days in the KGB archives and that Lowenthal had pushed him "to say things of which I was not fully convinced." Needless to say, the media did not welcome the retraction and paid it little heed, but worse was yet to come.

In that same year, 1992, Yale University Press secured access to a major Russian archive. The ensuing research resulted in the 1995 book, *The Secret World of American Communism,* which made clear that the American Communist Party had been fully controlled from Moscow. The book, though silent on Hiss, confirmed many of the details of Chambers's story. In July of 1995, the U.S. government opened its own files, the so-called Venona archives, a massive collection of the messages it had successfully decoded from the Soviet Union between 1942 and 1946. The files, however incomplete, were stunning. They showed that the Soviets had spies in every significant American military or diplomatic agency, no fewer than 349 in all. Among them was a particularly valuable agent, codenamed "Ales."

One message from a Washington-based NKVD agent to Moscow in March 1945 provided a good deal of detail about Ales. It told of how he had been working with the GPU since 1935, that he now managed a small group that included his own relatives, that it had been focusing on military information, that the whole group had just been awarded Soviet medals, and that Ales himself had gone to the Yalta conference and stopped afterward in Moscow to meet with the Soviet's deputy foreign minister. All details fit Alger Hiss, including the Moscow stopover after Yalta.

The Venona files led Weinstein and other researchers to look elsewhere in the Soviet archives, and almost everywhere they looked they found gold. Detail after detail confirmed Chambers's story and shot silver bullets into Hiss's undying heart. Now Weinstein could publish a new edition of *Perjury*, and the case was indeed closed.

Well, almost closed. On the very day of Hiss's death in November 1996, Peter Jennings reported on *ABC World News Tonight* that Hiss had "protested his innocence until the very end," and then added as an affirming, elegiac touch, "And last year, we reported that the Russian president Boris Yeltsin said that KGB files had supported Mr. Hiss's claim."

No evidence could or would ever breach the fact-proof barricades of the hardened left. In 1997, the same year he was declaring Mumia's innocence, Ward Churchill was declaring Hiss's as well. Specifically, Churchill attributed Hiss's perjury conviction to "doctored physical evidence and the almost certainly false testimony of former CP member Whittaker Chambers." Among the sources he cited for this bit of wisdom was Allen Weinstein's *Perjury*—an unwitting testament to the wide-ranging trumpery of Churchill's scholarship.

No Usable Political Meaning

In *Witness*, Whitaker Chambers tells a chilling story of a German diplomat who abandoned his Soviet sympathies literally overnight. His daughter, not comprehending the change, told Chambers how it happened:

"He was immensely pro-Soviet," she said, "and then—you will laugh at me—but you must not laugh at my father—and then—one night—in Moscow—he heard screams. That's all. Simply one night he heard screams."

Chambers did not laugh. He understood. Those screams don't just penetrate the mind. They penetrate the soul. The man who has not yet lost his humanity finally understands that those are the screams of another human "soul in agony." Chambers knew just where those screams had come from:

They come from husbands torn forever from their wives in midnight arrests. They come, muffled, from the execution cellars of the secret police, from the torture chambers of the Lubianka, from all the citadels of terror now stretching from Berlin to Canton. They come from those freight cars loaded with men, women, and children, the enemies of the communist state, locked in, packed in, left on remote sidings to freeze to death at night in the Russian winter. They come from minds driven mad by the horrors of mass starvation ordered and enforced as a policy of the communist state. They come from the starved skeletons, worked to death or flogged to death (as an example to others) in the freezing filth of sub-arctic labor camps. They come from children whose parents are suddenly, inexplicably taken away from them— parents they will never see again.

In progressive America, for the next fifty plus years, those screams would fall on shockingly deaf ears, none deafer than those of America's most internationally influential public intellectual, Noam Chomsky.

This calculated deafness speaks directly to the central deceit of Chomsky's career. "No party claims him," writes acolyte James Peck in the introduction of *The Chomsky Reader*. "He is a spokesman for no ideology." Peck perpetuates the fraud that the radical nature of Chomsky's dissent "fits nowhere" and that the real target of his righteous wrath is "the violence of the world."

This is nonsense. Chomsky has proven himself the world master of the Marxist shell game: deny Marxist horrors; imagine and expose Western ones. A week after 9/11, for instance, Chomsky was decrying America as a "leading terrorist state" whose "crimes against humanity" had left behind a "colossal number of victims." Yet two years after the onset of the most devastating mass slaughter post-Holocaust, the murderous ultra-communist rampage in Cambodia, Chomsky was publicly doubting whether it had ever happened.

Chomsky himself leaves no shortage of his clues as to how he came to despise the country into which he was born and in which has prospered. "In a certain sense," says Chomsky, "I grew up in an alien culture." He attended an experimental progressive school from infancy and felt fully estranged from the Irish and German Catholics in his Philadelphia neighborhood, whom he saw as fascist sympathizers. Although his parents were Roosevelt Democrats and Zionists, many of his uncles and cousins, especially those whom he loved to visit in New York, were communists or very nearly so.

Chomsky celebrated his thirteenth birthday on the day that the Japanese bombed Pearl Harbor. Given his precocious alienation, he might very well have blamed it on the United States. "I was rather skeptical about the Second World War," he observes. "I didn't know anyone who shared that skepticism." When he heard about the Hiroshima bombing at summer camp four years later, he walked off into the woods and stayed alone for hours. "I felt completely isolated." By this time in his life, the teenage Chomsky was deeply interested in radical politics "with an anarchist or leftwing (anti-Leninist) Marxist flavor."

At the age of sixteen, still living at home, Chomsky began his studies at the nearby University of Pennsylvania. There he received an unconventional B.A. that reflected his interest both in linguistics and philosophy. In 1955, he took his Ph.D. from Penn after having done most of his research at Harvard. With Ph.D. in hand, Chomsky headed off to MIT where he quickly and spectacularly made his reputation in linguistics, virtually revolutionizing the field with his theory of transformational-generative grammar. By the early 1960s, he was tenured, on top of his own world, and looking for new worlds to conquer.

In the early 1960s, David Horowitz seemed the least likely person to become Chomsky's future nemesis. At the time, Horowitz was moving through his political life on a parallel track, if anything even more swiftly than Chomsky. Both of Horowitz's parents were, in fact, Communist Party members, "loyal to the Soviet state" all the way through to Stalin's much lamented death.

In 1959, Horowitz graduated from Columbia University and left his native New York for the University of California at Berkeley. There, he joined up with other "red diaper babies," who more or less launched the movement that came to be known as the New Left. The New Left had embarked on much the same pilgrimage as the Old Left but without the baggage of Stalin and Stalinism. When the Israeli secret service, the Mossad, had slipped a copy of Khrushchev's secret speech denouncing Stalin out of the Soviet Union in 1956, the old Communist Party never fully recovered. With the brutal suppression of the Hungarian revolt that same year, the Party fell seriously out of fashion.

As his own contribution to the cause, Horowitz edited the first New Left publication, *Root and Branch,* and wrote the first book about the movement, *Student,* published in 1962. A month after the book's publication, he helped organize one of the earliest protests against a war most Americans were not even aware was being fought—the one in Vietnam.

On the east coast meanwhile, a newspaper strike in the winter of 1962-1963 left New York City's intellectual community without a suitable outlet for book reviews and discussion. In February 1963, a small group of publishing insiders filled the void with *The New York Review of Books (NYR).* With an all-star roster of contributors, NYR quickly emerged as the most influential intellectual publication in America. Lacking an established tradition, and feeding off the energy from the campuses, NYR could and did "progress" more quickly than its competitors. In his history of the publication, *Intellectual Skywriting,* Philip Nobile details how the publication turned almost overnight from a polite forum for literary discussion to a hotbed of radical politics. The cover headline of a late 1964 issue announced the bellwether review, "I.F. Stone on the Southeast Asia Mess."

Stone had achieved a unique niche in American journalism. When he died in June 1989, the reliable Peter Jennings of *ABC World News Tonight* described him as a "journalist's journalist." On the same occasion, the *Los Angeles Times* called him "the conscience of investigative journalism." Veteran PBS producer Bill Moyers accurately assessed his reputation fifteen years after his death as "America's premier independent journalist."

Philip Nobile, despite his New York intellectual credentials, was not afraid to question Stone's independence or his conscience. "There's no disputing that Stone was in love with Stalin's socialist paradise in the thirties," writes Nobile. And not just in the thirties—Stone faithfully followed the Stalinist line for the next twenty years. During the war, as the Venona files revealed, he attracted the attention of the NKVD who "greatly valued his work as a correspondent." According to Venona, the Soviets had approached Stone on several occasions. One cable suggests that the vacillating Stone was tempted by the extra income but feared jeopardizing the income he already had. Nowhere does he reject their overture outright.

In 1952, still in the thrall of the Soviets, Stone released *Hidden History.* The book served up the "then unappetizing view" that the United States had unilaterally launched the Korean War to advance its interests in Southeast Asia. In fact, Stone did not break with the Soviet Union until after a visit in the pivotal year of 1956. Eight years later, NYR laundered his reputation with front-page coverage.

From 1964 onwards, with Stone leading the charge, NYR grew

increasingly political and increasingly shrill. Nineteen sixty-seven marked what Nobile calls "the great leap leftward." By this time, Chomsky had finessed his academic capital into political credibility and was being taken seriously as a voice of the New Left. In February of that year, Chomsky contributed to NYR his own in-your-face manifesto, "The Responsibility of Intellectuals," a revised version of a speech he had given at Harvard a year before.

By this early date, long before the first serious public protests, Chomsky had thrown down the gauntlet before his more timid colleagues. "We can hardly avoid asking ourselves," Chomsky proclaimed, "to what extent the American people bear responsibility for the savage American assault on a largely helpless rural population in Vietnam." For the next four decades, Chomsky would continue to ask variations of this question. Given America's "utter disregard for the suffering and misery of the lower orders," the major variation in the re-asking would be the name of the country currently being squashed under the imperial U.S. jackboot.

Having reached the public stage after the Soviet Union had fallen out of fashion, Chomsky had to park his ill-disguised Marxist contempt for free enterprise and liberal democracy elsewhere. In this first flowering of his public career, he put his faith in Vietnam's National Liberation Front (NLF). "The facts are known to all who care to know," he pontificates in "The Responsibility of Intellectuals." The facts, as vetted by Chomsky, are that the NLF was an indigenous, purely political movement whose only weapons were "ideas" and whose only goal was to win "the minds and loyalties of the rural Vietnamese." Until mid-1964, Chomsky claims, help from Hanoi was limited to "doctrinal know-how and leadership personnel."

As leftists and as Frenchmen, the authors of *The Black Book of Communism* are not disposed to an easy pro-Americanism, especially on the subject of Vietnam. Rather, they let the facts speak for themselves. "The Indochinese Communist Party (ICP) got off to a bad start," report the authors. Soon after its creation in 1930, the ICP began executing its own dissidents and "liquidating local landowners by the hundreds" to create rural "soviets."

Heading up the ICP was Ho Chi Minh—"he who enlightens"—the nom de guerre for a man of many names. Born in Vietnam in 1890, Ho had moved to Europe as a young adult. He co-founded the French Communist Party in 1920 and went to Moscow in 1923 to train as a paid Comintern agent in which role he would return to Vietnam.

In the spring of 1945, the ICP launched a full scale armed struggle, paying less heed to the occupying Japanese than to "traitors" and "reactionaries" among its own ranks. After the Japanese surrendered, the ICP ramped up the terror, killing the leaders of the opposition parties and, as customary, Trotskyites of all ranks in the multiple thousands. When the French returned after the war, the ICP went underground and directed their energies against the colonialists.

It was only with the French capitulation in 1954 and the securing of the northern half of the country that the Vietnamese began to understand what terror was really like. "The scale of violence was extraordinary," reports the *Black Book*. Through a combination of lethal "land reform" and Stalinist intra-Party purges, the victorious "Democratic Republic of Vietnam" (DRV) executed an estimated 50,000 of its own citizens and imprisoned as many as 100,000 more. Millions meanwhile fled to the South, including at least 600,000 Catholics.

Chomsky, of course, claims that the North only began to send military aid to the NLF in 1964. This is wrong. As the *Black Book* reports, "In May 1959, the Vietnamese Communist Party made a secret decision to try to spread the war and support it by sending troops and arms, despite the immense cost, to the people of North Vietnam."

"It is the responsibility of intellectuals to speak the truth and expose lies," writes Chomsky imperiously, but he had no intention of doing that and never has. In the postwar period, disillusioned leaders from the North have confirmed that the Hanoi government essentially created the NLF

and controlled it from the beginning. The North's goal was never liberation but conquest. In other words, the United States was fighting a defensive war against a transparently Stalinist enemy from the very beginning,
not savagely assaulting rural innocents. An error of this magnitude should
have killed Chomsky's political career before it got untracked or at least
slowed it down, but it did neither. Chomsky was writing for an audience
that, to an increasing degree, cared as little about truth as he did.

To be sure, a few of the more moderate liberals resisted Chomsky.
Historian Arthur Schlesinger, for instance, scolded him for his "intellectual crookedness" and declared that "it has long been impossible to
believe anything he says." But the Schlesingers of that world had tolerated
too much intellectual dishonesty for too long to be effective.

Veteran CBS anchor Walter Cronkite had to be feeling the intellectual
heat on Martha's Vineyard and on the New York cocktail party circuits.
On February 27, 1968, after the Viet Cong's desperate Tet Offensive,
Cronkite gave his famous "we are mired in a stalemate" valedictory on
the CBS news. "My God," Lyndon Johnson is reported to have said on
hearing this, "if we've lost Cronkite, we've lost Middle America!"

"Truth is the first casualty of war," the old saying goes, and not
without justification. Nations typically sacrifice truth to promote victory.
But Vietnam represented the first major war in which a nation's cultural
elite sacrificed the truth to assure its own *defeat*. Cronkite's announcement represented not only a turning point in the war but also in the
culture. From that moment on, Cronkite and others would use the
literary-media complex to convince themselves and the millions of
impressionable Americans who heeded them that they were right in their
judgment. They would start by suppressing the truth about Tet—it was,
in fact, a military disaster for the North—and would end by suppressing
most inconvenient truths about the war and indeed about themselves.

Fortunately, military researcher B.G. Burkett has recovered many of
these truths. His efforts began innocently enough when he attempted to
raise money for a Vietnam memorial in Dallas in the late 1980s. A

Vietnam veteran himself, he found himself being rebuffed by one potential donor after another because of their perceptions of Vietnam veterans
as bedraggled, if not deranged. Using the Freedom of Information Act,
Burkett went to work addressing the myths surrounding the war, and
what he found is astonishing.

In 1972, for instance, Walter Cronkite and CBS showed a now classic
photo of a little Vietnamese girl running down the highway naked after a
napalm attack. As Burkett notes, this image "became the perfect illustration of America's 'indiscriminate' napalming of civilians." The incident
took place, however, in June 1972, when almost all American ground
troops had left. Nor were any American planes involved or American
advisors. The napalm was dropped by the South Vietnamese in response
to a brutal communist attack on a marketplace. After the war, the girl,
Kim Phuc, fled to the West.

It was a heavily promoted CBS documentary, *The Wall Within*, that
made Burkett aware of just how deeply fraud infected much, if not most,
expression about the war. Burkett tracked down the service records of the
six disturbed "trip-wire" Vietnam vets featured in the documentary only
to find that all six had concocted the grisly incidents that had allegedly
traumatized them. Some had not even been to Vietnam. Yet when the
men told the CBS producers and Dan Rather tales of assassinations,
civilian murders, and deaths of imaginary buddies, CBS aired their
stories without checking and refused to retract or apologize even when
confronted with the facts.

CBS was scarcely unique in its indifference to the truth. Burkett
reviewed the literature on Vietnam and found much the same indifference. In his and Glenna Whitley's book on the subject, *Stolen Valor*, he
cites one fraudulent account after another, many of which were best-
sellers and some of which have left a lasting impression.

Wallace Terry based his 1984 best-selling oral history, *Bloods*, which
was in turn made into a PBS documentary, on testimony that was often
fabricated and occasionally "wild fantasy." Terry recounts, for instance,

how one Air Force sergeant wiped out a troop of Viet Cong in black pajamas after they had seized the American embassy in Saigon. As it happens, the sergeant was never assigned to Saigon, no Viet Cong ever even entered the embassy, and the Viet Cong didn't wear black pajamas. Other tales in *Bloods*, says Burkett, were even "more ridiculous."

Terry also made the point that African Americans died disproportionately in Vietnam. Comparably, much of the furor around Mumia's death sentence centered on the disproportionate execution of blacks. Williams stresses this point in *Executing Justice*. Neither assertion is true. As Burkett shows, young black men died in Vietnam at a rate slightly less than whites. Likewise, as is easily proven, blacks convicted of murder are less likely to be executed than non-blacks.

In *Conduct Unbecoming*, his influential brief for the inclusion of gays in the military, the late Randy Shilts tells at length the story of Lt. Jerry Rosenbalm. As the story goes, Rosenbalm's enlisted man lover, Donald Winn, the "gay beret," was killed while heroically trying to rescue Rosenbalm during a Tet offensive firefight. So powerful was the story that Rosenbalm was asked to repeat it for a feature in *People* magazine and on ABC's *PrimeTime* Live.

With just a little checking, Burkett exposed the whole charade. Winn, in fact, entered the Army two years after Rosenbalm claimed to have met him, did not even attend OCS, let alone with Rosenbalm, was not a Green Beret, and died three years after Tet of cardiac arrest, much to the chagrin of his fiancée. "Apparently," writes Burkett, "Rosenbalm concocted the entire tale to present an episode of heroism and love by homosexuals in Vietnam." Winn's family was outraged.

Critics hailed Fred Wilcox's 1983 book about Agent Orange, *Waiting for an Army To Die*, as an ecological call to arms comparable to *Silent Spring*. For all the wrong reasons, the comparison is apt. What Wilcox failed to report is that this relatively benign defoliant has not shown any adverse impact even on the military aviators who were exposed to it as much as five or six days a week for up to twelve hours a day for a year. As an initiation rite, reports Burkett, new "ranch handers," as these aviators were called, had to drink a cup of the herbicide. In 1978, more than a thousand of these pilots entered a rigorous study on its effects. As of last count, they were healthier on the whole than the average American male of comparable age.

Perhaps the most influential war story to come out of Vietnam was the one told by Ron Kovic in his 1976 book *Born on the Fourth of July*, later made into a celebrated movie by Oliver Stone. Both the book and movie depict Kovic as a starry-eyed American teenager sent off by a duplicitous government to fight an immoral war only to be paralyzed for life. Kovic's military records tell another story altogether.

In fact, Kovic was wounded on his second tour of duty as a United States Marine. During his first tour, he had killed enemy soldiers and been commended for it. After that tour, he tirelessly campaigned to return to Vietnam and specifically into combat. "His writing about what happened to him," says Burkett of Kovic, "is dishonest at best and deliberately distorted at worst."

"I'm obviously telling Ron's story," Stone contended upon the movie's release, "I'm not screwing with the facts." But of course, Stone embellished upon an already disingenuous tale, adding a climactic police beating of the now anti-war Kovic at a Syracuse rally. In truth, there was no police violence at the Syracuse rally, and if there were, it would not have affected Kovic, as he was not there. Commenting on Stone's two Vietnam films, *Born on the Fourth of July* and *Platoon*, author and disabled Vietnam vet Richard Eilert commented, "They are saturated with so much hateful negativism that in the end the proper term to describe them is probably 'propaganda' or 'disinformation.'"

Oliver Stone's fellow dabbler in JFK conspiracy lore, attorney Mark Lane, wrote a book in 1970 called *Conversations with Soldiers*. Its full impact would not be felt for another thirty-four years. In the book, Vietnam veterans tell endless stories of atrocities and war crimes committed by themselves or their fellow soldiers. So absurd were so many of these tales that even establishment critics took Lane to task.

In a *New York Times* book review, for instance, Neil Sheehan showed that in case after case these presumed Vietnam vets had either not served in the capacity they claimed or not even served in Vietnam at all. When Sheehan asked Lane whether he had checked military records, Lane answered, "It's not relevant." Sheehan then asked an editor at Simon & Schuster whether he had checked their records. The editor had not, claiming that the military would just lie in any case and besides the book was published as an anti-war protest. "This kind of reasoning," wrote Sheehan, "amounts to a new McCarthyism, this time from the left. Any rumor, any accusation, any innuendo is repeated and published as truth."

Undaunted by the criticism, Lane helped a group called Vietnam Veterans Against the War (VVAW) organize what came to be known as the "Winter Soldier" investigation. A month after Sheehan's devastating review in the *New York Times,* "veteran" after veteran told Jane Fonda and other luminaries gathered in a Detroit hotel still more grisly Vietnam stories—many, if not most, fully imagined.

In April of that year, the VVAW staged a demonstration called "Dewey Canyon III," a "limited incursion into the country of Congress." This protest might have been lost to history save for the fact that among the protestors was aspiring Massachusetts politician John Kerry. After throwing what were presumed to be his own medals over a fence in front of the capitol, Kerry gave what seemed to be a spontaneous lecture to the Senate Foreign Relations committee on the various atrocities that Americans were committing in Vietnam.

In true JFK tradition, of course, John F. Kerry did not write his own speech. That, Burkett contends, was written for him by a Robert Kennedy speechwriter, Adam Walinsky, who also coached Kerry on how to deliver it. And of course too, those were not his own medals that Kerry threw over the fence. This he finally admitted when a reporter noticed his real medals on the wall of his Washington office. But this should not surprise.

Fraud defined the entire Winter Soldier operation. A decorated Air Force captain served as executive secretary for VVAW and penned the poem at the beginning of the book, *Winter Soldier Investigation.* He had apparently caught shrapnel in the spine while flying a plane into Da Nang in 1966, turned against the war, and helped organize the Winter Soldier protest. This was all well and good save for the fact that he was not a pilot, not a captain, had not served in Vietnam, and was, alas, not at all atypical.

As Kerry learned in 1971, and relearned in 2004, if one follows the progressive current, he can present almost any version of truth that he likes and get away with it. Critics outside the current like the Swift Boat veterans are irrelevant, and critics of conscience from within like Neil Sheehan can be ignored if the current is strong enough.

In January 1973, David Horowitz, by then the editor of the radical magazine, *Ramparts,* gave a memorable speech on Vietnam, a war that he described as "not so much a betrayal of American tradition, as its fulfillment." As to the execution of that war, he argued that it "ranks with the worst atrocities ever committed by one portion of the human race against another." When he finished, the listeners surged to their feet applauding. But this was not Berkeley Square. Those on their feet were not coffee house commandos. No, they were a thousand middle class professionals at a think tank symposium in the grand ballroom of the Shoreham Hotel in Washington D.C. The anti-war movement with all of its Marxist-inspired, anti-American dissembling had gone fully mainstream.

And then, unexpectedly, less than two years later, Horowitz heard his own silent scream in the night. His Moscow was Oakland, California. His NKVD were the Black Panthers, the revolutionary Marxist vanguard revered by the American left. Horowitz had recommended his friend, an unassuming forty-two-year-old mom named Betty Van Patter, to help the Panthers manage their business affairs. When she proved too honest, they fired her, then murdered her. "In my entire life, I had never experienced a blacker night," says Horowitz.

Worse was yet to come. When Horowitz sought justice for Van Patter, he found, much to his dismay, that no one cared. "There was only silence," writes Horowitz of his allies on the left. Van Patter had been swallowed by the "lacuna." She had joined the un-mourned millions of Lenin's crushed "insects" or of Stalin's "un-persons" or of Duranty's broken eggs. Horowitz would never blind himself to the truth again. "I began to ask myself," he recalls, "whether there was something in Marxism, or in the socialist idea itself, that was the root of the problem." And the answer, he concluded, was yes.

In 2004, he and his writing partner, Peter Collier, shed the light of truth on Noam Chomsky, whose uncorrected, Marxist-inspired vitriol had found a wider audience still in the wake of September 11th and the Iraq War. Their book, the *Anti-Chomsky Reader,* tracks his dissembling on issues ranging from Auschwitz to Afghanistan, from the denial of Holocausts that did happen to the promotion of those that did not. "These are not intellectual lapses for Chomsky," writes Horowitz, "but keys to a worldview that is shaped by one overriding imperative—to demonize America as the fount of all worldly evil."

In this regard, Cambodia proves instructive. As the *Black Book* notes, when the Cambodian capital of Phnom Penh fell to the Khmer Rouge in April 1975, the world witnessed "what was perhaps the most radical social transformation of all: the attempt to implement total communism in one fell swoop." This was obvious to all who wanted to see. Immediately after their victory, the Khmer Rouge ordered the evacuation of all major cities, including Phnom Penh with its two million plus population. Residents had twenty-four hours to leave their homes.

These "New People" were forced into the countryside. Here, they were made to wear blue clothes while everyone else was made to wear black. Their new masters not only starved them but systematically exterminated them, starting with the military, civil servants, and intellectuals and including even women and children. As testament to the madness and paranoia, in one district alone 40,000 of the 70,000 inhabitants were executed as "traitors collaborating with the CIA." Realistic estimates put the final death toll at about two million, most of the liquidated being men aged twenty to fifty. As late as 1990, nearly two-thirds of all Cambodians were female. Although obviously extreme, the Khmer Rouge "was indeed a member of the family," meaning the communist family. The Vietnamese communists, an eventual foe, had been the single greatest influence on the Khmer Rouge.

Although Chomsky would turn to the lessons learned in Southeast Asia again and again in his prolific career, a June 1977 article in the leftist magazine *Nation* shows his turn of mind most clearly. Entitled "Distortions at Fourth Hand," Chomsky and his writing partner, Edward Herman, essentially define those "distortions" as any accounts that suggest things have gone awry in Vietnam or Cambodia after the communist triumphs.

In essence, Chomsky sees "the tales of communist atrocities" coming out of Indochina as a way to "sustain the desired rewriting of American history." These "tales," by the way, were being repeated by the *New York Times* and other mainstream sources largely "to undermine the credibility of those who opposed the war." But, as Chomsky had to know, the major media had largely opposed the war since Tet. They would have had no interest in undermining the virtue of their own dissent.

Two years later, Chomsky and Herman would formalize their indictment of America in the book, *The Political Economy of Human Rights.* Indeed, they were prepared to announce in italics, *"Washington has become the torture and political murder capital of the world."* As to Cambodia, now that its horrors had become apparent beyond denial, the authors balanced the regime's "regimentation and terror" on the one hand against the "constructive achievements for much of the population" on the other.

In *The Anti-Chomsky Reader,* Stephen Morris, a senior fellow at the Foreign Policy Institute, asks incredulously what those "achievements" might possibly be. He cites as possibilities "the abolition of money, schools, modern medicine, religion, cultural life, and any communication with the outside world." In general, by all survivor accounts, "There was no forward progress anywhere in the economy and culture of the nation."

British historian Paul Johnson speaks of the four phases that Chomsky and Herman passed through in their obfuscations. The pair began with the premise that the massacres were a "Western propaganda invention" and ended by dismissing them as an intertribal traditional conflict that had nothing to do with Marx. "The Cambodian massacres could not be acknowledged to have taken place at all," writes Johnson, "until ways had been found that the United States was, directly or indirectly, responsible for them."

In the 1977 *Nation* article, Chomsky and Herman go to unwittingly absurd lengths to prove Johnson's point. They talk, for instance, about a *Washington Post* photo of a Cambodian man pulling a plow. "Quite a sensational testimonial to communist atrocities," the authors sniff.

"Even if the photographs had been authentic," they continue, "we might ask why people should be pulling plows in Cambodia. The reason is clear, if unmentioned. The savage American assault on Cambodia did not spare the animal population." Chomsky has "no ideology," his supporters repeat ad nauseam. Agreed, he has merely the parody of one.

In the final analysis, the massacres of two million innocent souls in Cambodia mattered no more to Chomsky than the murder of Betty Van Patter did to the Bay Area progressives. "The incident had no usable political meaning," remembers Horowitz of Van Patter's death, "and was therefore best forgotten."

3
Colors of the Wind

"The sense of innocence that is always entailed in feeling victimized filled us with a corresponding feeling of entitlement, or even license."

—SHELBY STEELE

THE ZONE OF DECENCY

The recently deceased firebrand Susan Sontag famously, if a bit hysterically, foretold the future of progressive cultural criticism and identified its principal target in her celebrated 1967 essay, "What's Happening to America":

The white race is the cancer of human history. It is the white race and it alone—its ideologies and inventions—which eradicates autonomous civilizations wherever it spreads, which has upset the ecological balance of the planet, which now threatens the very existence of life itself.

The Marxist attack on traditional Anglo-American values was about to mutate. Sontag did not just see it coming; she helped make it happen. The revelations of Krushchev in 1956 and the publication of Alexander Solzhenitsyn's *The Gulag Archipelago* in 1973 cost Soviet communism much of its progressive allure. The fall of the Berlin Wall and the collapse of the Soviet Union ended the fantasy altogether. Meanwhile, the other Marxist republics around the world were publicly malfunctioning in a variety of unseemly ways, if not imploding altogether.

What remained immune to the progressive meltdown was the Sontag scream, the full-throated attack on Western culture now revised and refined. The Marxist class struggle would not go away, but more and more, the class struggle would fuse with racial and environmental protest to create the dominant progressive paradigm of turn of the century America, often known as multiculturalism.

Like cholesterol, multiculturalism has a good kind and a bad kind. Books have been written about the distinctions among its various subsets in an American context: integrative pluralism, separatism, inclusionism, and on and on. The multicultural battle is also waged on an international level, where it has its own unique vocabulary.

The dominant intellectual strain, here and abroad, is unfortunately a "bad" one, the one voiced by Sontag. For the sake of expediency—and concision—this book will refer to it as zero-sum multiculturalism, or ZSM. In its purest form ZSM demands not only the recognition and elevation of the "marginalized" culture but also the debasement of the "dominant" culture.

Michael Moore captures the ZSM spirit with hyperbolic perfection in his sledgehammer bestseller, *Stupid White Men*. "It's not African Americans who have made this planet such a pitiful, scary place to inhabit," he says, complimenting the minority, albeit with his left hand. His right hand he reserves for a face slap to the majority: "You name the problem, the disease, the human suffering, or the abject misery visited upon millions, and I'll bet you ten bucks I can put a white face on it faster than you can name the members of 'N Sync." In the simple terms of transactional analysis, ZSM translates, "I'm okay. You're not."

Ward Churchill has elevated ZSM to near art form. He tells, for instance, of how in 1990 he served on an NEH grant as a "distinguished scholar" at Alfred University in New York State. Given his posturing as an Indian, he claims to have been "something of a curiosity" in this "primarily Euroamerican-staffed and attended institution." As such, journalists sought him out for his opinion on the upcoming Christopher Columbus quincentennial. He did not disappoint. His response was and remains that celebrating Columbus and European settlement "is greatly analogous to celebration of the glories of nazism [sic] and Heinrich Himmler."

Were ZSM mere intellectual chatter, it would not be worth discussing. In fact, however, it has gnawed its way into the very foundations of the culture. In 1967, who would have guessed that Sontag's self-hating discontents would be presented as truths to the next generation of schoolchildren? Skeptics might do well to consider the following bit of doggerel:

> You think you own whatever land you land on
> The earth is just a dead thing you can claim
> But I know every rock and tree and creature
> Has a life, has a spirit, has a name
>
> You think the only people who are people
> Are the people who look and think like you
> But if you walk the footsteps of a stranger
> You'll learn things you never knew you never knew

The above represents the musical scolding Captain John Smith receives from Indian princess Pocahantas in Disney's 1995 release of the same name. Hoping to win an Oscar, the Disney people passed on "Cancer of Human History" and called the song instead "Colors of the Wind." They won the award.

These two stanzas wonderfully capture the DNA of ZSM. The new settlers are cruel imperialists or, in ZSM lingo, "hegemons." They have no appreciation of the land, the "dead thing," (a claim easily refuted by the hundreds of deeply appreciative settler memoirs). Their religion is constrictive and unnatural. They are ignorant and racist. They are the only ones who need to learn anything, namely the alternative reality of the "colors of the wind."

No doubt, settlers like John Smith had their flaws. But ZSM advocates reject the notion that man's fallen nature might account for those sins. Indeed, they reject the very notion of "sin." They see evil instead as a byproduct of Western culture, and of the economic and religious traditions that sustain it.

The beauty of ZSM for white progressives like Sontag and Moore and War Churchill is that they can make a showy exclusion of themselves from that culture and its traditions. "White is a state of mind," claims Churchill in a stunning bit of post-exposure, intellectual jujitsu. "It's not a gene code, by the way. You've got to choose to act white in order to be white."

Black writer and social critic Shelby Steele describes the moral reserve progressives have set aside for themselves as the "zone of decency." Those within grant themselves the power to "decertify" those they choose to keep out. Nor does minority status translate into automatic certification. Racial minorities who ignore progressive dogma—Supreme Court Justice Clarence Thomas, for instance—face crueler exclusion and more hurtful labels (e.g., "Uncle Tom") than even their white counterparts.

Entire minority groups can be decertified if they deviate from the progressive line. Unknowingly, those multiple thousands of Cuban Americans who protested the dispatch of young Elian Gonzalez back to the workers' paradise of Cuba sacrificed their minority status by so doing. In *Stupid White Men,* Michael Moore describes them not as "Hispanics" or even as "Cuban Americans" but only as "a bunch of crazy Miamians." They are the one minority group in the book not identified as such or presented as victims.

On the other hand, minorities who heed the progressive line enjoy a special immunity from criticism by the cultural establishment. This immunity prompts some adventurous redefining of reality, a dynamic guaranteed to inspire serious intellectual misadventure. Sontag's accusations may be ugly, and Disney's silly, but they don't rise to the level of fraud. Fraud, real fraud, takes a good deal more work, all of it collaborative. As shall be seen, a great deal of such work would be required to get America's preteens humming progressive anthems.

AN ALMOST USEFUL HOAX

ZSM has spawned an international industry to help spread the good word. Largely based in the universities, the ZSM global enterprise generates as little controversy as it does only because its publications are written in a *lingua franca* too convoluted for ordinary people to understand. Generally speaking, this language and the philosophy behind it go by the name of "postmodernism."

In theory at least, postmodernism denies the existence of any one set of objective truths. It insists rather that the humanities, the social sciences, and even the hard sciences consist of nothing more than explanatory "narratives" or "myths" composed by those with the power to dictate them. Postmodern scholars attempt to "deconstruct" these myths—or "social constructions"—and in the process discover the true intentions of those who created them.

The abstract for an entirely typical journal article on a seemingly everyday subject—"Sunny Days on Sesame Street? Multiculturalism and Resistance Postmodernism" by Ute Sartorius Kraidy—will give the reader a feel for the Byzantine quality of the language. It also suggests the political uses of even preschool entertainment.

This article addresses the role of educational children's television as a contributor to the forging of the notion of multiculturalism by analyzing Sesame Street's suitability as a tool for multicultural pedagogy. Using McLaren's theory of resistance postmodernism (1994), this study argues that while Sesame Street does not directly provide a language for educators to critique social and cultural practices, it is a text that allows and invites multifaceted dialogues that critically discern an Other in the construction of identity.

In reality, many ZSM advocates are less keen on playing postmodern parlor games than they are on seizing the narrative power for themselves. They may use postmodernism to deconstruct the "myths" of the dominant culture, often with a vengeance, but they have little interest in deconstructing their own. They have even less interest in letting the adversary culture do the same. Despite all the relativist posing, their myths *are* the truth, and there can be hell to pay for those who suggest otherwise.

Having long observed the rough and tumble of postmodernism from the sidelines, NYU professor of physics Alan Sokal decided to join the scrum. In early 1996, he wrote an article entitled "Transgressing the Boundaries: Toward a Transformational Hermeneutics of Quantum Physics" and submitted it to *Social Text,* a journal that accurately describes itself as "a daring and controversial leader in the field of cultural studies."

In the article, Sokal argues that breakthroughs in feminist and cultural theory have caused him to rethink the "dogma" of the "Western intellectual outlook," namely that there is such a thing as an objective physical science. Although not a regular in such circles, Sokal phrases his argument in pitch perfect postmodern patois:

It has thus become increasingly apparent that physical "reality," no less than social "reality," is at bottom a social and linguistic construct; that scientific "knowledge," far from being objective, reflects and encodes the dominant ideologies and power relations of the culture that produced it; that the truth claims of science are inherently theory-laden and self-referential; and consequently, that the discourse of the scientific community, for all its undeniable value, cannot assert a privileged epistemological status with

respect to counter-hegemonic narratives emanating from dissident or marginalized communities.

The editors of *Social Text* were admittedly pleased to receive, in their
words, "the work of a progressive physicist committed to the critique of
science." The timing was convenient. They were about to publish a
double issue that would lay bare an alleged rightwing "scapegoating
crusade." Apparently, these right wingers were hell bent on exposing the
political motivations behind the kind of science studies that *Social Text*
and others were doing. The Sokal article offered added credibility to
Social Text's counterattack. Here was a respected physicist who shared
their views and was willing to say so publicly. Without any real peer
review, the editors published "Transgressing the Boundaries" in the
double issue. Says Sokal of the editors' rush to publish, "It was hard to
imagine a more radical way of shooting themselves in the foot."

In fact, as he quickly revealed, Sokal had written and submitted the
article as a hoax. He had pasted together a string of nonsensical quotes
from the leading postmodernist theorists, most of them French, and
added his own "whimsical" logic as glue. His revelation of the same
exploded into the major media with a force he had never anticipated and
played right into the hands of the very conservatives that this particular
issue of *Social Text* had been attacking.

Sokal's goal in the article, and in the subsequent book he coauthored
with French physicist, Jean Bricmont, was "precisely to say that the king
is naked (and the queen too)." "If the texts seem incomprehensible," write
the authors, "it is for the excellent reason that they mean precisely
nothing." This exposure of academic "charlatanism" seemed to everyone
but the ZMC crowd to be entirely admirable.

As much as conservative critics enjoyed the controversy, they did not
understand Sokal's motives. Although just forty at the time he entered
the fray, Sokal describes himself as an "unabashed Old Leftist." What
bothered him about postmodernism was that it had "seduced" many of

his fellow progressives and distracted them from pursuing "the ideals of justice and equality."

Sokal finds this all paradoxical. As he sees it, the left had defended science against the forces of irrationality for the last two centuries. Indeed, Marx and his followers saw themselves, with some justification, as the champions of reason and the rightful heirs of the Enlightenment. So did Darwin and his followers. The Scopes trial, after all, was a highly public display of the progressive commitment to science.

Sokal labors to understand why progressives have abandoned this tradition. He offers two possible explanations. One is the need for newly emerged cultural forces, like feminism and multiculturalism, to impose their own social-political paradigms on reality. The second is pure "political discouragement." Sokal argues that the collapse of communism and the collusion of the emerging nations with the agents of global capitalism have discouraged progressives. As a result, they have taken sterile refuge in "academic cults" like postmodernism. "In this way," Sokal laments, "the remnants of the left have collaborated in driving the last nail in the coffin of the ideals of justice and progress."

Overlooking for a moment his self-congratulatory idealism, to this point in the discussion Sokal would seem to be squarely on the side of truth and academic honesty. But like every other serious leftist in the last century, Sokal has developed a terribly narrow view as to what truth is. He reveals this myopia in one very telling sentence defending objective reality. If you throw out hard science, he argues, "you also throw out the Nazi gas chambers, the American enslavement of Africans, and the fact that today in New York it's raining."

Here, Amis's lacuna yawns wide once again. The one hundred million communist victims disappear as silently as David Horowitz's friend, Betty Van Tapper. So do the millions enslaved by virtually every other nation on earth since the beginning of human history, as well as those enslaved in Africa to this day. Like the death of Betty Van Tapper at the hands of the Black Panthers, these tragedies have "no usable political meaning" and are "therefore best forgotten."

A month after the horrors of September 11, Sokal could be found in the pages of *The New York Review of Books* warning readers against "the folly of a military assault on Afghanistan." Noam Chomsky, Sokal's avowed model of a truth-teller, would have been proud. Just ten days after September 11, Chomsky had shared with the world some new truths about that unfortunate country. As he claimed, the Bush administration had coldly suspended food convoys to Afghanistan's civilian population and was prepared to "kill unknown numbers, maybe millions, of starving Afghans" to root out the Taliban. History, of course, quickly proved Chomsky absurdly wrong once again. But Chomsky, like so many ZSM advocates, has little use for history. After all, it is merely a "myth" written by the winners, none more evil than "the cruel and vengeful superpower" of Chomsky's imagination, the United States of America.

Not Out of Africa

There is something ineffably sad about George G. M. James's book, *Stolen Legacy*. Published in 1954, the book makes one last anachronistic stab at finding respect for a distinctly black view of ancient history. "The aim of the book is to establish better race relations in the world," writes James eagerly, "by revealing a fundamental truth concerning the contribution of the African continent to civilization."

That truth was not a pretty one, but the Guyana-born James, then teaching at the University of Arkansas, Pine Bluff, did not shy from spelling it out. "The Greeks," he writes, "stole the legacy of the African continent and called it their own." He meant "stole" literally. The Greeks came, and they plundered. By depriving Africa of its rightful heritage, James argues, the Greeks have left the world with the erroneous opinion that "the African continent has made no contribution to civilization." This misrepresentation, he adds, "has become the basis of race prejudice, which has affected all people of color." James entertains the pathetically hopeful belief that by giving the Egyptians their due, he could eliminate that prejudice.

The book reads like a text written in the 1920s or 1930s. During those years, with no real sight of assimilation on the horizon, black nationalist leader Marcus Garvey was stirring African Americans with visions of the motherland. Like James, Garvey looked to Egypt as the center of civilization, claiming that "Greece and Rome have robbed Egypt of her arts and letters, and taken all the credit to themselves." Like James too, he derived his vision of Egypt through the Egypt-centered Masonic rituals that had been passed down over the centuries and that had found a receptive audience among West Indians and African Americans. Garvey's motives were much the same, namely to instill pride and self-respect in a people that had been largely deprived of both.

Times, however, were changing and quickly. Nineteen fifty-four witnessed not only the publication of *Stolen Legacy* but also the promulgation of the landmark Supreme Court decision ending formal segregation in the public schools, *Brown v. The Board of Education.* That same year, Martin Luther King Jr. moved to Montgomery, Alabama, to begin his historic mission. The next year, Jackie Robinson would lead the now fully integrated Brooklyn Dodgers to the World Series.

At the time of such change and obvious progress, many educators saw *Stolen Legacy* as a throwback to an earlier age. The reviewer for the *Journal of Negro Education* was among them. He gently dismisses James's thesis as "startling," one with which most readers, especially the Hellenophiles, "will strongly disagree."

Black America, however, was moving on two tracks, and James had unwittingly stepped on the fast one. Nineteen fifty-five, for instance, was the same year in which a minister for the Nation of Islam by the name of Malcolm X convinced nightclub singer Louis Eugene Walcott to join the organization. As was common among black Muslims, Walcott dropped his "slave" name and became known as Minister Louis X. He would later adopt the name Abdul Haleem Farrakhan and come to be known as Louis Farrakhan.

Within a decade, black nationalism had gained a surprisingly strong following in America's inner cities. In 1965, *The Autobiography of Malcolm X*, as told to writer Alex Haley, debuted to enthusiastic mainstream reviews and instant bestseller status. Among younger blacks, Malcolm was in, and Martin was out. The black nationalist movement quickly and embarrassingly found fertile ground in the cultural establishment. Writer Tom Wolfe famously captured the odd coupling of it all in his essay about conductor Leonard Bernstein's late 1960s Park Avenue duplex party for the Black Panthers. The title of the piece, "Radical Chic," has since become the definitive term to describe a phenomenon that has flourished at least since Sacco and Vanzetti.

If black nationalism played out as a fashion on Park Avenue, it took hold in the deeper, more intellectual circles of the cultural establishment, particularly on college campuses. Far from being an anachronism, James now seemed avant-garde. He had written what has been rightly called "the most influential Afrocentrist text," the seminal work in a field that barely existed but that would soon enough find a respected place for itself in every major university in America.

James was not exactly subtle about his attack on Western civilization. For him, the Greeks played the same role that America would play for Noam Chomsky: the evil "hegemon" that could do no right. James claims, in fact, that the Greeks did "not seem to possess the natural ability" to develop philosophy and science on their own. It was for this reason that Alexander, under the prodding of his mentor Aristotle, "ransacked and looted" the Royal Library at Alexandria and then carried off "a booty of scientific, philosophic, and religious books." To secure Western dominance, the Roman emperors Theodosius and later Justinian abolished the ancient culture system of the Egyptians and replaced it with Roman Catholicism. To "forever suppress" this same culture system, the Christian Church moved in to Africa with its only seemingly benign missionaries.

Stolen Legacy fit the 1960s better than it did the 1950s. It offered young African Americans, infused with the idea of black nationalism, a glimmering image of Africa as the center of civilization. It offered old Marxists and young sexual revolutionaries new ammunition in their attacks on Christianity in general and Catholicism in particular. And for the New Left, it presented Greece as a prototype of Western cultural imperialism. From James's perspective, it was not a question of reciprocal influence between Egypt and Greece. It was a question of theft. It was pure zero-sum. Just as America could prosper only at the expense of the developing world, so Greece and Western civilization could flourish only at the expense of the ancient civilizations of color—Asian, Native American, and especially African. James was just the first of many scholars to promote this view.

With zero-sum multiculturalism, if someone wins, someone else loses. The big losers in this battle were the classicists. Their whole world-view was under assault. A new and more powerful academic department was telling its students that the classicists had it all backwards, that what they had long presented as true was actually false. For the most part, the classicists did not dare fire back. They were morally and politically outgunned, and they knew it.

When resistance surfaced, it did so at a surprising place, Hillary Clinton's alma mater, Wellesley, a liberal women's college in Massachusetts. In February 1993, Dr. Yosef A.A. ben-Jochannan came to campus to deliver the annual Martin Luther King Jr. memorial lecture. The president of the college proudly introduced him as a "distinguished Egyptologist," and he lived up to his billing. Ben-Jochannan regaled the audience with a recitation of Western infamies, including the now stan-dard tales of how Aristotle robbed the library of Alexandria and helped Greece steal its civilization from Africa.

Wellesley professor Mary Lefkowitz, one of America's most respected classicists, listened in quiet horror. During the Q & A at the end of the talk she screwed up her nerve, rose up in all her five-foot four-inch glory, and asked ben-Jochannan a simple question. How is it, she asked, that Aristotle was able to plunder a library that was built only after his death?

Ben-Jochannan could not answer. Flustered, he told Lefkowitz that he resented "the tone of the inquiry." Afterwards, several Wellesley students accosted Lefkowitz, then nearing sixty, and accused her of racism and of being "brainwashed" by white historians.

For her part, Lefkowitz just wanted to know what evidence ben-Jochannan might have had that Aristotle had ever been to Egypt. She had never seen any. When she expressed her concerns to the dean about the lack of factual evidence for many Afrocentrist claims, she was served up the standard postmodern pabulum that every scholar "had a different but equally valid view of history." When she spoke about the same at a faculty meeting, one colleague dismissed her, saying, "I don't care who stole what from whom." Frustrated by their fear or indifference, Lefkowitz took matters into her own hands and wrote one of the boldest books by an American academic in recent memory, 1996's *Not Out of Africa*. "Universities are here for the dissemination of knowledge," says Lefkowitz in the way of explaining her motivation, "not for the spreading of falsehoods."

Mary Lefkowitz

Lefkowitz marches through James's evidence like Alexander through Persia. She traces his essential error to his use of Masonic ritual as historic text and follows the Masonic thread to its source. As she documents, Greek and Roman fabulists first imagined the famed "Egyptian Mystery System," and European novelists embellished it. "The Egypt of the myth of the Stolen Legacy is a wholly European Egypt," she writes. Indeed, if the Western world was so keen on erasing African civilization, one has to wonder why it sustained these glorious Egyptian myths for centuries.

As to more specific charges, Lefkowitz argues that "no ancient source says that Alexander and Aristotle raided the library at Alexandria." None. Nor is there any evidence that Aristotle ever went to Egypt. Besides, the celebrated library at Alexandria was built twenty-five years after Aristotle died. Indeed, the city itself was only about a year old at the time of his death. As to James's claim that Socrates had studied astrology and geology in Egypt and been initiated as a Master Mason, Lefkowitz painstakingly reveals that there is absolutely no evidence to support it and much to support the opposite. At his own trial, for instance, Socrates denies any knowledge of astrology or geology. His life, like Aristotle's, was well documented.

Lefkowitz has no use for the Afrocentrist "silence of history" argument, namely that the absence of specific evidence is the result of a convoluted Western conspiracy to deny Africa its due. "James introduced a new school of historical research," Lefkowitz concludes, "by demonstrating that anyone can say anything about the past."

Lefkowitz's argument, however, was less with James or even his academic heirs, but rather the postmodern assumption that there can be a diversity of truths. In too many universities, she notes, "It does not matter whether what is taught is true, or is supported by warranted evidence, because a diverse point of view, with a laudable social goal, has been presented." For all her courage and good intentions, Lefkowitz's protest could not stop truth from "diversifying" on campus. By the turn of the century, this mutant, diversified breed of the truth had spread more insistently than the ivy.

Stolen Legacy

In the very last sentence of the publishing phenomenon known as *Roots*, author Alex Haley expresses the wish that his story "can help alleviate the legacies of the fact that preponderantly the histories have been written by the winners." Although the dreadful syntax suggests the pressure that Haley was under to finish the massive book, his message is clear. The "winners," the historians of the majority American culture, have written all the "narratives."

With *Roots: The Saga of an American Family,* Haley set out to correct the record, and he intended to do it on the majority culture's own terms, in the form of a documented history. On the surface at least, he succeeded spectacularly. The book, first published in 1976, generated extraordinary reviews and spectacular sales, here and abroad. The mini-series based on the book captured more viewers than any series before it. 130 million Americans watched the final episode alone. And Haley won a special Pulitzer Prize for telling the true story of a black family from its origins in Africa through seven generations to the present day in America.

As a popular entertainment, *Roots* gave progressives a perfect "pedagogical tool" with which to instruct their less enlightened brethren in the quiet horrors of American culture. In fact, it quickly became *the* dominant narrative, a curriculum standard, a veritable sacred text, the reason that Alan Sokal could cite "the American enslavement of Africans" as a unique evil without feeling foolish. Given its centrality to the flowering multicultural movement, there would be precious little deconstructing of *Roots.*

The story that Haley tells goes down easily. There is nothing angry or radical about the book or about Haley himself, which helps account for *Roots'* success among white audiences. Working backwards through the book, Haley decides to trace his family's heritage to its African roots. All that he has to guide him are the tales his grandmother and great aunts have told him about "the farthest-back person" they could recall, "the African." According to his relatives, the African's master had called him

"Toby" after he first arrived by ship in "Naplis." Proud and defiant, Toby continued to call himself "Kin-tay." In time, Toby had a little girl named "Kizzy." Kizzy remembered that her father used to call a guitar a "Ko" and a nearby river the "Kamby Bolongo." Working from little more than this and the names of Kizzy's descendants, Haley finds his way back to the Gambia River, or "Kamby Bolongo." Here he learns firsthand from an old time "griot" the true story of his own ancestor, Kunta Kinte.

The story unfolds tranquilly enough. Born in 1750, Kinte grows up in a peaceful, sheltering community along the Gambia River in West Africa. He is well schooled in math and writing and the Islamic faith. Admittedly, there is slavery in this part of the world, but slaves were "respected people," whose rights were secured by the laws of Kinte's ancestors. Many of the slaves eventually bought their own freedom. There is also war, but it is fought under Marquis of Queensbury-like rules. Only the "greed and treason" introduced by white slave traders keeps Kinte's land from realizing its potential as an African Eden.

At age seventeen, Kinte is snatched from his youthful idyll by the evil, club-bearing "toubobs," or white people. When he finally regains his senses four days later, Kinte finds himself chained in the stinking, claustrophobic hold of an ocean-going vessel, manned by ugly toubobs, all of them seemingly British or American. After a hellish journey, he arrives in Annapolis, attempts to escape four times, and is subdued only after some poor white bounty hunters chop off half his foot. The year is 1767.

Not all "massas" are conspicuously evil in Haley's world, not even Kinte's. The book works because it has a sense of balance to it. And yet Haley is quietly laying out an indictment against the United States that is always loaded and often gratuitous. In Haley's tale, it is the whites who enter the forest and enslave the blacks, not Arab slave traders, not other blacks. Since Kinte is unconscious through the period of transaction, the reader has no picture of African participation in the slave market, nor of any Portuguese or Hispanic involvement in the slave trade.

As a Muslim, Kinte does not sense any virtue in Christianity. Indeed, it strikes him as crude and hypocritical. Coming of age during the revolutionary period in Virginia, Kinte sees the revolution as inherently fraudulent: "'Give me liberty or give me death,' Kunta liked that, but he couldn't understand how somebody white could say it; white folks looked pretty free to him."

To broaden the scope of subversion, Haley has an amusingly cynical fiddler friend of Kinte's provide an ongoing narrative on events and personalities from Christopher Columbus—"But if he foun' Injuns here, he ain't discover it, is he?"—to blacks fighting in Washington's army— "dem free niggers is crazy." When the fiddler is told that the war had ended, he discounts the news. "Ain't gon' be no peace, not long as it's white folks," he says, "cause ain't nothin' dey loves better'n killin'."

However unbalanced this might be, none of it really approaches fraud. No, fraud is the means Haley used to indulge his bias, and this he did in an extraordinarily reckless fashion. He may have thought he could get away with it by mimicking the emerging ZSM narrative and by mainstreaming it successfully. If so, he came very close to being right.

Unfortunately for Haley, at least one person in the cultural establishment was not about to give him a pass because of race or agenda. Approaching seventy when *Roots* debuted, Harold Courlander was shocked to read it. For the previous thirty years or more, Courlander had been traveling the world collecting folk tales and writing about his findings. He had a particular interest in Africa. Courlander, who himself was white, attributed his interest in African culture to the fact that he had grown up near black neighborhoods in Detroit. He had been well recognized in the field since 1947 when he coauthored *The Cow-Tail Switch and Other West African Stories.* In 1967, he wrote a more conventional novel titled *The African.* He had earned fourteen thousand dollars for it. Less than ten years later, Alex Haley flagrantly rewrote large sections of his book and made $2.6 million in hardcover royalties alone. Courlander was not a happy camper.

In 1978, Courlander sued Haley in a U.S. District Court in New York

for copyright infringement. The suit cited eighty-one passages that had
been lifted from Courlander's *The African* as well as the plot and certain
characters. Not unreasonably, Courlander asked for half of Haley's profits.
As is all but universal in such cases, the accused denied any wrongdoing.
Under oath, Haley went so far as to testify that he had not even read *The
African*. Throughout the six weeks of testimony, U.S District Court Judge
Robert Ward listened in disbelief to denial after denial. On one occasion,
he noted that Haley used "Yoo-hooo-ah-hoo" as a slave field call with
exactly the same spelling as Courlander had and wondered how that could
have happened by chance. It couldn't, and it didn't. Haley's defense fell
apart when, during discovery, the plaintiff's lawyers found three quotes
from *The African* among his typed notes, notes that he had apparently
failed to destroy. The examples are illuminating:

From *The African*
. . . but the hunter is not allowed to forget. All his senses must be
burning. He must hear what the farmer cannot hear. He must smell
what others cannot smell . . . his eyes must pierce the darkness.

From *Roots*
The hunter's senses must be fine. He must hear what others cannot,
smell what others cannot. He must see through the darkness.

From *The African*
. . . drifted into sleep . . . Hwesuhunu drifted into wakefulness
again. He felt his father's presence in the darkness. He reached out
his hand, but there was nothing there to be felt. He spoke aloud,
saying, "So it shall be, I understand. This is the meaning of things."

From *Roots*
One night when Kunta had fallen asleep but drifted again into wakefulness . . . he lay staring up into the darkness . . . feeling around him,

in some strange way, the presence of his holy-man grandfather, Kunte reached out in the darkness. There was nothing to be felt, but he began speaking aloud to the Alquaran Kairaba Kunta Kinte, imploring him to make know the purpose his mission here.

The last thing Judge Ward wanted to do was to undermine a newly ascendant black hero. Midway through the trial, he counseled Haley and his attorneys that he would have to contemplate a perjury charge unless they settled with Courlander. They did just that to the tune of $650,000, or about $2 million by 2005 standards. In return, Courlander agreed to keep quiet about the suit, which he did until he died in 1996.

The settlement got precious little media attention. In the press, only the *Washington Post* gave the case any ink of note, and even then it used a local hook—"Bethesda Author Settles 'Roots' Suit for $500,000"—to justify its coverage. Haley kept as quiet about the suit as Courlander, but when questioned, he sustained the fiction that he concocted at the trial, namely that only three brief Courlander passages had "found their way" into *Roots*. This oversight he attributed to his overwork during the twelve-year research phase of the book when he had to support himself on the lecture tour. "Often members of the audience would pass him slips of paper with suggestions," the *Post* reported with a straight face. "He said he dumped these in a carton and used some of them without knowing their source." In a quirky historical footnote, John F. Kennedy Jr. helped with the *Post* article. His father had also been accused, and with good reason, of winning a Pulitzer Prize for a book that he himself did not actually write, *Profiles In Courage*.

Like the other media who bothered to report on the settlement, the *Post* neglected to explore the real gist of the scandal: namely that the author of a "nonfiction" book plagiarized from a fictional one. "The uniqueness of *Roots* lay in the fact that it claimed to be painstakingly researched, and true," In reality, it was neither. Nobile calls it a "a hoax, a literary painted mouse, a Piltdown of genealogy, a pyramid of bogus research." As should have been obvious to any observant reader, Haley had learned his technique in the James' school of historical research, the "anyone can say anything about the past" school.

In the late 1970s, as Nobile would report, two leading genealogists, Gary Mills and Elizabeth Shown Mills, decided to follow up on Haley's work through the relevant archives in Virginia, North Carolina, and Maryland. They found that Haley, like most amateur genealogists, made mistakes. But they found too that his transgressions went well beyond mere mistakes. "We expected ineptitude, but not subterfuge," observed Elizabeth, herself the editor of the *National Genealogical Society Quarterly.*

The records showed that in the pre-Civil War period, Haley got virtually everything wrong. In *Roots,* for instance, Haley tells in great excited detail how he tracked down the very ship that Kunta Kinte had taken from the Gambia to 'Naplis, the Lord Ligonier in 1767, the very year that "the King's soldiers came" to the Gambia. In fact, as the Mills discovered, the man that Haley identifies as Kunta Kinte, a slave by the name of Toby in the possession of the John Waller family, could not have been Kunta Kinte or Haley's ancestor. Toby had been in America as early as 1762, five years before the Lord Ligonier arrived. Worse for Haley, Toby died eight years before his presumed daughter Kizzy was born.

Alex Haley himself died just as Nobile was beginning his research. Haley's unsuspecting archivists gave Nobile access to the various letters, diaries, drafts, notes, and audiotapes that Haley had kept. They were a veritable gold mine, theretofore unexplored. In working his way through them, Nobile came to understand the depths of Haley's "elegant and complex make-it-up-as-you-go-along scam."

Apparently, when Haley first conceived a family research project in 1964, he had no plans to find an African ancestor. That thought did not occur to him until much later when he met an exchange student from the Gambia. Together, they shared key phrases like "Kamby Bolongo" that Haley could pretend to trace. The student, who was from an influential family, helped Haley make contacts in the Gambia. As the correspondence and audiotapes revealed, these contacts then arranged for Haley to meet a "griot," who had been coached in advance to say what Haley wanted to hear. "It was sort of like Piltdown Man," says Nobile. "Haley would plant the evidence and then find it."

Not surprisingly, Haley puts another spin altogether on the encounter with the griot. "A sob hit me somewhere around my ankles." he writes in *Roots*. "It came surging upward, and flinging my hands over my face, I was just bawling, as I hadn't since I was a baby." True to ideological form, Haley was weeping "for all of history's atrocities against fellowmen." None of this weeping, however, is heard among the matter-of-fact exchanges on the tape.

What *is* heard on the tape raises further questions about Haley's motives. Through a translator, the imperfectly coached griot tells Haley that Portuguese soldiers helped capture Kinte and send him "back home to the Portuguese." To preserve the purity of his story, to remind his audience just who really is responsible for those "atrocities," Haley scrubs the Portuguese out of the picture and directs the audience towards America.

In truth, even if the griot had known a Kunta Kinte, there was no way Haley could have written anything approaching a "history" about the first seventeen years of his life, which he does in great length. The notion that an oral historian could recall the life of an ordinary young boy two hundred years prior surpasses the preposterous. "There was no Kunta Kinte," says Nobile bluntly.

Still, neither the lawsuit nor the unraveling of the genealogy dimmed Haley's star while he was alive. The Coast Guard named a cutter for Haley. His hometown erected a ten-foot bronze statue in his honor. The book and video remained a staple in history classes across America. The Pulitzer remained in his trophy case. And the awards and the money continued to roll in.

Black critic Stanley Crouch has suggested two reasons for the "durability of the hoax." One is the huge investment that Doubleday and David Wolper Productions have in *Roots'* continued viability. The second

Crouch traces back to the influence of Malcolm X, who taught black youth that "they were not Americans, but victims of Americanism." Their true identity, according to Malcolm, "was African and Islamic." *Roots* reinforced both. Indeed, given Haley's identification with Malcolm, one has to wonder whether he traced Kunta Kinte to an Islamic part of Africa by chance or design.

Nobile suggests a third reason for *Roots'* seeming immunity, one related to the second. This he lays fully on his progressive colleagues. "They were all too scared, or dishonest," writes Nobile, "to admit to the public that the most famous black writer had lied about his ancestry." Famed *Washington Post* editor and Pulitzer board member Ben Bradlee, who made his reputation at Watergate, was among those who gave Haley a pass. "No one wanted his ass," he told Nobile. Obviously, Bradlee's "let-it-all-hang-out" investigative style was somewhat selective in its targeting.

In 1993, a year after Haley's death, Nobile did his best to blow the whistle on what he calls "one of the great literary hoaxes of modern times." In February of that year, he published "Uncovering Roots" in the influential alternative publication, *The Village Voice.* The article brought to a larger public the story of the Courlander suit and the Mills' genealogy. Nobile also revealed that Haley's editor at *Playboy* magazine, the very white and Jewish Murray Fisher, did much of the book's writing.

In the British Isles, the Nobile exposé was a big story. It got serious coverage in all the major newspapers, and the BBC later made a documentary, *The Roots of Alex Haley,* confirming Nobile's charges. This author heard an hour-long interview with him on Ireland's major radio station, which actually prompted this book. The American cultural establishment, however, continued to turn its back on the story. (When I returned to America, I said to friends, "How about that Haley stuff!" They answered, "What Haley stuff?") Nobile and an African American coauthor put a book proposal together on the subject but, as Nobile ruefully admits, "Nobody wanted to touch it." A Lexis search shows shockingly little follow-up by the media, major or minor.

Not surprisingly, the black media paid more attention than the white. By and large, they did not appreciate Nobile's deconstruction. "Can anyone tell me," wrote Abiola Sinclair in the *New York Amsterdam News*, "what was behind that vicious, mean-spirited, ugly, and totally unnecessary attack on Alex Haley that appeared in *The Village Voice* that hit the stands last Wednesday, Feb. 17?" Likely fearing a similar attack, the *New York Times* buried the issue in a page 18, "Book Notes" column. There, in discussing whether Haley's new book, *Alex Haley's Queen,* should be shelved under fiction or nonfiction, the *Times* had exactly this to say about the controversy: "Two weeks ago, the charges about the authenticity of *Roots* and the integrity of Mr. Haley were raised anew in an investigative article by Philip Nobile in *The Village Voice.* Members of the Haley family have rebutted the accusations." And that was that.

Over the next decade, Haley suffered some posthumous setbacks. *The Norton Anthology of African American Literature* quietly dropped him. The Society of Journalists and Authors eliminated their now oxymoronic Alex Haley Excellence Award. *Reader's Digest,* with which Haley had long been associated, cancelled a tribute to Haley. But the big guns stuck in there. Although ABC passed on presenting a twenty-fifth anniversary special in January 2002, NBC stepped right in without a hint that anything might be amiss. Under the marketing slogan "a legacy of greatness," Warner Home Video rolled out its twenty-fifth anniversary DVD edition of *Roots*—"a winner of more than 145 awards, including nine Emmys, a Golden Globe, five Television Critics Circle Awards, and the George F. Peabody Award"—again, without a blush.

In an amusing open letter to two recently nabbed plagiarists, historians Doris Kearns Goodwin and Stephen Ambrose, Philip Nobile—writing as Alex Haley—offers some sage advice: "Deny, deny, deny." If an author can hold off the critics with some balderdash, advises Nobile, and continue to turn out profitable, politically correct books, he or she can always count on the publisher:

No plagiarist has ever had a more loyal publisher than mine. Even after the copying and fakery in *Roots* had been established beyond any literary or historical doubt, Doubleday refused to recall the book. Instead the company has continued to sell it under "nonfiction" with the original text intact!!! Like I said, don't worry, be happy. You can count on Simon & Schuster to do the unprincipled thing.

Your faithful correspondent,
Alex Haley

News from Indian Country

"There is nothing in this message that can make you happy," so wrote Paul DeMain, editor of *News From Indian Country* (NFIC) to his faithful readers in February 2002. He was preparing them for his and his staff's final conclusions about the case of the much-celebrated radical Indian activist, Leonard Peltier, still in prison after twenty-five long years.

DeMain expressed his regrets to a handful of people by name. One was Peter Matthiessen. If there were an encyclopedia entry for "cultural establishment," Matthiessen's picture would grace it. Well born and bred in New York City and educated at Yale, Matthiessen co-founded the influential *Paris Review* with George Plimpton just three years out of college. A prolific author and winner of the National Book Award, he had everything this establishment could offer including a home on Long island, lots of frequent flyer miles, and a contempt for the culture that spawned him. In 1983, that contempt took the shape of a book called *In The Spirit of Crazy Horse*, which details the arrest and conviction of Peltier for the 1975 murder of two FBI agents.

"The Peltier case, like that of Sacco and Vanzetti, had historic reverberations," writes Matthiessen accurately. Out of modesty perhaps, Matthiessen does not mention that it was largely his work—more so even

than Frankfurter's with Sacco and Vanzetti—that made the case rever-
berate. By investing his considerable reputation in Peltier, Matthiessen
rescued him from obscurity and elevated his plight to the level of international *cause célèbre.* "To a remarkable degree," confirms Scott
Anderson in a breakthrough 1994 article in the influential *Outside* magazine, "Matthiessen's version has been widely accepted as the definitive
account, as well as the starting point for most of those who have turned
their attention to the Peltier story."

With the exception of its climax, there is little dispute as to the nature
of that story. In 1975 and in the years preceding it, the Pine Ridge
Reservation in the southwestern part of South Dakota witnessed a good
deal of unusual mayhem. Taking their cultural cues from the black
nationalists then in vogue, activists from the American Indian
Movement (AIM) had turned militant and were testing that newly found
militancy in Pine Ridge.

The dispute attracted Leonard Peltier. Born in 1944 on a Chippewa
Sioux reservation, Peltier had bounced around the "red ghettos" of the
northwest in a variety of odd jobs before linking up with AIM. What
Peltier lacked in charisma or organizational skills, he made up for in
muscle and was hired on as a bodyguard. In late 1972, his path detoured
to Milwaukee. There he got into an altercation with two policemen and
was credibly accused of attempted murder. Peltier jumped bail in April
1973 and headed for Pine Ridge.

When Peltier arrived, AIM was locked in a veritable civil war with the
reservation's leadership. AIM forces had seized the iconic village of
Wounded Knee and were demanding the ouster of Pine Ridge tribal
president Dick Wilson. The siege of Wounded Knee by federal and state
authorities lasted seventy-one days, and Peltier left shortly after its incon-
clusive ending.

Although the siege was over, the guerilla warfare between the two
Indian factions went on and on. Peltier returned in 1975 when AIM
leaders put out a call for "warriors" allegedly to defend their people

against the rival Indian faction and the FBI. Accompanying Peltier were his ex-con cousin Bob Robideau and Robideau's friend, Dino Butler. The three set up camp in an enclave they called "Tent City." It did not take long for trouble to find them.

On June 26, 1975, two FBI agents in separate cars, Jack Coler and Ron Williams, were investigating a pair of politically motivated crimes on the reservation, one a murder. They were following at a distance a vehicle they thought was owned by a suspect named Jimmy Eagle, when it pulled off a lonely country road and stopped.

"They're getting out of the vehicle," FBI agent Williams cautioned over the radio. A moment later, Williams's voice became urgent: "It looks like these guys are going to shoot at us!" And they did just that. The two FBI cars took some 125 hits from high-powered rifles at a distance of roughly 250 yards. The agents, armed only with service revolvers, fired five futile shots in return. Both were quickly hit and wounded. As they lay helpless behind their cars, one or more of the gunmen approached. In a vain attempt to forestall the inevitable, agent Williams raised his hand to the barrel of an AR-15 now less than two feet from his face. Indifferent to his plea, the gunman let it rip. The shot blew off Williams's fingers before lodging in his face, killing him instantly. The gunman then put the semi-conscious Coler out of his misery with shots to the head and throat and fled the scene. Nearly two years later, in March 1977, Peltier was convicted of the double homicide in a federal court in Fargo, North Dakota. At the time, almost no one noticed.

Peter Matthiessen was among those with other things on his mind. In 1977, he was hard at work on arguably his finest book, *The Snow Leopard*. The book tells of his trip to Nepal in search of the elusive snow leopard and an even more elusive peace of mind following the death of his young wife from cancer. It would win him the National Book Award for 1978.

Yet for all the awards and honors, there was a hole in Matthiessen's soul, and he had no obvious way to fill it. Clearly, Christianity was not the answer. In his 1965 book, *At Play in the Fields of the Lord,* he attacked the faith and the missionary urge that spread it, from his perspective, like a cancer. In an earlier book, *Wildlife in America,* Matthiessen chronicled the devastation done to American fauna by the arrival of the white man. Doubly burdened by this cultural legacy, Matthiessen searched out his own "zone of decency," and in the mid-1970s that search took him increasingly to the Indian territories of the American west. It was in a California sweat lodge ceremony in the spring of 1979 that he first heard the radical take on the Leonard Peltier case. "At first I resisted the police-state implications in this idea," claims Matthiessen, but his identity issues seem to have overwhelmed his good judgment.

At the time, Matthiessen was not at all comfortable in his own skin, and *In the Spirit of Crazy Horse* shows it. In the words of one sympathetic critic, the book reflects a new "multicultural spiritual sensibility." The zero-sum nature of this sensibility is best expressed by Peltier's accomplice, Dino Butler: "You Christians," says Butler, "you are a lost people with no identity to this land, the only God you have is your technology which will destroy you because of the greed it demands."

Matthiessen uses Butler to voice his own elegy on a doomed culture. He marries the multicultural narrative to that of radical naturalism and identifies the white American as the villain in both. In effect, he is at play in the fields of both Rachel Carson and Susan Sontag and feels free to "decertify" those who are not, like Peltier's jurors. Indeed, their verdict means no more to him than the Sacco and Vanzetti jury's did to Felix Frankfurter. After all, these are ordinary white people from North Dakota, as ignorant and as excitable as those in 1921 Massachusetts. Matthiessen crudely stereotypes them as "very conservative rural jurors—mostly Lutherans of Scandinavian ancestry, with long faces and a long ruminative memory of nineteenth-century massacres in Minnesota." The Sioux uprising in a neighboring state 115 years earlier had apparently scarred the jurors and left them "ignorant about Indians, or prejudiced, or both." That Butler and Robideau, Peltier's accomplices, had been acquitted by an all-white jury in a separate trial some months earlier in Iowa, which also borders Minnesota, bought no grace for Matthiessen's benighted white man.

In the book's six hundred pages, Matthiessen adds little that the jury might not have known. In the realm of evidence, said Scott Anderson in his *Outside* piece, Matthiessen showed "a casualness toward documentation that bordered on the cavalier." The result is a TODDI defense that makes Mumia's look substantial. Yes, Matthiessen admits, Peltier did fire at the agents from a distance, and yes, he and his accomplices did take the dead men's guns after the massacre. But in the brief moments in between, an unknown "red pickup truck" pulled up to where the agents lay and administered the fatal *coup de grace*. The identity of the killers scarcely mattered in any case. "All the Indians who were there that day were warriors," Matthiessen writes, "and the nameless figures in the pickup truck were no more guilty than [Peltier] and Dino and Leonard, because no Indian that day was guilty." This was the Indian perspective on that fateful day and "increasingly" his own.

The gunmen were not guilty, Matthiessen suggests, because they, like their ancestors, were defending the land. At Pine Ridge, they were defending it from, among other dangers, a government that wanted to open up the uranium beds of western South Dakota to corporate exploitation. As Matthiessen saw it, the government had to eliminate AIM and Peltier before it could do so. Anderson, however, has more than minor problems with "Matthiessen's über-conspiracy theory." One is that there was scarcely any uranium worth extracting, and even if there were, AIM had no chance of restoring the treaty that would have protected it.

At the time, Viking did not sweat the details. It released Matthiessen's book to great, provocative fanfare in March 1983. The press release said it all: "This chilling, controversial book makes clear that Leonard Peltier is only one of the victims in the ruthless quest for land, minerals, and money that the government and industry have pursued at the expense of the Indians for the last 150 years." Although Viking had to soon pull the book for several years because of some well deserved libel suits, the genie was out of the bottle. The cultural establishment could not resist a cause so perfectly progressive in so many ways, no matter how dubious the evidence for Peltier's innocence.

Cries for Peltier's release came from all over the world, not just from the usual suspects like the French *Comité de Solidarité avec les Indiens des Amériques,* but from a former archbishop of Canterbury and Bishop Desmond Tutu of South Africa. Hollywoood, of course, was not far behind. In 1991, Robert Redford and Michael Apted produced a sympathetic documentary, *Incident at Oglala,* and Apted followed up a year later with a fictionalized feature film, *Thunderheart.* To round out the multimedia agitprop, rocker and *Sopranos* co-star Steven Van Zandt contributed the inevitable pop anthem, *Leonard Peltier:*

> June '75 Pine Ridge Reservation
> Two FBI trespass Lakota Nation
> Looking for trouble their army waiting outside
>
> And trouble they brought some
> They were pawns in the big game
> For stolen minerals and tourists
> They were sacrificed in profit's name
>
> And what would you do?
> As you stare into the face of
> The genocide of your people
> Put yourself in the place of
>
> Leonard Peltier
> Where is the justice for Leonard Peltier?

In prison, Peltier wrote his obligatory memoirs, which were published in 1999 by St. Martin's Press as *Prison Writings: My Life Is My Sundance.* The book quickly found its way into the multicultural curricula on campuses across America. The newly talented Peltier took up painting as well, his canvasses selling for as much as five thousand dollars apiece to Hollywood worthies like Peter Coyote, Jane Fonda, Val Kilmer, and Oliver Stone. Stone, not surprisingly, had optioned film rights to the Matthiessen book.

Stone, in fact, would play an important walk-on role as the case morphed from tragedy to burlesque with the emergence of a certain "Mr. X." As Matthiessen tells it, he was meeting in February 1990 with Peltier's cousin, Bob Robideau, when the hooded and "faceless" Mr. X slipped quietly into the room. Disturbed by Peltier's thirteen needless years in prison, Mr. X had volunteered to tell his story.

According to Mr. X, he and a nameless partner were delivering a red pickup truck full of dynamite to Peltier on that fateful June day in 1975 when they came across the two FBI agents. The agents allegedly fired at them, and Mr. X fired a shot over their heads to warn them away, but they persisted. When the other Indians from Peltier's tent city weighed in with covering fire, Mr. X drove his pickup behind the camp to unload the explosives. As the gunfire died down, Mr. X drove back to the seriously wounded agents. In the retelling, both were alert and alive. One allegedly tried to fire his revolver, and Mr. X blew them both away, shooting literally from the hip. "It was self-defense then," Matthiessen interjects. "There was no element of anger?" "I'm absolutely sure it was self-defense," Mr. X replies.

In August of 1990, Matthiessen brought in Stone to shoot a second interview. Matthiesen provided a tape of that interview to Robert Redford for his documentary and to *60 Minutes,* which broadcast it in 1991. "The death of those agents was brought about by their wrongful behavior, not mine," Mr. X told the twenty-six million people watching the *60 Minutes* segment. "I did not choose to take their lives. I only chose to save my own." *60 Minutes* reporter Steve Kroft all but vouched for the man's authenticity. "The man behind the mask seems intimate with every detail of the shoot-out," he told his viewers. What he did not tell them is that he could have gotten those details reading the Matthiessen book. Nor did he tell them that *60 Minutes* had not shot the videotape they had just seen.

The *60 Minutes* segment likely represented the high-water mark of the "Free Peltier" campaign. It energized a wide segment of the public, but it also introduced new facts that were capable of being disputed. Scott Anderson, for one, pointed out the "patent absurdity" of the story. Mr. X's shoot-from-the-hip scenario failed to account for the severed fingers of agent Williams. Nor did the authorities find any of the boxes of dynamite that Mr. X allegedly unloaded. Nor did any of the three accused ever mention a red pickup at any of their trials. When Matthiessen asked Robideau why the defense attorneys failed to introduce the red pickup truck story, he gave such a sorry excuse that even Matthiessen couldn't believe it, but no matter.

By 1995, one of the three, Dino Butler, had grown so weary of the lethal internecine warfare among AIM members that he came forward with the truth. "Well, there is no Mr. X," he admitted to a reporter from NFIC. "Those are all lies." He traced the origin of the Mr. X story to an AIM meeting that he had attended in California, where the idea was floated and rejected. Somehow, he claimed, the Mr. X scenario made its way to Stone and Matthiessen. "I lost a lot of respect for Peter Matthiessen as a writer and as a person I could trust," he admitted, "because he didn't verify this, and it put me and my family in jeopardy. He never made any effort to contact me and ask if this was true."

Scott Anderson had also begun to question Matthiessen's judgment and integrity. In a January 1992 *Esquire* article, Matthiessen made a number of seeming revisions to the story. Most glaringly, he transposed the site of the killings from a humble ranch in Oglala to the historically symbolic Wounded Knee twenty miles away. Anderson was stupified. "The Peltier story," he concludes, "has so entered the realm of myth that apparently its architects no longer feel the need to adhere to the most rudimentary of facts."

Although he had refused Anderson's request for an interview, Matthiessen inferred that Anderson had called him a "liar" and fired back with a scathing rebuttal. The fury and detail of it chastise any reader who might have doubted Matthiessen. Yet even the rebuttal is suspect. The following example speaks to its disingenuousness. Writes Matthiessen:

> Anderson begins with Peltier's "attempted murder" of a Milwaukee police officer, a trumped-up charge on which Peltier was speedily acquitted when the cop's own girlfriend testified that the whole episode had been a setup.

Matthiessen's rebuttal, however, is fully at odds with the account in his own book. In the book, the woman is a "former girlfriend," a different breed altogether. And there is no trial or acquittal because Peltier, "seeing no reason to expect justice," jumps bail, goes underground, and heads "west to the Dakotas." This is a critical distinction. The prosecution would argue that Peltier's fear of arrest on the fugitive charge made him uniquely dangerous that day in Oglala. As to the *Esquire* "botch," this Matthiessen writes off to a copyeditor's misreading of his own "scribbled editing." As Philip Nobile astutely advised, "Deny! Deny! Deny!"

The denial should have come to an end with Paul DeMain's brave editorial in a February 2002 edition of *News From Indian Country*. DeMain was right. His news was not going to make anyone "happy." "After many years of supporting and advocating clemency for Leonard Peltier," he writes, "the *News From Indian Country* editorial staff no longer believes Leonard Peltier is innocent of shooting the agents at close range as he has so often proclaimed."

DeMain had invested twenty-seven years in the case. He had read every document there was to read and interviewed every witness there was to interview. He acknowledged that he and his colleagues would have come to this damning conclusion sooner were it not for the "lies, deceptions, smoke and mirrors. Part of a charade."

That charade had begun with the nearly uncritical media acceptance of the American Indian Movement and continued with the celebrated martyrdom of Peltier. Tim Giago, an Oglala Sioux from Pine Ridge and the publisher of *Indian Country Today*, blames the "eastern liberal press" for ginning up the AIM mania. Although Giago is not at all off target, the press was just part of the problem. So was Matthiessen. To this day, in spite of the evidence, no major media outlet has dared to expose the Peltier hysteria. The charade continues.

OUT OF PLACE

Nineteen seventy-eight, the year that Peter Matthiessen won the National Book Award, proved triumphant for another member of New York's cultural establishment as well.

That was the year Edward Said (pronounced sigh-EED) published his masterwork, *Orientalism*, a book so influential that it changed the very direction of Middle Eastern studies. Like Matthiessen, Said had many of the proper establishment credentials. He had received his Ph.D. from Harvard, taught as a distinguished professor of comparative literature at Columbia University, played classical piano with style, and served for several years as the music critic for the progressive magazine, *Nation*.

Like Matthiessen, too, Said had absorbed a certain malaise, then epidemic among America's progressive intellectual classes, that is an almost complete sense of estrangement from the place he lived and people he lived with. Unlike Matthiessen, however, Said did not have to roam the world in search of his own personal "zone of decency." He found his in one very specific place, a house at 10 Brenner Street in Jerusalem.

This house and his Palestinian childhood became the central, compelling metaphor for Said's significant life work. "Mr. Said was born in Jerusalem and spent the first twelve years of his life there," confirms the *New York Times* in a flattering 1998 article. His family left the house and "fled" Palestine for Cairo in late 1947, "five months before war broke out between Palestinian Arabs and Jews over plans to partition Palestine."

Said's identity as a Palestinian and a refugee would inform everything he wrote, *Orientalism* most certainly. "*Orientalism* is written out of an extremely concrete history of personal loss and national disintegration,"

Said observes in the Afterword of the book's 1994 edition. It is this sense of loss that gives the book its spirit of righteous certainty. He needed it. The book's thesis was a bold one in 1978. Writing in full postmodern patois, then still cutting edge, Said argues that "Orientalism is more particularly valuable as a sign of European-Atlantic power over the Orient than it is as a veridic discourse about the orient." The postmodern "veridic" translates into English as "genuine." What Said means here is that "Orientalism," the Western study of the Middle East, is inherently corrupted by the position of power from which the observer writes. Such analysis is not genuine. By Said's lights, it inevitably tells us more about the people who are doing the writing than those who are being written about. In a nutshell, Westerners cannot credibly write about the East.

Said derived his moral power to devalue an entire academic field from his own "experiences." Indeed, these experiences inspired him to write the book. "The life of an Arab Palestinian in the west, particularly in America, is disheartening," he notes. "There exists an almost unanimous consensus that politically he does not exist, and when it is allowed that he does, it is either as a nuisance or as an Oriental."

Said set out to right past wrongs and succeeded brilliantly. His timing was impeccable. Multiculturalism was still in its embryonic stages, and by fusing it to postmodernism, Said helped to define it. As visible as he was influential, Said emerged, according to the *Nation*, as "probably the best-known intellectual in the world." For someone who allegedly did "not exist," Said did a masterful job of making his presence felt.

If the academic discipline was not fully formed in 1978, multicultural sensitivities certainly were. American universities had been protecting the voice of the "marginalized" from any serious criticism for at least a decade. More than any one person, Said extended that voice and that protection to the Arabic world. In true zero-sum fashion, British and American students of the Middle East would lose a good deal of their voice, and Israel would lose much of its protection. Said only profited. Upon his death in September 2003, the *New York Times'* obituary would describe him not only as "an exemplar of multiculturalism" but also, and perhaps more importantly, as "the most prominent advocate in the United States of the cause of Palestinian independence."

Said did not shy from using his influence to advance his cause. For fourteen years, he served on the Palestine National Conference, a kind of parliament-in-exile alongside the likes of the PLO's Yassir Arafat and still harder-core radicals from the Popular Front for the Liberation of Palestine, the terrorist group that hijacked the Achille Lauro. Although he denounced violence, Said was forever rationalizing its use and was once photographed on the Lebanese border throwing a rock at Israel as "a symbolic gesture of joy."

Throughout his career, Said returned again and again to the source of his own moral power—his forced exile from "my beautiful old house" in Jerusalem. So central was the house to his identity that the Palestinian Heritage Association presented him with a portrait of it during a ceremony in his honor. In early 1992, he paid a nostalgic visit to this house, a visit that was celebrated in a *Harper's Magazine* article, a longer one in the London *Observer* and eventually in a BBC documentary, *In Search of Palestine.* One scene in the film, shows Said and his son in front of the house "my family owned" while Said angrily talks about getting the house back from the Israeli authorities. Said, in fact, scripted and narrated this 1998 documentary to commemorate the fiftieth anniversary of the Palestinian "nakbah," or disaster.

Whether Said knew it or not, time was running out on the compelling saga of his own life that he had been at such pains to shape and share with the world. An Israeli scholar named Justus Reid Weiner had already done two years of hard-nosed, boots-on-the-ground background research on Said's life. As Weiner was learning, the narrative that Said had been successfully spinning was not so "veridic" after all, and he was about ready to deconstruct the heck out of it. "Virtually everything I learned," Weiner writes, "contradicts the story of Said's early life as Said has told it."

Weiner released his findings a year later in the September 1999 issue of the influential Jewish magazine, *Commentary.* In truth, Said had better establishment credentials than anyone suspected, right down to his Episcopalian upbringing. The son of an affluent, American immigrant father who had fought under General Pershing in World War I, Said attended the Mount Hermon School in Massachusetts and Princeton University before moving on to Harvard. It was the first twelve years of his life, however, that would truly raise eyebrows.

Justus Weiner

"I was born, in November 1935," Said writes in *Harper's* in 1992, "in Talbiya, then a mostly new and prosperous Arab quarter of Jerusalem. By the end of 1947, just months before Talbiya fell to Jewish forces, I'd left with my family for Cairo." After their forced departure, he writes in a 1998 *London Review of Books*, "... my entire family became refugees in Egypt."

Yes, Said was born in Jerusalem in 1935. He was born there because his mother had had a tragic experience with Egyptian health care—her first son, Gerald, died during childbirth. After Edward's birth, the family returned to Cairo where his father had been living for the last decade. There, Said's father continued to expand his extremely successful office supply business and moved the family through an increasingly luxurious series of apartments. A Christian and an American citizen from birth, Said attended the best British schools in Cairo before leaving for a pricey American prep school as a teenager.

The famed house, Weiner learned, belonged not to his parents, but to Said's Jerusalem relatives. During almost all of the years Said was alleged to be living there, the Said relatives rented the upstairs apartment to the Kingdom of Yugoslavia for use as a consulate. In a truly odd twist of fate, they rented the downstairs apartment to the renowned Jewish philosopher Martin Buber after he had fled Nazi Germany in 1938. In 1942, the Said relatives forced Buber out in a rent dispute and occupied the apartment themselves. One would think that in all his public recollections of this house, Said might have remembered sharing it with Buber or the Yugoslav consulate, but he did not. It is possible, in fact, that he never even stayed there. The apartment would have been too small for his Jerusalem relatives to share with their prosperous Cairo cousins if they had come to visit.

Said was busted big time. Weiner had proved beyond all doubt that America's most celebrated Palestinian refugee was not really a Palestinian or a refugee. Indeed, during the century's most turbulent years, 1935-1947, years that witnessed the death and dispossession of scores of millions of innocent people, Said had been living high on the hog in Cairo. The whole moral basis for his postcolonial posturing as a victim of Western injustice seemed shot.

Although its headline suggests a nationalist bias on Weiner's part—"Israeli Says Palestinian Thinker Has Falsified His Early Life"— the *New York Times* gave his exposé decent coverage. If Said could ignore Weiner, he could not ignore the *Times*. His comments are instructive and all too typical. "I have never said I am a refugee," he told the *Times*. "Never in my life. On the contrary, I go out of my way to say I had a very privileged life, we had a house in Cairo." Just a year earlier, remember, the *Times* had interviewed Said and written, "Mr. Said was born in Jerusalem and spent the first twelve years of his life there." Until caught by Weiner, this is what Said had told everyone.

To complicate matters, Said came out with a revisionist memoir, *Out of Place*, just months after the Weiner article appeared. Weiner knew the memoir was coming and suggests that his research, of which Said was aware, may have prompted it. In any case, the book papers over the difference between the story Weiner tells and the one that Said had been telling all his adult life.

Although acknowledging his Cairo upbringing—in boring and prurient detail—Said manages to place his parents, sisters, and himself in Jerusalem for "most of 1947." This is convenient timing as it allows him to experience the city's very real tensions before allegedly fleeing with family on the eve of partition. Why his father would abandon his Cairo business at this particular time and move to so obviously volatile a city, Said does not tell us. But he does provide detail of his days at St. Georges School in Jerusalem, an allegiance he had claimed dramatically in the BBC documentary. True, as Weiner showed, St. Georges had no record of his attendance, but truth no longer mattered. The cultural establishment was stuck with Said and would stick by him. He was too significant a force in the multicultural universe to cut loose.

By the time Said died four years later, the controversy had died as well. The *Guardian* of London does not even hint at one. Its obituary closes with a tribute from UN Secretary General Kofi Annan saying, "Both the Middle East and the United States will be the poorer without his distinctive voice." The *New York Times* does raise the Weiner objection, but it does so dismissively 2,000 words into a glowing 2,600-word obituary. In the beginning of the obituary, the "paper of record" had already decided to revive Said's imaginary past.

Edward Said was born in Jerusalem on Nov. 1, 1935, and spent his childhood in a well-to-do neighborhood of thick-walled stone houses that is now one of the main Jewish districts of the city. His father, a prosperous businessman who had lived in the United States, took the family to Cairo in 1947 after the United Nations divided Jerusalem into Jewish and Arab halves.

At the end of the day, even Said himself could not undo the much too useful myth that he himself had created.

LITTLE EICHMANNS

American universities, unfortunately, rarely hire people like Debra Burlingame. All too often, however, they do hire people like Colorado University professor Ward Churchill. Indeed, it is Churchill's status as "type," as a well paid, frequently rewarded academic bellwether that merits his inclusion in this study. Until recently, he has had more influence on the culture as part of this collective than as an individual. As the *Wall Street Journal* accurately observes, "His screeds usually attract little attention outside obscure Marxist Web sites and the like."

One of those screeds deeply offended Burlingame. Written on September 12, 2001, and titled "Some People Push Back: On the Justice of Roosting Chickens," Churchill's essay hailed the "gallant sacrifices" of the 9/11 terrorists and mocked the deaths of the victims. "If there was a better, more effective, or in fact any other way of visiting some penalty befitting their participation upon the little Eichmanns inhabiting the sterile sanctuary of the twin towers," wrote Churchill from his own tenured sanctuary in Colorado, "I'd really be interested in hearing about it."

Burlingame's brother Charles had piloted the American Airlines flight that had been hijacked and flown into the Pentagon. Churchill's essay offended her to the core. When in January 2005 she learned that Churchill had been invited to speak at Hamilton College in upstate New York, she swung into action. She called the president of the college and the chairman of the board of trustees and demanded that the invitation be withdrawn. Burlingame also talked to the *Wall Street Journal* and shared her Hamilton conversations with its editors. Without meaning to, she set in motion the exposure of one of the more successful frauds in academic history and the culture that enabled it.

Like Peter Matthiessen, Churchill sought his own zone of decency in the American Indian experience. Like Edward Said, however, Churchill built an entire career by pretending to be something he wasn't, in this case an American Indian. Indeed, in its perverse creativity, Churchill's lifelong masquerade makes Said's look almost honorable. Said at least had Palestinian roots. Churchill can make no such claims, although he often does and has.

He identifies himself on the infamous "Some People Push Back" essay as a "Keetoowah Band Cherokee" and "one of the most outspoken of Native American activists." In his book, *A Little Matter of Genocide*, Churchill describes himself as "an American Indian, as a twenty-five-year member of the American Indian movement." Perhaps more telling is the promotion of his book, *From a Native Son*. The cover is all Churchill: large sunglasses, long dark hair parted in the middle, shaded face, and slouching insouciance. He is the "native son." A prominent blurb on the South End Press Web site reinforces that impression, calling Churchill, "one of the Native world's most perceptive voices."

Native or otherwise, Churchill raised his voice often in support of a variety of bad actors, Mumia and Leonard Peltier chief among them. He insinuated himself into the Peltier case deeply and early. In fact, it was reportedly his home that was used for the famed videotaping of the Mr. X confession. If his activism impressed his Colorado University colleagues, it did not, however, impress all of his fellow Indians. "The American Indian Movement doesn't need whitemen [sic] wannabes claiming to be Indians, claiming to be AIM directors running around representing the movement," said AIM leader Vern Bellecourt in 1994, asking prophetically, "Who is Ward Churchill?"

To answer that question, the *Rocky Mountain News* did a little fact checking on Churchill and the man he claims to be his original Indian ancestor, Joshua Tyner, a Revolutionary War veteran from Georgia. The *News* discovered that in the 1820 census, Tyner listed himself as "white." The fact that Tyner's mother was killed and scalped by Creek Indians lends some credibility to Tyner's self-definition. Even if Tyner were a full-blooded Indian, Churchill would be only 1/64 Indian, not the kind of pedigree on which one typically builds an identity.

That identity has served Churchill well. With only a Masters degree from Sangamon State University—presuming that to be legitimate—he exploited the unspoken racial spoils system of the American campus and managed to become a tenured professor at Colorado University. Were he "white" he would never have been hired, let alone promoted.

This identity has also bestowed on him what he calls a certain "moral authority," or what Shelby Steele more accurately calls "the feeling of entitlement, or even license" that comes with victimization. When Churchill lashed out, in his September 12 essay, his colleagues at Colorado University respected his right as "victim" to exercise that license and/or authority. Indeed, it was *after* he published the essay that Churchill was named chairman of the Ethnic Studies Department. This one fact testifies as few others can to the unsalvageable state of the liberal arts in the American university.

Not surprisingly, Churchill's scholarship is as dubious as his identity. One area where he has had some influence is on the subject of genocide. The primary thesis of his book, *A Little Matter of Genocide,* is that "we" Native Americans are "one of the most victimized groups in the history of humanity" and that the "settler population" has and *continues* to shoot, stab, beat, burn alive, scalp, and "deliberately" infect Indians with infectious diseases "when deemed expedient." A strong secondary thesis is that Jews have no particular claim to victimization, their case not being one of deliberate genocide but rather an "erratic and contradictory hodgepodge of anti-Jewish policies." In ethnic studies departments, Churchill's dazzling lack of perspective hews to the norm.

Given his talent for self-invention, Churchill has few qualms about inventing history, and credit here goes to Thomas Brown, assistant professor of sociology at Lamar University, for rooting out at least some of his more egregious inventions, particularly on the subject of biological warfare. If, in academic circles, it is taboo to blame gays for spreading AIDS, it is entirely acceptable to blame Europeans for spreading disease. To make a case for "genocide," scholars like Churchill are at pains to present the infection of American Indians as purposeful. Given the crude state of medical knowledge five centuries ago, this is not an easy case to make.

If one dispenses with facts, however, the going is a good deal easier. In *A Little Matter*, Churchill asserts that the deliberate infection of the native population in North America may have begun with Captain John Smith and continued in the Massachusetts Bay Colony, but he cannot provide anything resembling evidence for either claim. Besides, like Noam Chomsky, a respected source, Churchill prefers to focus his anti-Western animus on the United States. Thus, he takes particular glee in being able to lay a specific charge of willful biological infection against the United States Army.

Churchill claims that in June 1837, the U.S. Army took blankets from a smallpox-infested infirmary in St. Louis, sent them up the Missouri on a steamboat, and gave them to the Mandan Indians gathered at Fort Clark in present-day North Dakota. As Thomas points out, Churchill first proposed this tale in 1992 as part of a legal brief justifying his disruption of a Columbus Day parade in Denver.

"Although the medical practice of the day required the precise opposite procedure," reads the brief, "army doctors ordered the Mandans to disperse once they exhibited symptoms of infection. The result was a pandemic among the Plains Indian nations which claimed at least 125,000 lives, and may have reached a toll several times that number." By the time *A Little Matter* was published in 1997, Churchill had revised the maximum casualty count from a possible several hundred thousand down to 100,000. According to the best estimates of the Smithsonian Institute, however, there were no more than 2,000,000 Indians in all of America north of Mexico at the time the Europeans arrived. For most scholars, a revision involving as much as 20 percent of total North American Indian population would merit at least a footnote of explanation, but not for Churchill.

In fact, no explanation will help this story. In his original drafts, the only source Churchill cites is Russell Thornton, author of *American*

Indian Holocaust and Survival: A Population History since 1492. When Thomas checked the Thornton source, he discovered an altogether different version of events. In Thornton's version, there is no mention of soldiers or blankets or a St. Louis infirmary or even a hint of intentional infection. Thornton also claims no more than 30,000 deaths.

The fatal steamboat stop in Thornton's version is not at the fort but at the Mandan village. "Some aboard the steamer had smallpox when the boat docked," writes Thornton. "It soon was spread to the Mandan, perhaps by deckhands who unloaded merchandise, perhaps by chiefs who went aboard a few days later, or perhaps by women and children who went aboard at the same time."

"If Churchill has sources that say otherwise, I'd like to see them," Thornton told the *Los Angeles Times.* "But right now I'm his source for this, and it's wrong." Churchill cites additional references in the book version of this story, but none of these references mention soldiers or blankets or a deliberate infection either. In fact, the epidemic horrified the white traders who worked through Fort Clark, and their letters communicated the same. Many of them lost their Indian wives and children as well as the trading partners upon whom they depended for a living. Some contracted the disease themselves. Other than pure evil, Churchill can suggest no motive for the elimination of an economically useful population many hundreds of miles and scores of years away from white settlement.

Despite his use of the word "holocaust" in the title, Thornton argues that Indian population rebounded in the twentieth century and grew steadily. In so saying, he absolutely undercuts Churchill's thesis. One cannot have both steady population growth and "continued" genocide in the same time frame. Demographics, however, do not deter Churchill and his fellow travelers from routinely accusing the United States not only of genocide but also of biological warfare against its own people. Students casually parrot this line. Given this indoctrination, professors and students are all but alone among their fellow citizens in willingly ceding the moral high ground to countries like Saddam's Iraq.

Meanwhile Churchill and his supporters have noisily manned the ramparts of free speech in demanding his right to be heard at the expense of Colorado's taxpayers. As with Mumia, however, Churchill's enthusiasm for the First Amendment is purely situational. Just a week before the Hamilton College blow-up, Churchill and his fellow defendants were acquitted in a Colorado court for attempting to block Denver's Columbus Day parade. They had argued that the parade, as an alleged celebration of genocide, was a form of hate speech unworthy of First Amendment protection. Turning the sophistry of his argument against him, Burlingame argued that Hamilton College should deny Churchill a platform. "I consider it hate speech," said Burlingame wryly, "which isn't protected at all by the First Amendment." Citing sundry "death threats," Hamilton College cancelled the Churchill event. Churchill's chickens had come home to roost.

The Public Burning

When the Nobel Peace Prize committee met to award its 1992 prize, the choices were many and good. With the collapse of the Soviet Union in 1991 and the fall of the Berlin Wall two years prior, committee members might have chosen any of the architects of that empire's demise—Ronald Reagan, for instance, or Margaret Thatcher or Pope John Paul II or the Soviet dissidents. They did not and never would. The committee passed as well on the heroes of Tiananmen Square.

No, this being 1992, the five-hundredth anniversary of Colombus's "discovery" of the Americas, the committee members took the opportunity to rub its thumb in America's eye. They awarded the Nobel Peace Prize for 1992 to a Guatemalan woman, an "indigena" by the name of Rigoberta Menchu.

No doubt, countless heads were scratched around the world at the time of the announcement: "Rigoberta who?" But there was little head-scratching on America's campuses. Her autobiography, *I, Rigoberta*

Menchu: An Indian Woman in Guatemala, had already become well known and well established in academe. *The Chronicle of Higher Education* accurately described the book "as a cornerstone of the multicultural canon."

What gave the book its power was not its literary quality, which was negligible, but its authenticity. "This has become *the* book one reads when one wants to learn about the problems of Indians in Latin America," Gene Bell-Villada, a professor of Latin American literature at Williams College, would tell the *Chronicle.* "Students are always impressed and very moved by it."

Conservative critic Dinesh D'Souza was neither moved nor impressed. In fact, he had dismissed *I, Rigoberta* as "bogus multicultural agitprop" when Stanford University included it in a new humanities course created in 1988 to replace its Western civilization requirement. On the very day of the Nobel announcement, *The Chronicle of Higher Education* called D'Souza. Its editors likely hoped that now at least he would have to eat some public crow. Although D'Souza did not exactly oblige, his response was still a bit defensive. "All I can say," he replied, "is that I am relieved she didn't win for literature."

The award was her "canonization," D'Souza admitted. She received fourteen honorary doctorates in its wake, and in that same year, 1992, she was nominated as a United Nations goodwill ambassador and special representative of indigenous peoples. In the two years following, she claims to have received some 7,000 international speaking invitations and was awarded the Legion of Honor by French president, Jacques Chirac. To criticize her inclusion in the canon now would seem churlish, if not downright racist.

In 1988, when the canon debate raged on the Stanford campus, David Stoll just happened to be there working on his Ph.D in anthropology. As an older student with a specific focus, he did not get involved. His area of interest, however, was Guatemala, and he knew Latin America well. As an independent scholar, he had spent nearly a decade studying it, specifically the role of Protestant missionaries in that part of the world.

For his Ph.D. dissertation, Stoll was researching the anthropology of civil war in the Latin American context, an entirely useful project if done conscientiously. He hoped to learn how Guatemalan peasants responded to insurgency and counterinsurgency. He had read Menchu's book and was unapologetically sympathetic with her people and her cause. It was hard not to be.

Menchu describes in heartbreaking detail how the light-skinned, Europeanized *ladino* ruling class used the government to steal the land of her father and other native peoples. And when the *indigenas* protested, that same ruling class called in the army to suppress even peaceful dissent with unspeakable brutality. Persecuted beyond endurance, Rigoberta's heroic father goes underground in 1977 and helps form the "legendary" Committee for Campesino Unity (CUC), which allies itself with the guerilla movement. Now about eighteen, Rigoberta gets involved in the struggle. Among other tasks, she teaches villagers how to make Molotov cocktails, dig stake pits, and capture vulnerable soldiers to defend themselves from army attacks.

In the book's most dramatic scene, the army hauls a crew of suspected dissidents to the square of the Maya town of Chajul in the western highlands of Guatemala. Among the twenty-three beaten and tortured prisoners is Rigoberta's sixteen year-old brother, Petrocinio.

Rigoberta and her parents had made a grueling journey to Chajul to seek his liberation. They sought in vain. First, the army forces them and the townspeople to listen to an anti-communist harangue. Then, they have to watch in horror as the soldiers pour gasoline on each of the prisoners and set them ablaze one by one. While the prisoners burn, the soldiers laugh and celebrate. Outraged by this ghastly spectacle, the townspeople, Rigoberta among them, rush at the soldiers, but they draw back for fear of being massacred. "I didn't think I might die," remembers Rigoberta, "I just wanted to do something, even kill a soldier. At that moment I wanted to show my aggression."

The following year, in January 1980, her father is among those protestors who occupy the Spanish embassy in Guatemala City to call attention to their increasingly desperate cause. In defiance of protocol and international law, riot police storm the embassy, and thirty-six people die in the fire that ensues, Vicente Menchu among them.

Soon after, the army kidnaps her mother, raping her and torturing her to death. Now about twenty-one, the unschooled Rigoberta becomes an activist with the CUC. "My job was to organize people," she recalls. "I had to learn Spanish and to read and write." As her leadership role grows, the authorities zero in on her, and she flees the country. In 1982, while in Paris, she tells her story to feminist Elisabeth Burgos-Debray, the ex-wife of international revolutionary and friend of Che Guevara, Regis Debray. "The world I live in is so evil, so bloodthirsty, that it can take my life away from one moment to the next," Rigoberta concludes her narration. "So the only road open to me is the struggle, the just war."

When Stoll first came to Rigoberta's region in 1987 to interview peasants about the cycle of violence, he was well aware of just how brutal the army could be. What the peasants were telling him, however, differed from Rigoberta's story in two critical ways. First, they seemed to fear the guerillas nearly as much as the army. They wished that both would go away. And secondly, they seemed to have a better relationship with their *ladino* neighbors than Rigoberta acknowledged, including a fair amount of open friendships and even intermarriage. Still, as Stoll admits, "I had no reason to doubt the veracity of *I, Rigoberta Menchu*. Nor did anyone else as far as I knew."

In 1989, he found himself in the infamous town of Chajul. He was interviewing an elderly gentleman named Domingo, when one of his questions left Domingo puzzled. "The army burned prisoners alive?" Domingo asked Stoll rhetorically. "Not here." Intrigued, Stoll interviewed six more townspeople, and they all told him the same thing. There had been no burning of prisoners in the town. This was the first of many discrepancies that Stoll discovered. "At this point," writes Stoll, "I did what any sensible graduate student does with a controversial discovery. I dropped the subject and scuttled back to my doctoral dissertation."

In 1993, Stoll published a book based on his dissertation, *Between Two*

Armies in the Ixil Towns of Guatemala, "Ixil" being a Mayan language spoken by a regional language-group. Stoll's "peers in the overlapping solidarity movement" did not take kindly to the book. They objected to the notion that the peasants were wary of the guerillas. Besides, as more than one person told him, "That's not what we read in *I, Rigoberta Menchu.*"

Then too, the postmodern, post-colonialist era was in full flower. A white, North American male judged a native woman's "narrative" at his own risk. For the very act of judging, any number of academics stood ready to denounce such a person for cultural imperialism, if not racism. Knowing this, Stoll was careful in choosing whom he talked to about Menchu and what he told them. At small academic gatherings as early as 1990 and 1991, he had begun to share his findings, and the response was, as he expected, often hostile.

"The reactions corroborate the final point of my 1990 talk," he notes, "that we have an unfortunate tendency to idolize native voices that serve our own political and moral needs, as opposed to others that do not." By constructing what Stoll calls "mythologies of purity," academics were able to isolate themselves from the reality of a situation often at the expense of the people they were mythologizing. And this is exactly what he thought was happening in Guatemala and why, despite the risks, Stoll felt the moral imperative to "deconstruct" Rigoberta's story.

It was not all that hard to do. Other than her age, twenty-three at the time of the narrative, just about every other contention on the very first page of the book is conspicuously false. "I must say before I start that I never went to school," writes Rigoberta, "and so I find speaking Spanish very difficult." (1) As Stoll quickly discovered, however, the one fact that all her fellow villagers recalled about Rigoberta was her education. She was esteemed for her learning. She was one of very few local girls chosen by the Catholic nuns for a select boarding school in Guatemala City. There she thrived in an accelerated program for older girls. "Spanish she spoke easily and well," remembered one particular teacher, a memory shared by others.

Nor did anyone in her town, however, remember Rigoberta as being a political leader, let alone a guerilla activist. The reason was simple. She did not live in the town in the late 1970s, the period of greatest unrest. She was away at school. In addition, she fabricated most other details of her childhood, like her having to work on the coffee plantations of the evil ladinos or her having witnessed the deaths of a younger brother from malnutrition.

The most problematic deceit involved her father. "My father fought for twenty-two years," recalls Rigoberta, "waging a heroic struggle against the landowners who wanted to take our land and our neighbors land." The reality was a bit different. In fact, Vicente Menchu was an army veteran and a relatively prosperous landowner, who shared in a community grant of 2,753 hectares of land. That's roughly 6,800 acres or about ten square miles of property. He even worked with the Peace Corps on its development.

Although most of that larger property was of little immediate value, Vicente Menchu laid claim to about 500 acres of cleared bottomland that was highly prized. The rapacious ladino plantation owners were not his problem. His own in-laws were. For years, much to his wife's consternation, Vicente and her relatives carried on a kind of Hatfield-McCoy dispute that occasionally spilled into violence and often spilled into court.

Stoll then raises the indelicate question of what the army was doing in this remote village in the first place. What he discovers is that a radical group called the Guerilla Army of the Poor (EGP in Spanish) showed up in the Ixil region in the spring of 1979. Few among them were indigenous. Most of the guerillas, in fact, spoke only Spanish and waved the heroic image of Che Guevara on their flag. They then proceeded to raise holy hell, beginning with vandalism and sabotage and ending with the harassment of missionaries and the murder of certain large landowners. Although these landowners had nothing to do with her father, Rigoberta portrays them as "thieves, criminals, and liars" and makes them the villains in her own morality play.

Understandably outraged by the murders, the families of these landowners cooperated with the army in hunting down suspects. To be sure, the army did respond with indiscriminate brutality and murdered Rigoberta's brother. One explanation Stoll heard is that the Menchus' feuding in-laws fingered Rigoberta's brother as a terrorist. His kidnapping helped spur her father to join the group that occupied the Spanish embassy. Although the siege by the riot police was irrational and illegal, the lethal fire was likely started by a Molotov cocktail misthrown by one of the protestors. The reign of terror from both sides had been swift. Vicente Menchu died in that fire only nine months after the EGP first showed up in his region.

Caught in the midst of all this mayhem were the generally peaceful, apolitical peasants. By the time Rigoberta's book was published in 1983, their region was a wasteland. "Blame that they had focused exclusively on the army for the obvious reason that it murdered their relatives," notes Stoll, "they now extended to the guerillas, for luring indigenas into a hopeless cause." Guerilla commander, Mario Payeras, likewise regretted this choice of battlefield. After leaving the EGP, he admitted that "the social backwardness of a marginal area of the capitalist system" made for a stubbornly infertile breeding ground for a progressive revolution. Had he read his Soviet history he might have known this in advance. For the Menchus, like most of their neighbors, were not without ambition. They saw themselves as small, petty capitalist landowners. In a word, they were "kulaks," not at all dissimilar to those wiped out in the Ukraine. Under normal circumstances, kulaks will resist a radical restructuring of society. They did in Bolivia. When Che Guevara tried to foment revolution there, they turned him in.

Unfortunately, the Marxist left mourns the kulaks' plight only when they are being murdered by the forces of the right. *I, Rigoberta Menchu* preserved that selective image and, Stoll argues, "protected revolutionary sympathizers from the knowledge that the revolutionary movement was a bloody failure." In fact, Stoll believes that the book firmed up international support for the insurgency and helped keep the revolution alive after it had lost most of its internal political support.

Appealing as it was to feminists, Marxists, multiculturalists, and supporters of indigenous rights—in other words, just about everyone in academia—*I, Rigoberta Menchu* had quickly become a sacred text. Stoll writes knowingly of Rigoberta's spiritual appeal. In North America, she often spoke in churches to packed audiences uncomfortable with their whiteness, their affluence, and their own government's real or imagined role in the civil war.

"Rigoberta's story of oppression is analogous to a preacher reminding listeners that they are sinners," observes Stoll. "Then her story of joining the left and learning that not all outsiders are evil makes it possible for the audience to be on her side, providing a sense of absolution." Many in the academic and human rights community, Stoll observes subtly, "felt that Rigoberta's account deserved to be interpreted literally."

When Stoll's not-unsympathetic book on the subject, *Rigoberta Menchu and the Story of all Poor Guatemalans,* came out in late 1999, the academic community would likely have ignored it save for one unexpected intervention. The *New York Times* sent a reporter to Guatemala to double check Stoll's research. To his and the paper's credit, reporter Larry Rohter told the truth about what he found, namely that "many of the main episodes related by Ms. Menchu have either been fabricated or seriously exaggerated." If Stoll could be ignored, the *Times* could not.

The article whipped up a firestorm in the academic community. That community's Bible, *The Chronicle of Higher Education,* did a 3,000-word follow up on the article and book. After interviewing numerous academics across the country, the *Chronicle* came to a bizarrely predictable conclusion about most of those who teach the book: "They say it doesn't matter if the facts in the book are wrong, because they believe Ms. Menchu's story speaks to a greater truth about the oppression of poor people in Central America." The Nobel Prize committee was not about to reconsider either. "All autobiographies embellish to a greater or lesser extent," Geir Lundestad, director of the Norwegian Nobel Institute, told the *New York Times.*

One can only imagine the internal pressure on the *Times* and Stoll. A month after the original article, the *Times* responded with a conciliatory piece, "Guatemala Laureate Defends 'My Truth.'" In it, Menchu smoothes over her deceits with half-truths and covers it all with the righteous indignation of the victim, "If anyone thinks I'm going to say I'm sorry because I was born Maya and am an ignorant Indian, they're wrong." Curiously, at the time she narrated the book seventeen years earlier, she never referred to herself as a Maya. That identity did not yet exist among indigenous Guatemalans.

In this second *Times* piece, Stoll helps by giving Menchu just enough wiggle room to keep her reputation intact. "You can understand and defend her narrative strategy, of folding others' experience into her own, making herself into a kind of all-purpose Maya," he comments generously. He adds that hers was an "emergency situation" that all but demanded a simple narrative.

Absent any explanation from Rigoberta, some have excused her prevarications as "magic realism." This is the school of alternative reality popularized by America's most celebrated student of the art, Carlos Castenada. In the 1960s and 1970s, Castenada wrote a series of bestselling books detailing his experiences with a Yaqui Indian shaman by the name of Don Juan. At the heart of each book is the presumption that Indians have a fully different way of seeing the world and interpreting facts.

Castenada submitted the "field notes" for one of these books as his Ph.D. dissertation at UCLA, and, incredibly, it was accepted. In 1973, just as multiculturalism was about to flower, he got his Ph.D. By 1973, however, it was becoming increasingly obvious that Castenada was writing fiction. As critic Richard DeMille has amply demonstrated, Don Juan was likely no more real than Kunta Kinte. Indeed, one noted sociologist called Castenada's work possibly "the biggest hoax in anthropology since the Piltdown Man." In the final analysis, his books proved too outlandish and insufficiently political to stay viable in academia. Still, the notion of the "separate reality" outlived his reputation and segued nicely into the postmodern perspective and the Disney cartoon.

A more likely source for Rigoberta's inventions was the Munzenberg-inspired repository of Marxist propaganda. The Rigoberta one meets in her book is less an all-purpose Maya than an all-purpose radical leftist. She creates for herself a studied multicultural reality that reflects popular trends as much as it does the traditional values of the Maya. As a tip of the hat to radical environmentalists, for instance, Rigoberta ascribes the death of one of her brothers to intoxication from pesticides sprayed from an airplane. There is no evidence that this happened.

More significant, Rigoberta goes to great pains to distance herself from the devout Catholicism that was customary in her region and to recreate herself along the lines of a Disney Pocahontas. "Our people have taken Catholicism as just another channel of expression," she tells the reader disingenuously, "not our one and only belief." The children of her world, she adds, "have more contact with nature" than "the white children" and worship "Mother Earth" among other "sacred" natural objects.

Historically, there has been no more riveting propaganda than the story of an enemy of burning people alive, often in public. "Tell the world how they run over prisoners with tanks," Comintern propagandist Willi Munzenberg exhorted Arthur Koestler during the Spanish Civil War, "how they pour petrol over them and burn them alive. Make the world gasp with horror."

In *I, Rigoberta Menchu,* the immolation of Rigoberta's brother takes place in the town square. Rigoberta did finally admit that she was not there to see it, but that it happened nonetheless. "If someone will give me his body," she tells the *New York Times* defiantly in her new postmodern accent, "I will change my view. My truth is that my brother Patrocinio was burned alive."

Curiously, a few years before Rigoberta's book was published, respected American novelist Robert Coover wrote a popular book called *The Public Burning.* In this satirical but sympathetic account of the conspicuously guilty Julius and Ethel Rosenberg, Coover has their execution take place in New York's town square, Times Square, thus the "public burning" of the title.

In fact, Rigoberta's family suffered real and horrific losses during the civil war. There is a larger truth here. But by fabricating the *istina,* one can create an alternative *pravda,* and for Marxists, that is the point of it all.

DISARMING AMERICA

In 1996, the world was Michael Bellesiles's oyster. He was a much admired young professor at a highly respected research university, Emory in Atlanta, the author of the year's best-reviewed journal article, and an up-and-coming, second generation "new historian."

For historians, the "new history" school was the place to be in 1996. It had emerged in and with the 1960s and steamrollered the old "consensus" approach into near oblivion. Within twenty years it had established itself as the reigning orthodoxy on American campuses. Not coincidentally, new history nicely complemented the multicultural movement. It did for the past what culture studies did for the present, replacing the search for "uniformity and progress" with the embrace of diverse perspectives and critical thinking.

In 1996, Clayton Cramer manned the opposite end of the history pecking order from Bellesiles. Indeed, it is hard to imagine a less prestigious posting than his as a graduate student working on his Masters thesis at the backwater Sonoma State University in California. A student of early American history, Cramer's thesis concerned the evolution of concealed carry laws in the early Republic.

Nineteen ninety-six was the year Bellesiles went public with a startling new thesis. He introduced it in one of the profession's most esteemed publications, the *Journal of American History* (JAH). Simply titled, "The Origins of Gun Culture in the United States, 1760-1865," Bellesiles flew in the face of conventional wisdom with his boldly stated thesis statement,

"We will find that gun ownership was exceptional in the eighteenth and early nineteenth century, even on the frontier."

As Bellesiles clearly understood, he was challenging not only historical assumptions, but political ones as well. Second Amendment supporters read that cryptically worded amendment as an intrinsically individual right. Gun control advocates, on the other hand, believe that the right to bear arms derives from the state for the limited purpose of establishing a "well regulated militia." If gun ownership were rare on the frontier, and the state were the primary dispenser of weapons as Bellesiles argued, then gun control forces would acquire a powerful new rhetorical weapon. Bellesiles's colleagues obviously liked the thesis. The Organization of American Historians named his JAH piece "Best Article of the Year."

Back at Sonoma, Cramer recoiled in amazement when he read the article. It challenged everything he knew about gun ownership, and he knew a lot. He was particularly piqued by Bellesiles's probate data suggesting that only 14 percent of early American households had guns. More confident than his lowly station might seem to warrant, Cramer sent a letter to the JAH citing a number of anecdotal accounts that refuted Bellesiles's thesis. He concluded with a bold bit of effrontery, "If the probate data shows that guns were owned by a small minority of white males, then I conclude that the data suffers some serious selection bias problems."

As was customary, the JAH showed Bellesiles a copy of Cramer's letter before they published it and invited his response. "I could add a few more quotes to Cramer's list," Bellesiles harrumphed in reply. "Such would be an easy task, since my source would be the same as his: the 'Firearms Alert' internet site run by the National Rifle Association." In reality, Cramer had taken none of his citations from the NRA's site. He had put them there.

The conflict then moved to the H-Net, an electronic message board for historians. For several years, the conflict remained in cyberspace, which is where respected historian Peter Charles Hoffer stumbled upon it. Although he was an early champion of Bellesiles and an unapologetic gun control advocate, the tone of Bellesiles's responses disturbed him.

"Bellesiles did not refute, indeed did not attempt to refute, the substance of Cramer's criticism," Hoffer writes in his fair-minded book, *Past Imperfect*, "he belittled it by associating it with a partisan, nonscholalry Internet source, and dismissed Cramer as a gun nut and crank."

In late summer 2000, as the presidential campaign headed into the homestretch, Alfred A. Knopf released Bellesiles's book on his research, *Arming America*. Hoffer rightly describes it as a "major publishing event." The response from the cultural establishment was pure gush. "The early reviews," he adds, "ran from favorable to ecstatic." And the reviews ran everywhere.

Historian Garry Wills's 2,000-word review in the *New York Times*, "Spiking the Gun Myth," nicely captures the establishment embrace of Bellesiles's thesis. Although guns are a "holy object" in American mythology, writes the happily reeducated Wills, "they were barely in existence" before the Civil War. Those few guns that did exist—here he quotes Bellesiles—"were state-controlled." The joy in Wills's review is unmistakable. "[Bellesiles] provides overwhelming evidence," he writes in summary, "that our view of the gun is as deep a superstition as any that affected Native Americans in the 17th century."

In April 2001, Bellesiles capped his season of honors by winning Columbia University's highly coveted Bancroft Prize for American history. But while the rest of the history world cheered, Clayton Cramer busied himself checking facts. To say the least, they weren't checking out.

Clayton Cramer

"I could flip his book open

at random and find a significant error," says Cramer. He discovered that many of Bellesiles's quotations were so out of context that they reversed the author's meaning. The same was true for laws that Bellesiles quoted. Dates had been changed as well. As Cramer notes wryly, "It took me twelve hours of hunting before I found a citation that was completely correct."

Cramer upped the ante. After reviewing a number of Bellesiles's sources, he blasted him on the H-Net, "I have changed my mind. He's not just wrong; he's intentionally deceiving people." The first specific challenge that Cramer posted on the Internet was a critical one and a typical one. It involved the Militia Act of 1792, which required free white males between the ages of eighteen and forty-five to enroll in the militia. What follows is how Bellesiles quoted it:

Further, "every citizen so enrolled, shall . . . be constantly provided with a good musket or firelock, a sufficient bayonet and belt, two spare flints," and other accoutrements.

What follows is the actual text from the Library of Congress Web site:

That every citizen so enrolled and notified, shall within six months thereafter, provide himself with a good musket or firelock, a sufficient bayonet and belt, two spare flints, and a knapsack, a pouch with a box therein to contain not less than twenty-four cartridges, suited to the bore of his musket or firelock: or with a good rifle, knapsack, shot-pouch and powder-horn, twenty balls suited to the bore of his rifle, and a quarter of a pound of powder.

As Cramer points out, Bellesiles substituted the active "shall within six months thereafter, provide himself" with the passive "shall . . . be constantly provided." He makes the direct implication that Congress would do the providing not the individual. This is a critical switch, and it is not an accident. If ordinary citizens were capable of arming themselves then guns could not have been all that scarce.

What troubled Cramer from the beginning as well were the travel documents that Bellesiles cited. Many of these he had read himself, and his memory did not square with Bellesiles's presentation of them. Bellesiles, for instance, had reviewed numerous travel accounts written in America from 1750 to 1800 and claimed that none of the travelers noticed "that they were surrounded by guns and violence." In rechecking the accounts Bellesiles cited, Cramer found that at least eight made specific reference to hunting, guns, and violence. One that he posted was Isaac Weld's *Travels through the States of North America:*

> The people here, as in the back parts of the United States, devote a very great part of their time to hunting, and they are well skilled in the pursuit of game of every description. They shoot almost universally with the rifle gun, and are as dexterous at the use of it as any men can be.

As he continued to fact check, Cramer found "hundreds of shockingly gross falsifications." He wasn't the only one. After the wave of enthusiasm subsided, historians began to notice the work of critics outside their community like Cramer and James Lindgren, a Northwestern University law professor. And the historians too began to enter the fray, however tentatively.

In January 2002, *The William and Mary Quarterly* staged a special print forum to examine Bellesiles's work. The historians featured were not kind, and more and more the criticism centered on the probate records that Bellesiles had cited. Disturbed by the controversy, Emory University convened a three-scholar panel to review Bellesiles's documentation. When pressed for his notes on the probate records, Bellesiles claimed that they had been lost in a campus flood. Emory wasn't buying. The panel found "serious deviations from accepted practices" including "evidence of falsification." In October 2002, Emory accepted his resignation. In December 2002, Columbia University withdrew the Bancroft Award. In January 2003, Knopf cancelled Bellesiles's contract.

Bellesiles was clearly a conflicted individual. Although he claims to have been a registered Republican and McCain supporter as late as the year 2000, he had at an earlier date proudly posted on H-Net, "I make no apology for being a political activist as well as an historian." His public activism, particularly in the area of gun control, suggested a decidedly non-Republican tilt. So does the tone of *Arming America*. One cannot read a page of the book without confronting Bellesiles's *contempt*—there is no better word—for traditional American culture and values. His zero-sum animus perfectly captures the multicultural ethos *au courant* on campus, an animus particularly evident in his oddly ironic chapter, "Creation of the First American Gun Culture: Indians and Firearms."

The bias in this chapter borders on the Churchillian. Indians, for instance, humiliate the hapless white settlers in "daring nighttime raids." By contrast, when the settlers attack at night, they do so by "sneaking among their sleeping prey." Every single portrayal of a white man in this chapter is negative: settlers are cowardly, brutal, unskilled, mendacious, and dishonorable. "Militia companies throughout New England demonstrated little skill in battle against Indian warriors," writes Bellesiles in a typically grotesque generalization, "finding themselves best able to defeat women and children, and far too willing to throw aside their muskets for a quick retreat."

In his analysis of Mary Rowlandson's well-known captivity narrative, Bellesiles is at his dishonest best. In 1675, Indians had descended upon Rowlandson's sleeping settlement in Lancaster, Massachusetts. The reader does well to recall Bellesiles's thesis, namely that guns were something of a rare and useless extravagance on the American frontier. Indeed, in the first paragraph of the book, he quotes Benjamin Franklin on the supremacy of bows and arrows over guns. Mary Rowlandson, however, has a different take on their relative utility.

At length they came and beset our own house, and quickly it was the dolefulest day that ever mine eyes saw. The house stood upon the edge of a hill; some of the Indians got behind the hill, others into the barn, and others behind anything that could shelter them; from all which places they shot against the house, so that the bullets seemed to fly like hail. . . .

In their courageous defense of the household, three of the male defenders are shot down. Although Rowlandson makes no specific reference to their firing back, it is certainly implied. Here is how Bellesiles summarizes the event:

But as Mary Rowlandson's famous account makes clear, setting the houses on fire proved the most effective weapon. As the New Englanders fled the flames they were cut down by Indian hatchers and arrows, both of which were more accurate than guns. Oddly, Rowlandson saw no settlers returning fire, apparently the surprise and panic were too extreme.

"Oddly" is a good choice of words. For somehow the homesteaders, with "two flankers at two opposite corners," managed to hold off the Indians off for "about two hours." Nor does Rowlandson make a single mention of arrows in the horrific aftermath that follows the burning of the house. When she and her children attempt to flee, "The Indians shot so thick that the bullets rattled against the house." Rowlandson is shot. The child in her arms is shot dead as is Rowlandson's sister. Rowlandson describes the twelve dead with her typical sober detail—"some shot, some stabbed with their spears, some knocked down with their hatchets." Not one has been killed by arrows.

In fact, Rowlandson's account deflates Bellesiles's entire thesis. For good reason, Indians and settlers alike highly valued guns, and this a full century before the American Revolution. Indeed, were it not for the superiority of their weapons, one cannot imagine how Bellesiles's cowardly and incompetent settlers could have ever triumphed as they quickly did.

Rowlandson also shows why self-defense was so necessary. Indians presented a real and omnipresent threat, and it was terrifying. "It is a solemn sight to see so many Christians lying in their blood," she writes, "some here, and some there, like a company of sheep torn by wolves, all of them stripped naked by a company of hell-hounds, roaring, singing, ranting, and insulting, as if they would have torn our very hearts out." Writing at a safe remove, new historians could dismiss settler fears as paranoia and xenophobia. Indeed, Churchill writes off Rowlandson's account as "anti-Indian propaganda." On the frontier, the settlers had no such luxury.

A decade earlier Bellesiles would likely have gotten away with his inventions. Although Bellesiles's defenders like progressive historian Jon Wiener trace his demise to a "politically motivated effort by the gun lobby and its supporters," they overestimate the enemy. Bellisles was undone not by the NRA but by determined individuals empowered by the Internet. They exposed his deceits to the point where historians could no longer ignore them. The self-motivated Cramer expected no rewards for his exceptional efforts and got none. As with so many whistleblowers, the academic establishment turned its back on him. "I would not bother to apply to a doctoral program," says Cramer, now a software engineer in Boise, Idaho. "I don't think I could get in."

If in late 2002 Michael Bellesiles's career was moribund, his essential message was alive, well, and about to saturate the culture. Although revising some of Bellesiles's finer points, filmmaker Michael Moore was spreading Bellesiles's larger anti-gun, anti-American message to a much wider audience, and he was doing so, if possible, even more dishonestly. The vehicle was Moore's new film, *Bowling for Columbine*. It had received a special prize and a standing ovation at Cannes and was on its way to mega sales and Oscar glory.

An animated section of *Bowling*, called "A Brief History of the United States of America," nicely distills the ZSM take on American gun ownership into a toxic little brew. Fleeing Europe out of fear, America's early settlers meet the cartoon's cute Indians. Alas, they "get scared all over again" and "killed them all." Next, the settlers "started killing the British so they could be free." Along the way, they enslave Africans, which makes America "the richest country in the world." Slave uprisings drive Americans to a new level of fear, and Samuel Colt invents the revolver "just in the nick of time."

After the Civil War, the NRA is founded in the same year the Ku Klux Klan is declared illegal. "Just a coincidence?" asks Moore. The viewer is led to believe exactly the opposite. By advocating "responsible gun ownership," the NRA somehow facilitates the lynching of blacks in the south for the next century. The civil rights movement frees the black man anew, and this prompts white America to flee to the suburbs in fear and buy a quarter of a billion more guns.

Moore counts on the ignorance of his audience to enable him to rewrite history as he pleases. This he does with particular deceit in the case of the NRA about which the audience would know little at all. Yes, the National Rifle Association was formed in 1871 the same year that President Ulysses S. Grant signed the federal Ku Klux Klan Act into law. Left unsaid, however, is that the NRA was created by an act of the New York state legislature at the request of a pair of former Union officers. After the Klan-busting Grant left the White House, the NRA elected him president. From the beginning, the NRA contested the gun control laws that denied guns to blacks as they do to this day.

Undeterred by facts, Moore carves a zone of decency out for himself and his fellow progressives. Beyond the zone is a nation of xenophobes, their dread of the black man having driven them deep into anxiety, hate, and eventually the NRA. Moore tars NRA President Charlton Heston with the same implied charge of racism that he does all the other "gun nuts" shown in *Bowling*. It doesn't matter to Moore that Heston was

leading civil rights marches with Martin Luther King when such activities could actually hurt an actor's career or that he was personally responsible for breaking the interracial romance barrier on screen when he
picked actress Rosalind Cash for his film, *Omega Man*.

"I want to live," says one of Moore's cartoon whites, "don't kill me, big
black man." This is the underlying drumbeat of *Bowling*. In a classic
Moore touch, the film shows a 1988 George Bush ad that attacked
Michael Dukakis for allowing convicted murderers weekend leave. The
Bowling version of the ad features the photo of Willie Horton and the
caption, "Willie Horton released. Then kills again." A sloppy propagandist, Moore inserted the caption into the ad unaware that Horton did not
kill upon his infamous weekend leave. He merely raped and assaulted.
Nor did the George Bush ad show or name Willie Horton.

So nasty and numerous are Moore's deceptions that they unnerved
many of his ideological allies. Film critic and gun control advocate
Richard Schickel defined Moore as "the very definition of the current
literary term, 'the unreliable narrator.'" The liberal magazine *New
Republic,* in a piece titled "Dishonest White Man" described *Bowling* as
being "riddled with errors and misrepresentations." British socialist and
critic Christopher Hitchens admitted to being "appalled" by Moore's
popularity in Europe after *Bowling for Columbine*.

Moore's conservative critics are less kind and more specific in their
criticisms. Former Interior Department attorney, David Hardy, questioned whether *Bowling* even qualified for the Oscar as a "documentary"
given the Academy's "nonfictional movie" definition. "The point is not
that *Bowling* was biased," writes Hardy. "No, the point is that *Bowling* was
deliberately, seriously, and consistently deceptive." In the best-selling
Michael Moore Is a Big Fat Stupid White Man, Hardy and coauthor, Jason
Clarke, meticulously document those deceptions.

Moore targets no one more slyly than he does Heston, then nearing
eighty and in the early stages of Alzheimer's. The Heston that the viewer
meets is stunningly callous. He comes to Denver just ten days after the

killings at nearby Columbine High School and holds "a large pro-gun rally for the National Rifle Association." There, brandishing a musket, he shouts, "I have only five words for you: 'from my cold, dead hands.'" When a six-year-old girl is shot in Moore's hometown of Flint, Michigan, Heston exploits her death as well. Says Moore, narrating the movie, "Just as he did after the Columbine shooting, Charlton Heston showed up in Flint to have a big pro-gun rally."

What the viewer does not learn is that the annual NRA convention had been scheduled years in advance for Denver and that by law it could not be cancelled, even after the shooting at Columbine. The NRA did, however, cancel all events other than its mandatory members' voting. By cobbling together five different parts of Heston's Denver speech and adding the "cold, dead hands" section from a speech given a year later in North Carolina, Moore turns Heston's conciliatory address in Denver to a provocative call to arms. Moore's editing would have made Willi Munzenberg proud.

As to Flint, Heston passed through there as he did many other cities in battleground states a full eight months after the killing of the little girl. This was not a pro-gun rally, but a get-out-the-vote drive a month before the 2000 presidential election. No one but Moore connected Heston's visit to the girl's murder. Moore himself was there hustling votes for Ralph Nader. Al Gore was there at the same time.

Given his zero-sum multicultural grounding, Moore could not begin to give an honest answer to the question the movie pretends to address: namely, why does America seem uniquely troubled by gun violence? At first, the movie steers the audience to the conclusion that the problem is too many and too available guns, but then it detours to Canada where guns are just as numerous and available but where gun violence is negligible.

Moore shames the audience from even contemplating race as a possible factor in gun crime. No issue can be made of it. The fact that the little girl in Flint was white and her killer black and that he found the gun at his uncle's crack house goes unmentioned. Moore is above that. Instead, he parades through South Central Los Angeles and piously declares the irrelevance of race from the seemingly peaceful corner of Florence and Normandie, the epicenter of 1992 Los Angeles riots.

This self-righteous bit of grandstanding could not have offered much in the way of consolation to the mothers of South Central. In 2002, the year the movie was released, blacks in America were six times more likely than whites to be homicide victims and seven times more likely to be perpetrators. For gun crimes, the disparity was higher still. Taking race off the table in discussing crime is much like taking sexual orientation off the table in discussing AIDS. It makes the creative person feel better about himself, but it fully ignores the plight of those who are suffering most.

Moore could not have succeeded, however, were it not for the indulgence of the mainstream media. Although most serious reviewers chastise Moore for what A.O. Scott of the *New York Times* calls his "slippery logic, tendentious grandstanding and outright demagoguery," few, if any, challenge the dishonest foundation on which the logic is built. This is the ZSM logic that informs his animated "brief history" of America. Conditioned to believe that history themselves, critics fail to see the corrosive nature of his dissembling and dismiss it as mere mischief from a "cheerful rabble-rouser." They can then recommend the movie for what Scott of the *Times* calls "its disquieting insights into the culture of violence in America."

Indeed, few movies have been as widely honored as *Bowling*. Not only did it win an Oscar for best "documentary" it also received top honors at a score or more of film festivals from Chicago to Sao Paolo. Its success prompted Moore to make *Fahrenheit 9/11*, an even more subversive and deceitful look at America, released in the middle of a war.

"To describe this film as dishonest and demagogic would almost be to promote those terms to the level of respectability," writes Christopher Hitchens of *Fahrenheit 9/11*. His, however, was a voice in the wilderness. In full collaborative spirit, the cultural establishment cheered *Fahrenheit* even more enthusiastically than it did *Bowling*. In an election year, it seemed so very useful.

Borrowed Dreams

On October 5, 1990, acting Boston University president Jon Westling sent one of the least truthful missives in the history of American letters. It was directed to the editor of the *Chronicles: A Magazine of American Culture,* and it concerned the doctoral dissertation of BU's most famous graduate.

"Not a single instance of plagiarism of any sort has been identified," Westling wrote. Later in the letter, he got even more definitive: "Not a single reader has ever found any nonattributed or misattributed quotations, misleading paraphrases, or thoughts borrowed without due scholarly reference in any of its 343 pages."

The *Chronicles'* managing editor Theodore Pappas knew that Westling's response was pure hokum. In the same October 25 issue in which Westling's letter appeared, he said as much. Unknown to him at the time, and unbelievable even in retrospect, the Westling letter would launch Pappas on a long and difficult critical odyssey, one that would result in several death threats, a physical assault, unending rejection, and his own deep disillusionment with the academic mission.

As it happens, the plagiarist whose career Pappas would document is something of an anomaly. He is the only unapologetic Christian covered in this book, the only one whose fraud did not advance a progressive agenda, the only one who spoke reverentially about the American dream and the creed that secured it. And yet, after his death at least, no one was more firmly embraced by the progressive establishment than Martin Luther King. Indeed, King had become all things to all people, and everyone wanted to protect his piece of the action.

By way of background, King graduated from the largely white Crozer Theological Seminary in Chester, Pennsylvania, in 1951. Given his humble scores on the Graduate Record Exam, Pappas argues that it was "clearly on the basis of race and class, not scholarship" that King was recommended for doctoral studies at Boston University. Complicating matters, King did not have an adequate grasp of German, the language in which much of the philosophy he would be researching was written.

If these were not handicaps enough, King was already working full time as a pastor when he started writing his dissertation in 1954. Still, despite these drawbacks, he finished the dissertation and submitted it to BU in 1955. It was entitled "A Comparison of the Conception of God in the Thinking of Paul Tillich and Henry Nelson Weiman." Upon reviewing the dissertation, King's panel recommended corrections. Although King never made them, he somehow received his doctorate and immediately thereafter began his life's great work.

In 1962, six years before his death, King had donated many of his papers to Boston University but not all of them. For reasons likely known to him but not others, he left some papers in his private study and others still in church filing cabinets around the country. In 1984, King's widow, Coretta Scott King, decided to gather all the papers together. To manage what came to be known as the Marin Luther King Jr. Papers Project, she selected a respected Stanford University historian, Clayborne Carson.

In reviewing his papers and assembling them into a two-volume collection, Carson and his staff came to a disturbing conclusion: King had throughout his career, and especially in his doctoral dissertation, lifted passages wholesale from other people's work—"on a scale so vast," says distinguished historian Eugene Genovese, "as to leave no room for excuse or exculpation."

The primary victim of King's pilfering was a Boston University student named Jack Stewart Boozer. A few years ahead of King at BU, Boozer had written his dissertation on a similar subject, "The Place of Reason in Paul Tillich's Concept of God." As the editors of King's papers soon became aware, King had mined Boozer's dissertation deeply. "It is not merely that King's argument, language, and choice of words run parallel with Boozer's," writes Pappas, "but that whole phrases, sentences, and even paragraphs are lifted verbatim from Boozer's text." The examples that Pappas provides are many and damning. Writes King on the subject of the Trinity:

It is a qualitative . . . characterization of God. It is an attempt to express the richness and complexity of the divine life. . . . It is the abysmal character of God, the element of power which is the basis of the Godhead, "which makes God God."

Writes Boozer on the same subject:

. . . It is a qualitative characterization of God. It is an effort to express the richness of the divine life. . . . It is the abysmal character of God, the element of power, which is the basis of the Godhead, "which makes God God."

There are scores more of comparably egregious examples, none of which King attributed to Boozer. The dissertation, however, was just part of the problem. Further research showed that King purloined other people's work freely throughout his career. He plagiarized his Nobel Prize lecture from the works of a Florida minister, J. Wallace Hamilton, and he swiped key passages of his famed "I Have a Dream" speech—including the "from every mountainside, let freedom ring" part—from an address to the 1952 Republican convention by black preacher, Archibald Carey.

Had this story surfaced before King's death, it might not have troubled the incipient multicultural movement. In the last few years of King's life, black nationalists and their progressive allies had little use for him or his traditional "I have a dream" ethos. In these more radical quarters, King was seen as something of a dinosaur, if not an Uncle Tom, a man whose integrationist approach to race relations seemed outdated, even obsolete.

King's assassination changed all that. In death, his very traditionalism made King something Malcolm X could never be, an unassailable, universal symbol of righteousness. In their ongoing effort to depict traditional America as racist, progressives would use King's memory as a weapon. They would demand not just respect from the rest of America, but worship. Failure to worship would have consequences. Those states, for instance, which were slow to adopt King's birthday as a holiday faced boycotts and other economic sanctions for their presumed racism. This drive was in high arm-twisting gear when the plagiarism controversy surfaced. If King were revealed to have foibles like the rest of humanity, to be less than a saint, the drive would lose much of its moral momentum.

In October 1989, Coretta Scott King first learned that this symbolism was in jeopardy. At an awkward meeting of the King Papers Project's advisory board, the project's senior editor Clayborne Carson laid out the problem that he and his researchers had known about for at least two years. Breaking the news was not going to be easy. One could expose the flaws of Washington or Jefferson or Lincoln with impunity—indeed, new history encouraged that kind of critical analysis—but there was no deconstructing King, the most sacred figure in the multicultural pantheon. As the board understood, iconoclasts challenged his memory at their own risk.

After much discussion, the board authorized Carson to publish the papers with explanatory footnotes and to write a separate scholarly article explaining the nature of the problem. It would be nearly two years before that article made its way to the *Journal of American History*. It would be another year still before the first volume of the King papers was published, an inexplicable seven years of public funding after the project started. In the meantime, Carson remained tight-lipped.

While Carson kept his silence, some of his former researchers began to leak the story. In December 1989, the *London Sunday Telegraph* ran a piece on the plagiarism charges only to have Carson deny them. "There is no fraud," he told the *Telegraph*. "What we're talking about is whether there was adequate citation of all sources."

True to form, the mainstream American media hesitated to publish anything. When the *Washington Post*'s Dan Balz inquired in the spring of 1990, Carson put him off and held him off through the summer and fall, telling him that his researchers needed more time before they could say anything conclusively. Balz didn't push. The *Post's* ombudsman would later tell Pappas, "I suspect that we pursue more rapidly and vigorously things about some people than we do about others."

The various researchers and government officials who knew vowed to remain silent and did. So did the *Atlanta Journal-Constitution,* the *New York Times,* and the *New Republic,* all of which had the story in early 1990 and sat on it. "Everybody suddenly got palsied," admitted the *New Republic* editor, Martin Peretz. "The King plagiarism story," writes Pappas, "was suppressed for one simple reason—fear—fear of the massive retaliation that would be visited upon anyone who attempted to set the historical record straight."

In September 1990, *Chronicles'* editor Thomas Fleming ran a small article on the brewing controversy, which prompted the heated response from Boston University cited at the beginning of this section. In November 1990, the *Wall Street Journal* finally broke the full story by telling Carson that it had a copy of Boozer's dissertation and was going to run an article with or without his cooperation. He reluctantly cooperated. After the *Journal* article, however, there was almost no media follow-up. Soon the *Journal* itself began to soft pedal the charges. Boston University convened a committee to investigate the case but did not go public with its findings until October 1991. Even then, BU pulled its punches. Committee member John Cartwright—ironically, the Martin Luther King Jr. Professor of Social Ethics at the university—told the Associated Press that "there is no obvious indication in [King's] dissertation that he inappropriately utilized material."

Although ideology did not inspire King to commit fraud, it drove the cover-up by Boston University and its accomplices. "They lied," writes Genovese, "they told half-truths, they made up fables, they did everything they could but address facts. . . . They called into question the very standing of the university as a place where cheating is penalized and misrepresentation condemned."

Soon enough, friendly academics hit upon a new strategy in the protection of King's reputation. If they could no longer deny his plagiarism, they could do the next best thing: diminish it through postmodern analysis. Chief alchemist in this effort was King scholar Keith Miller of Arizona State University. His 1992 book *Voice of Deliverance: The Language of Martin Luther King Jr. and Its Sources* popularized a dozen new euphemisms for King's plagiarism, among them "mining," "welding," "quarrying," "yoking," "intertextualization," and most notoriously, "voice merging."

In a 1993 article, "Redefining Plagiarism," Miller made the case explicitly for "voice merging," arguing that scholars needed to "appreciate the difficulties that some [minorities] have in negotiating the boundaries between oral and print traditions." This argument appalled Pappas. Miller talked about King as though he were a "grunting savage just snatched from the jungle," writes Pappas. In fact, King was an obviously gifted rhetorician with eleven years of higher education and three advanced degrees to his credit. Whatever his motives for plagiarizing, he did not deserve Miller's kind of condescension.

As Pappas attempted to move the story of the King plagiarism forward, he became more and more aware of just how uniformly the cultural establishment could respond to a perceived threat. Despite his excellent credentials, publisher after publisher, forty in all, rejected Pappas's proposal for a book on the subject. One "reader's recommendation" revealed with unwitting candor the rationale for this wall of silence. "I recommend against publishing this book," observed the reader ingenuously, "because such honesty and truthfulness could only be destructive."

Orwell could not have said it better himself.

"In decades past," writes Genovese, "it was books that disturbed liberal complacency that were abused or made to disappear; in these days of the Culture War, it is books that rankle the complacency of the multicultural left." Genovese is in a position to know. One of America's great historians, he was an avowed Marxist until his conversion to Catholicism in 1996. Like Whittaker Chambers, he understood that an intellectual had to choose one side of the barricade or the other, God or man.

For the past century, the preponderance of America's intellectuals have chosen man. Unanswerable to any higher authority, they have inundated America with a steady stream of unvetted invention. To date, fortunately, just enough of their fellow citizens have chosen God to protect them from the full weight of their folly. Other nations, alas, have not been so blessed.

4
Darwin's Heirs

"Although it is developed in the crude English style,
this is the book which contains the basis in
natural history for our view."

—MARX TO ENGELS: ON THE *Origin of Species*

A ROYAL PAIN

Eugenie Scott had a problem on her hands. Literally.

In early November 2000, she held that problem up in front of a class at the University of California at San Diego and said to the wide-eyed students, "This book will be a royal pain in the fanny." The book was the just released *Icons of Evolution* by Jonathan Wells, and Scott was righter than rain.

As executive director of the National Center for Science Education, Scott had no more pressing task than to keep Darwin in the classroom and to keep the challengers out. Wells's book, as Scott knew, was about to make that task a whole lot more difficult.

Icons didn't question Darwinism per se (nor will this book). It did something much more problematic for the Eugenie Scotts of the world. It challenged the evidence for Darwinism that had been presented to generation after generation of America's high school and college students like those at San Diego where Scott was guest lecturing. As Wells knew, and as Scott feared, much of that evidence was conspicuously fraudulent, and virtually all of it was suspect.

169

To be clear, Charles Darwin was not a fraud. At least in 1859, when he published *On the Origin of Species,* he believed what he wrote. And although bold and provocative in its thesis, *Origin* was admirably restrained in its tone.

Darwin's elegant and timely work made several essential claims. One was that living things experience what Darwin called "variations" or what we call "mutations"—genetic changes that occur randomly. The second was that a blind, automatic process Darwin called "natural selection" preserved favorable variations and rejected harmful ones, and thus living things changed for the better over long periods of time.

In and of themselves, these claims were not terribly controversial. There was not a man jack alive in this still largely rural world who did not know at least something about variation and change as they related to the breeding of domestic animals. It was the third idea, the one implicit in the title of the book, which shook the world, namely that variation and selection account for the origin of new species—in fact, of every species, at least after the first.

If Darwin had stopped at this point, there still might have been room for compromise between his position and that of the theistic naturalists then still highly influential in the world of science. But he didn't stop.

"There is no obvious reason why the principles which have acted so efficiently under domestication should not have acted under nature," deduces Darwin. This is a subtly loaded sentence. Here, Darwin introduces a new and all-powerful change agent: not man, not God, but "nature," raw and unguided. If "domestication" implies an active and caring intelligence, "nature" implies just the opposite.

"The purpose of *On the Origin of Species,*" confirms Louis Menand in his Pulitzer Prize-winning book, *The Metaphysical Club,* "was not to introduce the concept of evolution; it was to debunk the concept of supernatural intelligence—the idea that the universe is the result of an idea." Richard Dawkins, Britain's leading Darwinist, elaborates: "For Darwin, any evolution that had to be helped over the jumps by God was not evolution at all. It made nonsense of the central point of evolution."

For those Enlightenment souls who had been bristling under the restraints of a Judeo-Christian God, and all the fuss that entailed, *Origin* was their "get out of jail free" card. Now, Darwin fans had their own creation story, and no one to account to at the end of the day except for a hugely indifferent "nature." This was the essence of "naturalism"— nature is all that there is. And with a good deal of guidance from friends, the age of naturalism was about to blossom into a full, giddy flower.

Even while Darwin's theory remained "highly speculative," the cult of naturalism swept the intellectual world like the Spanish flu. Darwin knew that the evidence to support his thesis was scant—he was hopeful it would be found in the future. But his more reckless acolytes, and they were legion, did not much trouble themselves with evidence. They were, generally speaking, more interested in self-justification than in science. Their eagerness to prove what they thought to be true was a dangerous prescription for fraud.

A TEXTBOOK CASE OF FRAUD

Among the earliest and, at the end of the day, the most embarrassing heirs of Darwin was embryologist and philosopher Ernst Haeckel. Born in Potsdam, Germany, in 1834, Haeckel read *Origin* the summer it was first published in German, 1860, and fell immediately under its sway. He could see straight off that Darwin offered a useful exit strategy from a God-dominated cosmos.

Once liberated, Haeckel created his own secular religion called "Monism." Obviously not lacking for confidence, he imagined Monism as nothing less than a unified, naturalistic understanding of the entire universe. One marvels at Haeckel's *chutzpah*. He blithely evicts from his new universe the Christian God of his own heritage, the creator of heaven and earth.

"The modern science of evolution has shown that there never was any such creation," claims Haeckel, "but that the universe is eternal and the law of substance all-ruling." As would become painfully evident, Haeckel's philosophy quickly corrupted his science, and his science, such as it was, would help undo twentieth century Western civilization, starting in Germany.

Given this book's focus on America, Haeckel's continuing influence on the nation's academic culture demands his inclusion. The man who has made that continued inclusion immensely awkward for the science establishment is none other than Jonathan Wells. When *Icons* was published, Wells expected a rough response. What he got was even rougher than anticipated. Indeed, one review in the *Quarterly Review of Biology* compared him to the talented Mr. Ripley of movie fame, a charlatan and murderer.

If, however, the Darwinists and their allies thought "The Talented Mr. Wells" would go away, they obviously hadn't taken full measure of Wells. "I spent a year and a half in prison defending my principles," says Wells. "I wasn't about to back down now."

Jonathan Wells

More like Forrest Gump than Mr. Ripley, Wells has often found himself at the intersection of destiny and history. Born in New York City in 1942, Wells grew up in suburban New Jersey, excelled in high school, and narrowed the post-*Sputnik* space race by sending his homemade missiles as much as a mile skyward. A go-as-you-please Protestant by upbringing, Wells majored in geology at Princeton where he found Darwin and lost whatever faith he had. A born rebel, Wells dropped out in his junior year while in the top 1 percent of his class.

On August 28, 1963, he happened to be visiting friends in Washington when he all but stumbled on Martin Luther King's famed march on Washington. So inspired was Wells by the marchers' peaceful discipline that he began his own study of Ghandian pacifism. He would need all the peace of mind he could find. With the Vietnam War heating up and his own draft imminent, he could land no better a job than driving a New York City taxi. As Wells expected, his number came up quickly, and he spent the next two years in Germany as guest of the U.S. Army.

Encouraged by the many leftist Germans with whom he came into contact, Wells began to question the war effort. After his discharge in 1966, he headed to Berkeley both to finish his education and to advance the cause of pacifism. When the Army insisted he report for reserve duty, Wells, with TV cameras whirring, read a defiant letter of refusal on the steps of Berkeley's Sproul Hall, the ultimate radical platform. Needless to say, the Army was not pleased. Shortly thereafter, Wells was grabbed off the Berkeley streets by a pair of plainclothes MPs and imprisoned, still defiant, for four months of solitary confinement at the Presidio stockade and for another eight months at Leavenworth.

Upon release from prison, Wells returned to Berkeley and graduated in 1970 with a major in geology and physics and a minor in biology. Put off by the coldhearted drift to violence of the Berkeley left, he fled the Bay Area first for a commune and eventually to the California hills where he built a small, solitary cabin. There, he immersed himself in nature, much as Thoreau had done more than a century earlier, and soon began to intuit a sense of design in the grandeur of it all. This discovery informed his spiritual reading, and he found himself coming back time and again to the Bible.

Never one to shy from controversy, in 1974 Wells joined the one organization that offered the mix of physical and spiritual he had been seeking, the Reverend Sun Myung Moon's Unification Church. Under Moon's guidance, Wells attended the Unification Church's theological seminary in upstate New York. While praying for direction, he received a veritable calling to study Darwin. This calling took him to Yale where he got his doctorate in religious studies and wrote a book on nineteenth century Darwinian controversies. Not sufficiently armed for the battle to come, he took his mission a major step further. In 1989, now a husband and father, the forty-seven-year-old Wells headed back to Berkeley to get a Ph.D. in molecular and cell biology.

Two years later, a friend alerted Wells to a provocative new book called *Darwin on Trial* by Phillip Johnson. Wells consumed the book in a gulp and, in still another Gumpian moment, discovered that Johnson was a law professor there at Berkeley. Wells called Johnson immediately and invited him to lunch. Intellectual historians may one day trace the beginning of the influential anti-Darwinian movement known as "intelligent design" to that very lunch, a coming together that Wells does not think was merely a matter of chance.

If at Yale Wells grew to understand the philosophical holes in Darwinism, at Berkeley, he began to see the scientific ones, none of which was blacker than the one opened by Ernst Haeckel. Wells's chapter on Haeckel in *Icons of Evolution* stands out.

For the record, Haeckel is the fellow who coined the phrase, "ontogeny recapitulates phylogeny," a phrase that gets quoted much more often than it gets understood. Simply put, "ontogeny" means the development of the fetus—human or animal—in the womb. "Phylogeny" refers to the presumed evolution of this being over time. "Ontogeny recapitulates phylogeny" thus means that the development of the fetus in the womb mimics the evolutionary development of that same being stage by stage.

As to the predictive power of embryos, Darwin and Haeckel were on much the same page. In *Origin,* Darwin argues that early embryos "show us, more or less completely, the condition of the progenitor of the whole group in its adult state." In other words, the original parent of, say, the human race would have looked very much like a tiny embryo before it evolved into a full-blown human. Darwin took this assertion seriously, as would Haeckel. Both believed that embryos provided what Darwin called "by far the strongest single class of facts" in favor of Darwinian evolution.

In a later book, *The Descent of Man,* published in 1871, Darwin made another powerful claim about embryos. He now argued that since all vertebrate embryos look more or less alike and pass through the same early stages of development, one "ought admit frankly their community of descent." In other words, the fact that embryos look alike was more proof still that all animals, humans included, descended from a single ancestor.

To help visualize this phenomenon, what he called the "Biogenetic Law," Haeckel drew up a series of illustrations. These drawings compared the embryonic development of fish, amphibians, reptiles, bird, and mammals, including humans. They have had exceptional lasting power. More than a century later, as Wells demonstrated, nine of the ten most popular high school and college textbooks in current use in America were showing Haeckel's drawings or reproductions of the same. Inevitably, the textbook authors used these drawings to make the case for Darwinian evolution.

Wells cites, among others, the 1994 edition of *Molecular Biology of the Cell* by National Academy of Sciences President Bruce Alberts and his colleagues. According to Alberts, neo-Darwinian mechanisms explain "why embryos of different species so often resemble each other in the early stages, and, as they develop, seem to replay the steps of evolution." Burton Guttman's 1999 textbook, *Biology,* makes much the same point with a redrawn version of Haeckel's embryos. Says Guttman, "An animal's embryonic development holds clues to the forms of its ancestors."

In none of the ten textbooks is there any hint of a problem with Haeckel, his theory, or his illustrations, but in fact there are severe problems with all three. The most obvious problem is that biologists have long since rejected the Biogenetic Law of Haeckel and Darwin. Wells traces the theory's fall from fashion back a century or more, and it did not fall silently or unseen. Historian of science Nicholas Rasmussen observes, "All the important evidence called upon in the rejection of the Biogenetic Law was there from the first days of the law's acceptance." This is common knowledge and has been for a long time. Wells would not have had to look further than the UC Berkeley Museum of Paleontology Web page to read that the "law of recapitulation has been discredited since the beginning of the twentieth century."

The earliest stages in vertebrate embryos are clearly *not* the most similar. Just the opposite is true. Embryos of these different vertebrates grow to look *more* alike until the midpoint of their development, a fact that plays utter havoc with both the Darwinian theory of common descent and of Haeckel's theory of evolution being mimicked in the womb. Indeed, there never was any empirical evidence that either of these theories was valid. Haeckel merely deduced his argument from Darwin's evolutionary theory.

Bad science, however, is not necessarily fraudulent. Haeckel crossed that line when he faked his drawings. For starters, he biased his sample by drawing only those embryos that looked somewhat alike. He chose not to draw those that looked different enough from one another to challenge his thesis. Worse, he drew his embryos to look much more alike one another than they actually are.

"These famous images are inaccurate," observed leading British embryologist Michael Richardson in 1995, "and give a misleading view of embryonic development." In 1997, a team of international experts, Richardson among them, compared Heackel's illustrations with actual embryos of the relevant classes of vertebrates. The comparisons, Wells notes, show "quite clearly that Haeckel's drawings misrepresent the truth." Interviewed by *Science* after publishing his comparisons, Richardson admitted, "It looks like [the Haeckel illustration] is turning out to be one of the most famous fakes in biology." In fact, however, accusations of fraud had dogged Haeckel even during his own lifetime.

Stephen Jay Gould came clean about the Haeckel problem in a March 2000 issue of *Natural History* article, "Abscheulich! Atrocious!" Gould charged that Haeckel had "exaggerated the similarities by idealizations and omissions" and chided him for his "inaccuracies and outright falsifications." In the article, Gould admitted that he had known that Haeckel had faked his drawings for more than twenty years.

This is no small admission. In fact, as early as 1973, Gould was writing that "the whole theory of recapitulation" had collapsed with the rediscovery of Mendelian genetics in 1900. If Gould knew that Haeckel's science was foolish and that his drawings were fakes, other eminent biologists surely knew as well. Why then did they not try to stop the textbook publishers from passing this fraud along to one generation after another of unwary students? The answer seems fairly obvious: Darwinism is the most important prop not only in the progressive house of cards, but also in the career of many a biologist.

NAZIS IN THE WOODSHED

There is still another problem with Haeckel, a darker one, and one that speaks to the deeper uses of fraud in corrupting Western culture. Although Jonathan Wells does not explore this topic, others have, most notably Daniel Gasman, a longtime professor of European history at John Jay College in New York.

The unhappy fact is that Haeckel, in addition to being a fraud, was also a proto-fascist. In *The Scientific Origins of National Socialism,* first published in 1971, Gasman shows the "decisive" role that Haeckel played in the development of the German "Volkish" movement, a revival of pre-

Christian German culture and spiritualism that found its eventual political outlet in the rise of none other than Adolph Hitler.

As it happens, many of the most influential Volkish writers and
spokesmen were tied in with either Haeckel or his Monist followers.
These were the semi-respectable zanies that found common cause in
National Socialism, and they were problem enough. But it was in the field
of eugenics and racial science that Haeckel had the most direct and lethal
impact. Germany's leading advocates of racial anthropology and
eugenics, notes Gasman, "were deeply and consciously indebted to
Haeckel for many, if not for most, of their ideas."

Otto Ammon, (1842–1916), a Haeckel disciple, went public with what
many Darwinists prefer to keep private, and that is the oddly spiritual
nature of the Darwinian experience. "In obvious imitation of Haeckel,"
writes Gasman, "Ammon taught that Darwinism had to become
Germany's new religion. It had to be accepted as a complete
Weltanschauung and its ideas had to be encouraged in every facet of life."

Haeckel's co-editor at the leading Darwinian journal *Kosmos,* Ernst
Krause, introduced still another unhinged idea, one that proved to have
serious geo-political consequences. It was Krause who transformed
Germans into "Aryans." In his two influential books, he labored to trace
the origin of his imagined Aryan race back to classical Greece and to
show the superiority of this race of people over time. When the Nazis
came to power, their narrow reading of just who was and who wasn't an
Aryan might have even seemed comic were it not so catastrophic.

For all their grandiosity, Haeckel and his colleagues worked within the
then respectable pale of Germany's scientific establishment. Beyond that
pale, feeding on their ideas and their respectability, was a rogue class of
theorists who propagandized for the creation of a racially pure Germany
and often got scarily specific as to how that might occur.

One such theorist was a popular author by the name of Willibald
Hentschel. Among his more ambitious plans was to create a breeding
colony for pure Nordics. One imagines a kind of Club Med where contra-

ception and blond jokes are strictly *verboten*. Here, through scientific methods of procreation, Hentschel hoped to spawn an Aryan elite. The cities, meanwhile, would be left to rot at the hands of the biologically unfit.

The German eugenicist movement might have been written off as just another eruption of crackpot science had it not eventually used humans as lab rats. Not surprisingly, Haeckel has blood on his hands. As Gasman observes, Haeckel was "one of the most vociferous opponents of the Jews" and arguably the first to assess the "Jewish problem" as one of biology. Having subjected Jews to "scientific" analysis, he came to the unhappy conclusion that their perceived shortcomings were inborn and resistant to change.

To be fair to Haeckel, he never proposed anything like a final solution. Indeed, his plan was to absorb the Jewish population through coerced assimilation so that its less desirable characteristics would be swallowed by the much larger "Aryan" gene pool. To be fair to Darwin, the future national socialists knew him largely as interpreted by Haeckel. It's just that in posing "Judaism" as a scientific and technical problem in a godless world, Haeckel invited others to suggest technical solutions, and history records that they did just that. Haeckel directly, and Darwin indirectly, most assuredly contributed to the rise of Hitler and the coming of the Holocaust.

In one of his few specific references to Haeckel, Hitler spoke of their shared opposition to Christianity. Both resented the faith because it competed with what Gasman calls "a holy conception of nature." Haeckel had, in fact, inspired Hitler and Hitler's Germany with Darwin's cosmology, the story of the world as told by Nature. For Haeckel and Hitler both, Gasman writes, "The great defect of modern Western society was that man was in constant violation of nature." Given this perspective, it should not surprise that Nazi and proto-Nazi propaganda depicted Jews as pollutants: poisoning wells, drinking blood, spreading disease, and, ultimately, defiling the Aryan race.

In his own inhuman way, Hitler set out to address this seeming violation. In this regard, he was merely the first, and most lethal, of a long line of activists who would stand the "Great Chain of Being" on its head by putting "nature" ahead of man and man ahead of God. (Indeed, the term "eco-Nazi" is not without its historical roots.) And in their war against God, truth would, as usual, be the first casualty.

The First Cricket Bat

In 1861, just two years after the publication of *On the Origin of Species*, Hermann von Meyer announced the discovery in Germany of an extraordinary fossil. This large, bird-like creature sported wings and feathers, but it also had teeth and claws on its wing and a long, lizard-like tail. Although von Meyer gave this find a suitably unpronounceable name, archaeopteryx, meaning "ancient wing," Darwin's champions throughout the world were soon shouting that name from the rooftops.

Archaeopteryx seemed to solve one major problem for the Darwinists, that of the "missing links." In *Origin*, Darwin argues that all evolutionary change had taken place in the tiniest of increments. As a result, adds Darwin, "The number of intermediate and transitional links, between all living and extinct species, must have been inconceivably great."

But if there were so many, just where were they? Darwin had to admit that there were no transitional links running wild, certainly not in 1859 England. Nor could he identify any in the then existing fossil record. An optimist, he presumed that such fossils would soon be found, and— eureka!—he did not have to wait long. Archaeopteryx! For decades, this genuine fossil appeared to be the perfect link between reptiles and birds.

With this transition seemingly accounted for, the more ambitious fossil hunters set their sights on the greatest find of all, the missing link between ape and human. Among the hunters was Charles Dawson, a British lawyer and an avid amateur paleontologist. In 1909, the fiftieth anniversary of *On the Origin of Species*, a laborer working in a gravel pit on a farm near Piltdown Common in Sussex found a small piece of skull and gave it to Dawson. Two years later, Dawson himself went to the site and found another piece of the same skull.

Dawson promptly brought his finds to Arthur Smith Woodward at the British Museum. In the summer of 1912, Woodward joined Dawson in the search, and they found additional prehistoric animal fossils, some human tools, and an ape-like lower jaw with two molars. The jaw did not appear to have derived from any known European ape, and the teeth appeared to have worn down in human fashion.

Woodward reconstructed a skull from the fragments and went public with "Dawson's Dawn Man" before the best and brightest of Britain's science establishment at a packed Geological Society of London meeting in 1912. Needless to say, Woodward's announcement rocketed around the world, making headlines even in non-scientific publications like the *New York Times*.

"Darwin's Theory Proved True," screamed the *Times*' banner headline. "English Scientists Say the Skull Found in Sussex Establishes Human Descent from Apes." The scientific world and its accomplices in the major media were eager to see Charles Darwin vindicated, and so he seemed to be.

From the beginning, to be sure, some paleontologists had their doubts. If anything, the Piltdown Man fit prevailing theories of human evolution *too* well. Piltdown's enlarged brain and primitive, ape-like jaw made too good a case for man's brain-first emergence from his monkey ancestors. Additional finds at the site and Woodward's undeniable authority, however, quieted the skeptics, at least for a while.

A full thirty-six years later in 1948, dictating from his deathbed, Woodward published a book celebrating the discovery called, appropriately enough, *The Earliest Englishman*. To be sure, the tone of the book was a wee bit defensive. Over the intervening years, other paleontologists with other finds had begun to challenge Piltdown Man, not so much on the grounds of its legitimacy but on the basis of its relevance. They had come to see Piltdown Man not as the missing link but as an "aberrant offshoot." Still, Woodward died with his reputation largely intact.

Five years later, the British Museum's Kenneth P. Oakley ran a chemical analysis on Piltdown Man. Obviously, someone should have looked more closely much sooner. The fraud was transparent. The skull, however old, proved to be that of a modern human. The jaw came from an orangutan. Both skull and jaw had been carefully stained to look ancient, and the teeth had been filed to look human. Someone had planted the surrounding artifacts, including an elephant bone mischievously carved to look like a cricket bat, all the more in keeping with the "Earliest Englishman" theme.

It remains something of a mystery as to who faked the evidence. Initial suspicion fell upon Charles Dawson, no longer around to defend himself when the fraud was revealed. Others accused included everyone from the famed Jesuit paleontologist Teilhard de Chardin to Sherlock Holmes's creator, Sir Arthur Conan Doyle, who lived nearby.

A 1996 *Nature* article reported the first hard evidence in the case. Apparently, a trunk discovered under the roof of London's Natural History Museum was found to contain bones that had been stained and carved in the same way as the Piltdown fossils. The trunk bore the initials of Martin A. C. Hinton, a curator of zoology at the museum at the time of the fraud.

"The evidence," writes Henry Gee, chief science writer for *Nature*, "appears to identify Hinton as the sole fraudster—and Dawson as his unwitting dupe." The most likely scenario has the skilled forger Hinton planting the faked remains in Piltdown and steering the ever hopeful Dawson to find them. His apparent motive was to get even with "the pompous, stuffy keeper of paleontology, Smith Woodward."

"The real victim seems to have been Smith Woodward," writes Gee, "and the motive an argument about money." But Gee and the editors of *Nature*, the world's most prestigious journal of the biosciences, miss the point. The identity of the trickster is not particularly relevant. The real fraud here lies in the British Museum's failure to submit the evidence to the most basic of tests, and in this regard, Woodward is more victimizer than victim.

The museum's partners in fraud include everyone within the scientific community who trumpeted these finds without challenging the evidence. So eager were they all to validate Darwin and the naturalist worldview that they closed their eyes to the obvious.

One could argue, as many scientists have, that in this instance science corrected itself. But if so, science took its own sweet time. In fact, the scientific establishment let the Piltdown Man crash only after Piltdown had ceded what Wells aptly calls its "iconic status." By 1953, paleontologists had mustered enough other presumed evidence of man's transition from the apes that Piltdown Man was no longer needed or wanted.

SLIPPERY PARTNERS

At the same time the science establishment was surrendering its skepticism before the altar of the Piltdown Man, it was showing just how scrupulous it could be about evidence when that evidence threatened Darwin. In *The Case of the Midwife Toad*, Arthur Koestler tells the story of the most notorious such case and in the process sheds a good deal of light on the politics of biological science.

As Koestler relates, the controversy first went public in 1910, two years before the Piltdown discovery. At that time, British biologist William Bateson began to challenge the work of Austrian scientist Paul Kammerer. Kammerer had made the political mistake of championing something other than Darwinism, namely a theory introduced a century earlier by French scientist Jean-Baptiste Lamarck.

Lamarck had proposed two related concepts. The first was that of "use and disuse," by which he simply meant that those parts of an organism that get used grow larger. Those that don't get used wither away. Lamarck's second theory, and his best known, was that improvements in the body structure or skill sets that parents acquire in their struggle to overcome their environment are passed on to their offspring through direct inheritance.

A classic example is that of the blacksmith. By using his biceps, the blacksmith enlarges them. Since the father's acquired characteristics can be inherited, the son is likely to be born with more robust biceps than those, say, of an accountant's son.

In his most hotly contested experiment, Paul Kammerer induced a midwife toad, which normally breeds on land, to breed in water like most frogs. To do this successfully over succeeding generations, without help, the midwife toad's little toad sons would have had to develop dark horny pads on their hands to grasp their slippery partners. Within two generations, Kammerer claimed, the little toads were being born with this innate capacity.

If this theory seems implausible now, it did not seem so at the time. In the last decades of the nineteenth century, many biologists, including Darwin himself, had begun to lose confidence in Darwinian evolution. Many had turned back to Lamarck and his theory of the inheritance of acquired characteristics to help find their way through the seemingly impenetrable maze of evolution.

And then along came Gregor Mendel, an Augustinian monk whose 1865 paper on plant hybridization was rediscovered thirty-five years later. Mendel pioneered what we know today as "genetics," a word coined by Mendel's leading champion in England, the aforementioned William Bateson.

Mendel argued correctly that genes did not "blend" and become diluted as was then commonly believed, but rather they were passed intact to the next generation to combine into new patterns. The clearest example of this genetic transfer is the sex of a newborn. Save for the occasional aberration, a baby inherits either male or female characteristics, blue eyes or brown eyes, but not a blend of both.

Unwittingly, more than fifteen years after his own death, this humble man of God had breathed new life into a withering, godless revolution. The fact that Mendel fudged his statistics—as was soon and easily enough proved—bothered almost no one in the science establishment. Indeed, as the following passage from a respected horticultural journal suggests, some found Mendel's sleight of hand, here concisely explained, rather amusing:

In the beginning there was Mendel, thinking his lonely thoughts alone. And he said: "Let there be peas," and there were peas and it was good. And he put the peas in the garden saying unto them, "Increase and multiply, segregate and assort yourselves independently," and they did and it was good. And now it came to pass that when Mendel gathered up his peas, he divided them into round and wrinkled, and called the round dominant and the wrinkled recessive, and it was good. But now Mendel saw that there were 405 round peas and 102 wrinkled ones; this was not good. For the law stateth that there should only be 3 round for every wrinkled. And Mendel said unto himself "Gott in Himmel, an enemy has done this, he has sown bad peas in my garden under the cover of night." And Mendel smote the table in righteous wrath, saying "Depart from me, you cursed and evil peas, into the outer darkness where thou shalt be devoured by the rats and mice," and lo it was done and there remained 300 round peas and 100 wrinkled peas, and it was good. It was very, very good. And Mendel published.

"It is rare to find this historical scandal mentioned in the literature," observes Koestler. The principle behind Mendel's statistics looked right, and better still, that principle seemed to reaffirm Darwin's theory.

There is, as they say, no zealot like a convert. A burned out Lamarckian himself, William Bateson dedicated himself to exposing Kammerer and his midwife toads. If World War I did not completely ruin Austria and Kammerer with it, Bateson moved in after the war to finish the job. To assist him in his efforts, he marshaled the same Anglo-American forces that were protecting the Piltdown Man.

Still, Kammerer was not about to yield without a fight. As everyone had to acknowledge, Bateson included, Kammerer was a uniquely skilled biologist. Before the war destroyed his lab, he had been able to create genuine experimental conditions that no one else could match. When he challenged Darwinists and others to duplicate his experiments, as was appropriate, they typically blanched at the difficulty of recreating the lab conditions.

Rampant inflation in post-war Austria had eroded his resources, and so in 1923 Kammerer hit the lecture circuit to raise the money needed to continue his research. The popular media in England and America embraced the charming and provocative scientist. The headlines that followed Kammerer around the world—"Transformation of the Human Race," "Race of Supermen," "Vienna Biologist Hailed as Greatest of the Century"—hyped his achievements well beyond what the modest Kammerer would ever have claimed for himself.

Even the *New York Times* heralded his accomplishment, albeit a bit more accurately. "Scientist Tells of Success Where Darwin Met Failure," reads a May 1923 headline. A subhead adds, "Evolution Would Be Speeded Up If Best Characteristics Could Be Transmitted."

As often happens in the world of science, Kammerer's public acclaim only antagonized his opposition. Since Kammerer believed in evolution, reporters failed to note the rift between the often spiritual neo-Lamarckians and the agnostic neo-Darwinian establishment. Bateson's son, Gregory, later explained to Koestler the reason why this rift was so intense. Note the religious imagery:

I think [William Bateson] always knew there was something very wrong with *orthodox* Darwinist theory, but at the same time he regarded Lamarckism as a *tabooed* pot of jam to which he was not allowed to reach. I have his copy of *The Origin of Species*, sixth edition, in which he listed on the fly-sheet the pages on which Darwin slipped into Lamarckian *heresy*. (italics added)

As young Bateson implies, Darwin provided the West with an alternative faith, one no less fervent but a good deal less fixed than the Judeo-Christian tradition it replaced. As happens all too often in faith communities, the orthodox establishment reacts more harshly to heretics than it does to nonbelievers.

Kammerer was feeling the heat from a second source as well. His evidence for the inheritance of acquired characteristics troubled the Haeckel school, then in its ascendancy in Germany and Austria. If Kammerer's theories were right, then Aryans had no exclusive genetic claim to racial superiority. With a near civil war raging in Austria between the national socialists and the international ones, Kammerer insulted the nationalists, especially when he announced his impending move to Moscow.

Kammerer paid the price for seeming to be a self-annointed "second Darwin" as an advertisement for his 1924 book, *The Inheritance of Acquired Characteristics*, claimed. In 1926, Kammerer gave Dr. G.K. Noble, an American ally of Bateson, permission to examine the one remaining preserved specimen of a genetically transformed midwife toad. Noble quickly struck gold—black gold that is. The dark coloration of the toad's horny pad proved to be nothing other than India ink. Six weeks after Noble went public with his scandalous findings, Kammerer shot himself.

It is possible that some proto-Nazis in Vienna sabotaged Kammerer's work. But the real story here is not whether or not Kammerer perpetrated a fraud. The real story is whether the Darwinian establishment did. These were sophisticated people. In the Kammerer case, they showed just how probing and persistent they could be. In the Piltdown case, they rolled over.

"Indeed, the real mystery is not who did it," write Broad and Wade of the Piltdown Man in their book about scientific fraud, *Betrayers of the Truth*, "but how a whole generation of scientists could have been taken in by so transparent a prank." This comment comes in a chapter titled "Self-Deception and Gullibility."

The Kammerer incident seems like it could have happened yesterday. The Piltdown incident reads like a page out of some long ago science history. And yet the two incidents were fully contemporaneous, save that *Nature* magazine exposed the midwife toad fraud twenty-seven years before it exposed Piltdown and busted Kammerer seventy years before it did Martin Hinton. No, these scientists weren't the naïve souls the literature makes them out to be. They were crusaders on a mission.

"When men have suffered their imaginations to be long affected with any idea," observed political philosopher Edmund Burke, "it so wholly engrosses them as to shut out by degrees almost every other, and to break down every partition of the mind which would confine it." Just how much of the Darwinian argument depends on this collective breakdown remains to be seen.

Inherit the Spin

One hesitates to use the word "fraud" when discussing a work of fiction. But when a play declares itself "the tense drama of the most explosive trial of the century," that play has ambition enough to deserve an exemption.

The play in question, *Inherit the Wind,* mirrors the celebrated Scopes monkey trial of 1925. Its authors, Jerome Lawrence and Robert E. Lee, stake their claim to poetic license, but they cannot back out of their flirtation with history all that easily. Despite their disclaimer, they have consciously trucked with the cultural record. The events that take place in their fictional Hillsboro are much too close to the real life events in Dayton, Tennessee, to be written off as merely the "genesis" of the play. And the deviations from history are too conscious and consistent to be seen as anything but a knowing effort to reshape reality.

"[*Inherit the Wind*] may not have been accurate history," writes Edward Larson in his Pulitzer Prize-winning account of the Scopes trial, *Summer for the Gods,* "but it was brilliant theater—and it all but replaced the actual trial in the nation's memory." Fortunately, Larson's definitive book has shed needed light on the increasingly cloudy progressive mythology about the trial. And unlike, say, Jonathan Wells, Larson has no dog in this fight. His follow-up book is the Darwin-friendly, *Evolution: The Remarkable History of a Scientific Theory.*

Publicly at least, the authors have professed more interest in attacking McCarthyism than creationism. The play, after all, was produced in 1955, the year after Senator Joe McCarthy's official inquiry into American communists and fellow travelers in government had come to an end. But for the authors, fervent anti-communism and anti-Darwinism seem to derive from the same source, the hysterical hinterlands of traditional Christian America, what Michael Moore has taken to calling "Jesusland." Over the last fifty years, in fact, the cultural establishment has conspired to make *Inherit the Wind* a case study in primitive Christian opposition to progress and science, Gallileo redux.

Although examples abound, the evolution battle that embroiled the Kansas School Board in the summer of 1999 showed just how this establishment wields its power. That very summer the leading repertory theater in Kansas City quickly changed its schedule to feature the play and use it as a veritable teaching device. Kansas University imported Hollywood actors to stage a highly public reading of the play. High school science teachers in Kansas showed the movie in class as an example of the kind of opposition science faces. And journalists, print and broadcast, used the play as a template from which to fashion their typically inaccurate and often defamatory reporting.

The Hillsboro of Lawrence and Lee's imagination is a subtly scary place, America's heart of darkness. A largely anonymous, fully irrational crowd of townspeople always seems to be gathering, surging, and implicitly threatening the progressive forces of science and sweet reason. These are the kind of people who have cast a pleasant young teacher into a dark prison below the courthouse where he defiantly broods as the play opens.

The real Dayton, Tennessee, was not like this—not at all. In fact, East Tennessee was one of the more modern parts of the whole South.

Although William Jennings Bryan, the real life protagonist in the trial, swept every Southern state in each of his three presidential runs, he never carried Dayton's largely Republican Rhea County. Most Christians in Dayton belonged to the relatively liberal Methodist Church, not to the Baptist Church dominant elsewhere in the South.

"The town, I confess, greatly surprised me," wrote the famed "boob-baiting" reporter H. L. Mencken, "I expected to find a squalid southern Village, with darkies snoozing on the houseblocks, pigs rooting under the houses, and the inhabitants full of hookworm and malaria. What I found was a country town full of charm and beauty."

What happened in this town in real life has nothing to do with the imagined terrors of a McCarthyist purge. In May 1925, after the state of Tennessee passed an anti-evolution law, the fledgling ACLU went looking for a test case. A young engineer from New York, newly moved to Dayton, saw the ACLU ad in the *Chattanooga Times* and recognized an opportunity. He headed down to the local drug store, a kind of ad hoc chamber of commerce, and shared his vision with a few other leading citizens.

These drug store go-getters agreed that if they could find a willing teacher to test the law, they could drum up some much needed publicity for this hustling little hamlet. They found their man in John Scopes, a science instructor and football coach who had filled in for an ailing biology teacher and, in that brief window, had taught a little evolution.

Single and restless, Scopes figured he had nothing to lose from what Larson calls a "summertime caper." An easy-going agnostic and socialist, he subscribed to Darwinism and never much cottoned to the anti-evolution law. After the town boosters convinced him to play along, they got the prosecutor to arrest him. Once arrested, Scopes went not to jail, but to the tennis courts to get in a set or two. One of the boosters, now brimming with enthusiasm, promptly called the *Chattanooga News*. "Something has happened," he told the reporter, "that's going to put Dayton on the map."

"Everything about this case appeared upside down," writes Larson, "and no one seemed to care about upholding the law." Indeed, the prosecutors were working under the "auspices" of the ACLU, the ACLU was defraying the prosecution's expenses, the accused were conspiring with the prosecution, and the school district was eagerly publicizing the whole enchilada, including the criminal charges against one of its teachers.

Lawrence and Lee, however, launder all of this wonderfully Main Street American mischief out of their progressive morality play. They locate the urge to punish the Scopes figure, named Bert Cates in the play, in the town's fulminating Christian bigots, incited by the most predictably narrow-minded of them all, the town minister, a fully fictional character.

"The Reverend Jeremiah Brown, a gaunt, thin-lipped man strides on," read the unintentionally comic stage directions. "He looks around, scowling." As if the reader needed to be told!

From his first appearance on, Brown is total bad news. He, in fact, serves the play as Lawrence and Lee's surrogate McCarthy. Before the congregated townspeople, including his sympathetic daughter Rachel who has been quietly seeing Cates, Brown calls down some spectacularly over-the-top hellfire on the forlorn schoolteacher.

"Let him feel the terror of Thy sword!" Brown prays in a frenzy, his eyes looking skyward. "For all eternity, let his soul writhe in anguish and damnation." At this point, Rachel rushes toward him and implores, "No, Father. Don't pray to destroy Bert!" But the Reverend Brown will have none of it. "Lord," he rages, "we call down the same curse on those who ask grace for this sinner—though they be blood of my blood, and flesh of my flesh!"

There is something going on here. Although Larson and Lee have professed to be targeting McCarthyism by proxy, they have, in reality, targeted the proxies, the progressive world's most entrenched enemy, conservative Judeo-Christian America. In *Inherit the Wind,* they zero in on its supposed Achilles heel, Southern fundamentalism.

The attack is fully gratuitous. In the 1950s, Christian fundamentalists had little public connection to anti-communism or McCarthyism.

McCarthy, after all, was a boozing Catholic from Wisconsin. His number two man, Roy Cohn, was a Jewish homosexual from New York. Richard Nixon was a Quaker from California. Arthur Koestler, author of the anti-communist classic, *Darkness at Noon,* was a Hungarian and a recovering communist. Whittaker Chambers was an atheist from Long Island who also abandoned communism, in his case for a quiet Quaker Christianity.

So blinding is progressive contempt for conservative Christianity that Lawrence and Lee fully strip the play's central character, Matthew Brady, of the impressive progressive credentials of the real life William Jennings Bryan. Known as "the boy orator of the Platte," the young Bryan ascended to national prominence with his fiery "cross of gold" speech at the 1896 Democratic convention. The speech won him his party's nomination for president over the incumbent conservative, Grover Cleveland. At the time, Bryan was thirty-six years old.

The populist Bryan secured the nomination twice more and lost the general election each time. His attacks on American militarism and imperialism, and his calls for increased public control over private business, failed to resonate in the age of Roosevelt. In 1912, he helped secure the presidency for Woodrow Wilson who rewarded Bryan by making him secretary of state. A sincere Christian pacifist, Bryan recoiled at the horrors of World War I and resigned his cabinet position in protest as Wilson prodded the nation towards war. In fact, Bryan began speaking out against evolution only after he located the origins of that war in the dog-eat-dog, Social-Darwinism then popular.

When the "Great Commoner" descended on Dayton in the summer of 1925 to aid the prosecution of Scopes, he had a variety of motives for doing so. To be sure, he did believe that Darwinism contradicted the biblical account of creation. But he also believed that the survival-of-the-fittest explanation for human behavior eroded both faith in God and love for one's fellow man. He saw Darwin's grim determinism as an obstacle to social reform, and he believed that the study of evolution distracted students from socially useful pursuits.

The Matthew Brady who descends on Hillsboro is a buffoon. As Larson notes, "The writers transformed Bryan into a mindless, reactionary creature of the mob." In the course of the play, Brady voices no social concerns about Darwinism and attacks it only on narrow biblical grounds. Although not as severe as the Reverend Brown, Brady is scarcely more sophisticated in his attacks on "Godless" science.

In the play, Henry Drummond stands in for the famed attorney Clarence Darrow, who, in fact, managed Scopes's defense. The play's presumably liberal audience is invited to see its reflection in Drummond— a skeptical, shrewd, fearless, and tirelessly rational seeker of justice.

"I hold that the right to think is very much on trial," says Drummond in court, cutting to the chase. For Drummond, religion may serve its purpose but reason trumps all. "An idea," claims Drummond, "is a greater monument than a cathedral."

Before his arrival, the townspeople whisper that Drummond is an "agnostic." Upon first seeing him, a young girl thinks he's "the devil." And although Drummond does his share of Christian baiting—dismissing Christian tradition as "medieval nonsense" and "fairy tale notions"—he proves himself at the end of the play to be as fair-minded as a good progressive could hope to be.

When the play's H.L. Mencken character, E.K. Hornbeck, tells Drummond that Matthew Brady has died of a "busted belly" and proceeds to ridicule him, Drummond scolds Hornbeck: "You smart-aleck! You have no more right to spit on his religion than you have a right to spit on *my* religion! Or my lack of it!" In real life, of course, it was the profane and insensitive Darrow who claimed that Bryan had died of a "busted belly."

The play's most disingenuous moment comes at the very end. Drummond spots a "copy of Darwin" on a courtroom table. He picks it up and weighs it in his hand. Then he spots a Bible on the judge's bench and weighs that in the other. "He half-smiles, half-shrugs," read the stage directions, and then he puts them both in his briefcase "side by side."

The progressive, at least in fiction, is kind and non-judgmental. He respects both Christianity and Darwinism, each in its place. In one of the play's more memorable scenes, Drummond cross-examines Brady on the witness stand about the origins of life. Having established that Brady has not read Darwin, Drummond scolds him. "How can you be so sure that the body of knowledge systematized in the writings of Charles Darwin is, in any way, irreconcilable with the spirit of the Book of Genesis?" The play's end suggests that they can indeed be reconciled, and that Drummond is just the man to do it.

The real Clarence Darrow knew better. Not a rumored agnostic but a self-avowed atheist, Darrow considered Christianity a "slave religion" and had no use for its Bible. "Where does man get the [selfish] idea of his importance? He gets it from Genesis of course," claimed Darrow in his autobiography. "In fact, man was never made. He was evolved from the lowest form of life."

Darrow's view squares with that of the neo-Darwinian movement. Like all honest evolutionary biologists, Stephen Jay Gould admits that Darwin's theory is a "basically atheistic" version of evolution. "Darwin made it possible," notes Richard Dawkins cheerfully, "to be an intellectually fulfilled atheist."

In the actual Scopes trial, as in the play, Darrow/Drummond attempts to persuade the jury that there is no inherent opposition between Darwinism and Christianity, but in real life, Darrow understood this reconciliation to be no more than a courtroom tactic.

"Darrow, of course, believed that the theory of evolution flatly contradicted the Bible," writes Larson, "but the defense planned to present Christian scientists and theologians who professed otherwise." Eighty years ago, as today, there was no shortage of clergy who were intent on proving their modernist credentials by ignoring the undeniably godless infrastructure of Darwinism. These clergy may simply be ignorant. Scientists have no such excuse. By encouraging this charade, evolutionary biologists and their knowing supporters perpetrate an ongoing cultural fraud.

The final scene in *Inherit the Wind* strikes one other major false note. When Rachel Brown, the minister's daughter, departs with schoolteacher Cates, she leaves her "copy of Darwin" behind. This is the book Drummond balances with the Bible. But when Rachel entered that final scene, suitcase in hand, she did not have a copy of Darwin or any reason to have one. It would have made much more theatrical sense for Drummond to balance the Bible with the textbook in question, *Hunter's Civic Biology,* the book from which both Scopes and Cates taught.

By 1955, however, George W. Hunter's book had lost much of its innocence. A classic example of post-Darwinian scientific racism, the book could not have borne much scrutiny just ten years after the opening of Auschwitz. In addition to its claim that the Caucasian race represented the "highest type of all," Hunter's text aggressively championed the then flourishing eugenics movement.

Hunter had little use for the "eugenically unfit"—the retarded, the mentally ill, epileptics, and the like—and was not afraid to say so in his best-selling textbook. "If such people were lower animals, we would probably kill them off to prevent them from spreading," observed the coldhearted Hunter. "Humanity will not allow this, but we do have the remedy of separating the sexes in asylums or other places and in various ways preventing intermarriage and the possibility of perpetuating such a low and degenerate race." It was specifically to check this kind of reasoning that Bryan launched his anti-evolution crusade. Needless to say, Lawrence and Lee spare the audience these trifling details.

For the record, John Scopes lost his case and was fined a hundred dollars. It didn't much matter. The trial was all just a game, and he knew it from the beginning. At the end, the Dayton school board offered him his job back, but by then he had better opportunities. Sympathetic scientists had pooled their resources to offer Scopes a graduate scholarship in whatever field he chose to study. He eventually settled on the University of Chicago where he studied geology on his way to a career as a petroleum engineer.

For Bert Cates, the end of the trial was a good deal more unsettling. "Do you think they'll send me to prison?" asks a worried Cates before the jury returns its verdict. "They could," responds Drummond somberly. But they don't. As in the Scopes case, the jury finds him guilty, but a prudent judge elects not to send Cates to prison and instead just fines him a hundred dollars.

Here, however, the parallel between fact and fiction ends. At this point in the play, the unlikely—and loaded—stage directions read, "The mighty Evolution Law explodes with the pale puff of a wet firecracker." Sensing this pale puff of an implosion, Brady "thunders" that Cates deserves a "more drastic punishment." Frustrated and filled with rage, he soon thereafter falls over dead before a large crowd.

In real life, Bryan died a few days after the trial, but he did so peacefully in his sleep after a hearty lunch. If the anti-Darwin movement had self-destructed, no one had told him about it. He thought he had won. But now, with his majestic voice silenced by death, progressive mythmakers could set about having him lose. And this they did. By 1955, the year of *Inherit the Wind*, they had streamlined the conflict to a one-sentence synopsis: Forceful Darrow humiliates foolish Bryan before the world.

"Millions of people will say you won," Drummond consoles Cates minutes after receiving his guilty verdict. "They'll read in the paper that you smashed a bad law. You made it a joke!" Millions did just that. In his influential book, *The Age of Reform: From Bryan to F.D.R.*, Richard Hofstadter confirms the judgment of history. The home stretch of Bryan's career—his years fighting against war and eugenics and for local control of schools—represented to Hofstadter nothing more than "the collapse of rural idealism and the shabbiness of the evangelical mind." So reflexive were progressive prejudices by this time—*The Age of Reform* and *Inherit the Wind* were both released in 1955—that Hofstadter's transparent bigotry passed unnoticed.

By the time playwright Jerome Lawrence died in 2004, elite cultural attitudes had, if anything, hardened. As testament, Lawrence's obituary in *Playbill* casually describes *Inherit the Wind* as "even-handed." To be sure, literary fraud is always a collaborative exercise.

That collaboration was entirely evident in the reverse-Scopes case of Burlington, Washington, high school teacher Roger DeHart. Following the publication of *Icons of Evolution,* DeHart shared with his biology class articles from mainstream science publications that exposed Haeckel's embryos and other frauds. The biology establishment was not amused. It brought in its muscle, the always-reliable ACLU and Eugenie Scott's National Center for Science Education. For no other offense than DeHart's sharing of these criticisms, they intimidated the school district with veiled threats of legal action unless he cease and desist. The school district yielded. DeHart was not allowed to continue teaching biology, and orthodox Darwinism triumphed once again.

THE PILTDOWN BIRD

As archaeopteryx approached the 150th anniversary of its discovery, the winged dinosaur was losing his charm. It's not that this dino-bird fossil was a fake. It's just that he didn't seem to go much of anywhere. No two schools of paleontology could quite agree just what this original "missing link" was linking from or to.

The "cladists," the most prominent Darwinian school, were convinced that all birds were "card-carrying dinosaurs." This being so, cladists and others were eager to wrap up the loose ends. They wanted to find a transitional specimen that had the "right stuff," one that could actually fly, a talent that seems to have eluded the earthbound archaeopteryx.

In November 1999, *National Geographic Magazine* breathlessly announced the finding of just such a fossil. Amazingly, amateur enthusiast Stephen Czerkas had come across this new "missing link" at an Arizona mineral show. He called it "archaeoraptor." The *National Geographic* editors were thrilled. They were convinced that the archaeoraptor had exactly the combination of features that one would expect to find "in dinosaurs experimenting with flight." This link established, they were now just as confident that birds were dinosaurs as they were that "humans are mammals."

For a variety of reasons, none of them having to do with the Bible, the science establishment in the People's Republic of China has resisted Darwinism. Thus when Chinese paleontologist Xu Xing examined Czerkas's find, he was not hesitant to announce the obvious, namely that some rascal had merely glued a dinosaur tail on to the body of a primitive bird, and voila, archaeoraptor!

The finger pointing began immediately and in earnest. Storrs Olson of the Smithsonian Institution scourged the National Geographic Society with misplaced religious rhetoric, claiming that it had allied itself with a "cadre of zealous scientists" that had become "outspoken and highly biased proselytizers of the [dino-bird] faith." That a public squabble about "Piltdown Bird" could be unfolding 140 years after the debut of *Origin* speaks to the unsteady state of the Darwinian belief system and the willingness of the faithful to embrace it regardless of the evidence.

As Jonathan Wells relentlessly shows, "the icons of evolution," the classic proofs presented to generation after generation of school children, consciously and consistently "*misrepresent* the evidence."

One icon (the Miller-Urey experiment) gives the false impression that scientists have demonstrated an important first step in the origin of life. One (the four-winged fruit fly) is portrayed as though it were raw materials for evolution, but it is actually a hopeless cripple—an evolutionary dead end. Three icons (vertebrate limbs, archaeopteryx, and Darwin's finches) show actual evidence but are typically used to conceal fundamental problems in its interpretation. Three (the tree of life, fossil horses, and human origins) are incarnations of concepts masquerading as neutral descriptions of nature. And two icons (Haeckel's embryos and peppered moths on tree trunks) are fakes.

The Darwinian paradigm may one day prove its validity beyond the shadow of even an entrenched creationist's doubt. Its advocates believe this to be so. In the meantime, however, their shameless use of fraudulent props does not inspire confidence in the enterprise.

THE AGE OF POISONS

If there is any one man who defined the word "environmentalist" it is the recently deceased J. Gordon Edwards. Edwards was an author, a park ranger, a legendary mountain climber, and an esteemed entomologist.

In fact, it has been the work of people like Edwards that makes it inappropriate to create a separate category in this book for environmentalists. The environmental movement does not need fraud to justify itself. The problem, as Edwards observes, derives from the "pseudo-environmentalists." Much to his own surprise, Edwards would one day confront the most powerful one of all.

Trained as a mountaineer during World War II, Edwards never lost his affection for the out of doors. After the war, he worked as a ranger and naturalist in Montana. For the next forty years, he taught biology and entomology, the study of insects, at San Jose State University. So valued was his contribution that in 1990 the university named its entomology museum after him. Edwards was a member of the Glacier Mountaineering Society, the prestigious Explorers' Club in New York, and the Sierra Club as well.

More to the point, Edwards had an interest in honest science as passionate as his interest in nature. As someone used to surmounting obstacles, he was not easily deterred once he began his search to find the truth. The search in question, one that Edwards did not anticipate or welcome, began in 1962 when Rachel Carson published her breakthrough book on the environment, *Silent Spring*.

At the time of the book's release, Edwards was delighted. Wary of corporate designs on nature, the young scientist read the condensed version of *Silent Spring* in the *New Yorker* as if it were the revealed word.

He then rushed out to buy a copy of the book as soon as it hit the book-stores.

Edwards eagerly raced through the first several chapters, but as he did, his anticipation eroded into uneasiness: "I noticed many statements that I realized were false." Attracted by Carson's message, Edwards tried to overlook the misstatements or to rationalize them away, but increasingly he could not. "As I neared the middle of the book," he adds, "the feeling grew in my mind that Rachel Carson was really playing loose with the facts."

A stickler for documentation, Edwards had no appetite for Carson's obvious mischief. When not just making stuff up, she was wording many of her sentences to mislead the reader. In addition, remembers Edwards, "She was carefully omitting everything that failed to support her thesis that pesticides were *bad,* that industry was *bad,* and that any scientists who did not support her views were *bad.*"

In 1962, however, Edwards was doing fieldwork in Wyoming. He was scarcely in a position, either through prestige or geography, to challenge Carson's book, one that Supreme Court Justice William O. Douglas was hailing as "the most important chronicle of the century for the human race." Predictably gullible as Douglas may have been, his was just one voice in a seemingly universal chorus.

The tune had obviously changed over time. Old-school environmental-ists could not have followed its rhythm. They had operated under the naïve assumption that God had created the earth for man's use and enjoyment. A year after Rachel Carson's birth in 1907, President Theodore Roosevelt had set aside 800,000 acres in Arizona, which would soon enough become known as Grand Canyon National Park. That same year, he staged a White House conference on the conservation of natural resources to which flocked governors, university presidents, businessmen, and scientists eager to preserve the nation's resources for future generations.

Rachel Carson had little apparent interest in those generations or their pleasures. As she proceeded through her academic career, first as an

English major, and then in biology, she absorbed the neo-Darwinian synthesis as it matured. Indeed, she helped pioneer it, especially in its popular application. By the time Carson published *Silent Spring* in 1962—her fourth and easily most influential book—her radical naturalism was on full display.

There is no God in Carson's world, no hint of one. It is "the environment" that has done all the "shaping and directing" of life on earth. This life has taken "hundreds of millions of years to produce" but is now threatened by that most reckless of nature's creatures, man.

There is no mistaking Carson's position on man's attempts to assert his mastery. "The 'control of nature' is a phrase conceived in arrogance," writes Carson, "born of the Neanderthal age of biology and philosophy, when it was supposed that nature exists for the convenience of man." Today, Carson's geocentric smugness is the stuff of science fairs and after-school specials, but then it had the power to shock the system.

Carson derived much of that power from her Gothic literary flair. In 1962, the year of the Cuban missile crisis, she served up her own vision of apocalypse. The title of the book derives from an opening "fable" in which a "strange blight" has crept over an imagined American town, casting its "evil spell" and spreading a "strange stillness" across the land.

"No witchcraft, no enemy action had silenced the rebirth of new life in this stricken world," writes Carson. "The people had done it themselves." Indeed, *Silent Spring* reads like a novel from Anne Rice or Stephen King. The chapters have titles like "The Elixir of Death," "Rivers of Death," and "Beyond the Dreams of the Borgias." The Borgias, it seems, were mere dabblers in the art of poison. Ours is the "age of poisons." Indeed, Carson uses words like "toxins," "contaminants," "hazards," "death-dealing materials," and the inevitable "poison" where others might use "chemical" or "insecticide." And she never lets up.

As Edwards and others have argued, millions of people might be alive today who aren't if Carson had turned her talents to fiction or identified her work as such. For the one "poison" that truly provoked her literary rage was dichlorodiphenyl-trichloroethane or, as it is more commonly known and reviled, DDT.

A German chemist by the name of Othmar Zeidler had first composed this chemical compound in 1874 but did not suggest a use for it. In Switzerland in 1939, Dr. Paul Müller was looking for chemicals that might kill insect pests when he came across Zeidler's written directions for preparing DDT. Müller perfected it, applied it, and in 1948 received the Nobel Prize for his work with it.

Had Gordon Edwards been in a position to cast a vote that year on Müller's behalf, he surely would have done so. While on duty in Italy in 1944, he and the other soldiers in his company had been plagued by body lice. This lice was spreading typhus among the troops, a disease that had killed three million people in Europe during and after the previous war. To check the developing epidemic, the chemists at Merck & Company in New Jersey produced the first five hundred pounds of American-made DDT, rushed it to the airport, and flew it to Italy.

There, Edwards got the order to dust every soldier in his company with the DDT powder. For two weeks straight, he did just that, breathing the fog of white dust as he did so. Much to everyone's relief, the DDT worked, and the epidemic was checked. The surgeon general estimated that the DDT had saved the lives of five thousand soldiers. After the war, inspired by this experience, Edwards went on to get his Ph.D. in entomology from Ohio State and eventually headed out to San Jose State where he taught medical entomology courses for more than thirty years.

So when Edwards read *Silent Spring*, he did so more knowingly than almost anyone in America. His first reading, in fact, shocked him into reading it again and more closely, checking references as he went. What he found now appalled him. The book went consciously wrong with the very dedication.

"To Albert Schweitzer," writes Carson, "who said 'Man has lost the capacity to foresee and to forestall. He will end by destroying the Earth.'"

Edwards had also read Schweitzer's autobiography. He knew that the great doctor was referring to nuclear war, not insecticides. In fact, in dealing with the "wicked insects" that plagued him, Schweitzer boasted of having found "a ray of hope, in the use of DDT."

The body of the book fulfilled the dedication's false promise. Edwards combed through the book page by page, noting literally scores of "deceptions, false statements, horrible innuendoes, and ridiculous allegations." Edwards did so with some reluctance and great care. As Marcel LaFollette accurately observes in his book on scientific misconduct, *Stealing into Print,* "Exposing fraud and deception in professional conduct brings no applause, few rewards, and little public satisfaction." The risks are even higher when one takes on an icon.

Carson's iconic status never slowed Edwards down. In a series of articles and very public presentations, he exposed Carson and others like her who would deceive the public to advance their cause. When Carson alludes to increased bird deaths during the DDT era, Edwards responds, "Is it possible that Carson was unaware of the great *increases* in mammals and game birds?" Her claim that robins were on the verge of extinction because of DDT and related chemicals he reveals to be transparently untrue. Observers, he points out, spotted twelve times more robins in the DDT era than before. As to her claim that DDT was originally tested as an "agent of death" for man, this he calls "despicable." At the end of the day, beyond all reasonable doubt, Edwards revealed Carson's claim that DDT is "deadly" to be "completely false."

Not afraid to put his mouth where his moxie was, Edwards took to swallowing a tablespoon of DDT on stage before every lecture on the subject. In September 1971, *Esquire* magazine pictured Edwards doing just that. The accompanying text explained that Edwards had "eaten two-hundred times the normal human intake of DDT, to show it's not as bad as people think." He did not even consider this gesture risky. In the one year of 1959, for instance, unprotected workmen had applied 60,000 tons of DDT to the inside walls of 100 million houses. Neither the 130,000 workmen or the 535 million people living in the sprayed houses had experienced any adverse effects.

Edwards was not at all alone in his quest. When hearings were held to determine the fate of DDT, he was gratified to find that many esteemed scientists and health officials were ignoring the anti-pesticide hysteria and testifying in defense of DDT. Still, it was not easy to fight a movement like the one Carson inspired. This was especially true in an era when three major networks called all the broadcast shots. In April 1963, *CBS Reports* presented a feature called "The Silent Spring of Rachel Carson," which greatly amplified her message. A month after that show, sensing the prevailing winds, the chairman of the President's Science Advisory Committee declared that pesticides were potentially more dangerous than radioactive fallout.

In 1964, with the momentum behind her movement still building, Carson died. She was just fifty-six years of age. Her death of breast cancer only aggravated the nation's fears of a mass poisoning. This excerpt from a nearly 3,000-word *New York Times* obituary shows how thoroughly her DDT phobia had infected the general culture:

> It was not until 1942 that DDT, a synthetic compound, was introduced in the wake of experiments that included those with poison gas. Its long-term poisonous potency was augmented by its ability to kill some insects upon contact and without being ingested. This opened a new era in pest control and led to the development of additional new synthetic poisons far more effective even than DDT.

Here, the *Times* repeats the canard about DDT and poison gas. The writer also employs the loaded word "poison" and its derivatives where "chemical" would have done nicely. If nothing else had been poisoned, Carson's careless hysteria had surely contaminated the culture. The political fashions followed the cultural ones. On the last day of 1972, William D. Ruckelshaus, the head of the newly formed Environmental Protection Agency, issued an order ending the general use of DDT in the United States after nearly three decades of application.

Today, more than forty years after Carson's death, the struggle over DDT use continues. One Western country after another followed America's lead and outlawed the chemical. Only a valiant effort in the late 1990s, led by Harvard's Amir Attaran, a biologist and former lawyer, thwarted a potential worldwide ban. As Attaran pointed out, no two studies have shown that DDT increases the risk of cancer or any other disease. Studies have shown, however, that judicious use of DDT can cut malaria deaths by as much as 99 percent and at much less cost than any alternative pesticide.

Attaran's approach was shrewd. In the leftist precincts of the environmental movement, he employed the one agent capable of checking the self-indulgence of scientific naturalism, and that was the moral force of race. Historically, and relentlessly, progressives have used this force against the right. They even created the spurious new phenomenon of "environmental racism" to fight corporate power. Almost never have they had to face race- and class-related charges themselves. Attaran turned the tables on them. He accused the would-be DDT banners of the World Wildlife Fund of "eco-colonialism" and scolded them for imposing "Western environmental values, written by the rich and healthy, on the backs of the sick and poor." And he seems to have shocked them into submission.

In his bold and meticulously documented 2004 novel, *State of Fear*, Michael Crichton shares the eco-colonialism message with a much larger public than had ever heard it before. A Harvard-trained M.D., Crichton takes particular aim at the banning of DDT. He describes it as "arguably the greatest tragedy of the twentieth century" and provides the mortality statistics to back up his claim. Interestingly, in the appendix, Crichton draws a detailed comparison between the growth of the eugenics movement and that of global warming, each a "social program masquerading as a scientific one."

Like Attaran and Crichton, J. Gordon Edwards was not afraid to tackle the naturalist establishment. He attacked it not for its insensitivity to the third world but for its indifference to humanity. He cited the 500 million saved lives that the National Academy of Sciences attributed to DDT. He echoed the World Health Organization's affirmation that no substance had ever proved more beneficial to man. And then he dared to question publicly why Rachel Carson and her followers chose to ignore the undeniable human benefits of DDT.

In Carson's case, the answer is apparent on every other page of *Silent Spring*. Straightforward as always, Edwards describes the Carson philosophy as a "lack of concern for human lives." She could vividly describe the death of a bird, notes Edwards, but nowhere in the book does she even think to describe the death of a human by an insect-borne disease.

For the record, the research activities of this DDT-eating scientist finally caught up with him. Edwards died of a heart attack while climbing Divide Mountain at Glacier National Park, where he held the unofficial title as the patron saint of climbing. He was eighty-four years old.

THE BET

In one of the more intriguing ironies of modern science, famed ecologist Paul Ehrlich and the man who would forever haunt his career, economist Julian Simon, were born three months apart and grew up less than three miles apart, each in Jewish households in neighboring Newark, New Jersey, suburbs.

From his childhood on, Ehrlich was an avid butterfly collector. Indeed, in another irony, he would emerge as his high school's second most famous collector of insects after Alfred Kinsey, also featured in this book. By Ehrlich's own recollection, what first prompted him towards his career as an ecologist was "finding out that there was so much DDT sprayed around New Jersey in the late 1940s that I couldn't raise caterpillars to get butterfly and moth specimens." This insight pre-dates *Silent Spring* by more than a decade. Given his precocious indifference to humanity, it should come as no surprise that Ehrlich would one day cite Carson as his personal "environmental hero."

Ehrlich followed a conventional career course through academia getting his Ph.D. from the University of Kansas and then hiring on as an assistant professor of biology at Stanford University where he has been ever since. Long interested in nature and evolution, Ehrlich taught evolutionary biology courses when he first arrived at Palo Alto. "In the first nine weeks I told students where we'd come from," remembers Ehrlich, "and in the last week told them where we were heading."

Where we were heading was essentially nowhere. "My belief," Ehrlich once told an interviewer, "is yes, that after I'm dead it'll be exactly like it was before I was born." A thoroughgoing materialist, Ehrlich rejected the notion of a soul and disavowed all organized religion. One of the crueler ironies of his life, and the admittedly worst moment of his professional career, came when Northwestern University rejected him for a teaching position because of his presumed allegiance to a faith he did not profess.

Despite the rejection, Ehrlich enjoyed a remarkably successful career as the late twentieth century's best-known neo-Malthusian. Nearly two centuries before Ehrlich, British scientist Thomas Robert Malthus had argued that humans, like plants and animals, were capable of overproducing. If left to his own devices, man would generate far more children than could survive. Thus, family size had to be regulated. If not, famine would sweep the globe and eventually destroy England and the rest of mankind. Indeed, it was from Malthus's imagined struggle for survival that Charles Darwin deduced the basic principles of natural selection.

For all his debt to Malthus, Ehrlich makes his predecessor look positively prudent. For Ehrlich, the very idea of "growth" appalls him, and he warns his followers to treat it "as the cancerlike disease it is." He begins his breakthrough 1968 book *The Population Bomb* with the startling claim, "The battle to feed all of humanity is already lost." A hardcore Darwinian, Ehrlich blames this disaster on the simple fact that there are "too many people," a condition he traces to "an urge to reproduce. . . . fixed in us by billions of years of evolution."

Even at the time of its release, *The Population Bomb* had to read a wee bit hyperbolic. Today, it just seems flat-out silly. Ehrlich lays out three possible scenarios that could define the earth "in the next decade or so." In the most "cheerful" of these scenarios, Americans assume an unexpected "maturity of outlook," a new Pope "gives his blessing to abortion," and only half a billion people die of famine. In the least cheerful scenario, worldwide famine leads to nuclear war, and the most intelligent creatures that survive are cockroaches.

In an amusing *Stanford Review* article, Mike Toth gathers up some of Ehrlich's more ambitious, post-*Population Bomb* projections:

> In 1969, Ehrlich added, "By 1985 enough millions will have died to reduce the earth's population to some acceptable level, like 1.5 billion people." That same year, he predicted in an article entitled "Eco-Catastrophe!" that by 1980 the United States would see its life expectancy drop to 42 because of pesticides, and by 1999 its population would drop to 22.6 million. In the mid-seventies, with the release of his *The End of Affluence*, Ehrlich incorporated drama into his dire prophesies. He envisioned the president dissolving Congress "during the food riots of the 1980s," followed by the United States suffering a nuclear attack for its mass use of insecticides. That's right, Ehrlich thought that the United States would get nuked in retaliation for killing bugs.

In an odd way, Ehrlich's over-the-top style helped insulate him from his own folly. He could be wrong a thousand times, and no one would much notice amidst the environmental hysteria that he himself helped whip up. His frequent TV appearances—twenty on Johnny Carson alone—and the success of *The Population Bomb*—three million copies sold—helped radicalize young America and its conservationist organizations like the Sierra Club and Greenpeace. Not surprisingly, Ehrlich was a founding father of Earth Day.

Perhaps even more alarming, *The Population Bomb* established

Ehrlich as a rising star within an increasingly radicalized academy. He capped a lifetime of prestigious environmental awards with a $345,000 MacArthur Foundation grant and the Crafoord Prize from the Swedish Academy of Sciences, the Nobel equivalent for environmentalists.

In his naturalist faith, and rejection of God, Ehrlich hews to type. Giving Ehrlich the benefit of the doubt, his is not the conscious fraud of the bunco artist, but rather the self-deception of the blowhard. He appears to have drunk often at the well of his own snake oil. What pushes Ehrlich's contribution up the fraud continuum is his failure to take stock, to reassess his science, to atone for past mistakes. This he could not bring himself to do, and so it was left for Julian Simon to do it for him.

For all the parallels, the arc of Simon's early career did not track nearly as smoothly as Ehrlich's. Still, it seems to have been better grounded. Simon attended Harvard on a naval ROTC scholarship and shipped out after graduation as a junior officer. Upon completion of his duty, Simon went to work in advertising in New York, headed off to the University of Chicago for a Ph.D. in business administration, and then returned to New York to work in direct marketing. Bored, he headed back to academia, ending up at the University of Maryland as a professor of business administration where he taught until he died in 1998.

Simon called himself an "unconventional economist" with good reason. He was largely self-taught in the field and never sought professional advancement within it. In fact, in his 1991 book, *The Population Explosion,* Ehrlich would dismiss Simon namelessly as "an economist specializing in mail-order marketing."

If Simon needed confirmation of his status as an outsider, he got it in spades when he attempted to commercialize a brainchild of his own devising—the voluntary auction system for airline overbooking. It took him nearly thirteen years and countless rejections every step of the way before the head of the Civil Aeronautics Board (CAB), Alfred Kahn, also an economist, finally learned of Simon's proposal and implemented it.

Prolific and persistent, Simon would write thirty-seven books and monographs before he died at sixty-five, as well as more than 330 articles on a wide variety of subjects. For all his publications, however, Simon would be most remembered for his optimistic rejection of Malthusian gloom and his very public bet with Paul Ehrlich that put his optimism to the test.

In the way of background, Simon had an economist's flair for hard data and a direct marketer's faith in results. Freed of academic cant, his analysis led him to believe that life on earth was getting better, not worse. The signs were everywhere and undeniable. "Length of life and health are increasing," he writes, "supplies of food and other natural resources are becoming more abundant, and pollutants in our environment are decreasing."

On the famine front, the evidence seemed to Simon transparent. The only reliable data recorded in the years after World War II had been kept by the United Nations and the United States, and the trend could not have been clearer. "The record of food production entirely contradicts the scary forecasts," Simon observed in 1996. "The world trend in recent decades shows unmistakably an increase in food production per person."

For Simon, like any good scientist, the proof was in the data, specifically those for earth's natural resources. If mankind were running out of resources, as Ehrlich contended, then why weren't the prices on these resources climbing? In fact, prices had declined throughout history. Simon saw this decline as evidence of greater abundance, not increasing scarcity.

Simon also argued that, over time, the environment had been getting cleaner, not dirtier. The ultimate proof of this trend was the spectacular increase in life expectancy across the globe, which Simon considered "the best overall index of the pollution level." He insisted that Ehrlich's "population bomb" was not a "bomb" in any real sense of the word, but a "boon."

Simon centered his economics on the idea that newcomers to a society, either children or immigrants, represented a good deal more than additional mouths to feed. "The ultimate resource," he wrote, "is people—skilled, spirited, and hopeful people who will exert their wills and imaginations for their own benefit, and inevitably they will benefit not only themselves but the rest of us as well." He saw each new human as a future contributor and producer who would continue the effort to enhance life and improve the environment.

For Simon, too, progeny meant more than just progress: "If we also consider the non-material aspects of children—their meaning for parents and others who enjoy a flourishing of humanity—then the case for adding children to our world becomes even stronger." True to form, Simon had three children; Ehrlich had one and a vasectomy.

Paul Ehrlich has a decidedly more mixed view of mankind. Although he defines man as one "animal" out of many, he does not deny humanity its big-brained cleverness. He seems to applaud man as he existed in the beginning of the agricultural age for his "increasingly efficient use of both renewable and non-renewable sources." He even comments favorably on the industrial revolution with its "generally improving living conditions" and its declining death rates. But he is not at all enthused with contemporary Western man, the one "species," he scoffs, "with the hubris to call itself 'homo sapiens.'" With a straight face, Ehrlich describes the advances in medical science that have allowed this population to grow and flourish "as the straw that broke the camel's back."

Most progressives nurse a quiet disdain for the great unwashed, but in Ehrlich's case, there is nothing quiet about it. "Our population consists of two groups," he writes, "a comparatively small one dedicated to the preservation of beauty and wildlife, and a vastly larger one dedicated to the destruction of both (or at least apathetic toward it)."

Ehrlich has a particular grudge against Americans, and this takes us to the heart of his obsession with population. As Ehrlich sees it, an area is "overpopulated" when it can no longer maintain its citizens without depleting "nonrenewable resources" like oil and minerals or without degrading the environment. For Ehrlich, the "grossly overpopulated" South Florida is a striking example of the same.

Unlike Simon who sees man essentially as a producer, Ehrlich sees him as a consumer and despoiler and none more of either than *homo Americanus*. In an entirely revealing section of his book, *The Population Explosion,* Ehrlich shows his hand when addressing the question of Mexican migration.

Ehrlich admits grudgingly that immigration has enabled millions to improve their standard of living and that Mexican immigration, in particular, has been useful for the United States. Still, he hopes to shut down the flow of immigrants into the United States. The reason? "The world can't afford more Americans." Here, he is likely projecting from his own circumstance as an affluent Californian whose "environmental vices" include flying his own airplane. It doesn't seem to matter, as Ehrlich notes elsewhere, that North America produces three quarters of the world's grain and supports a hundred countries in the process; Americans consume too many nonrenewable resources.

Ehrlich presents a straightforward three-step approach to solving America's population that could have come out of the Khmer Rouge playbook. We simply "halt human population growth as simply and humanely as possible," lower per-capita consumption, and convert to more benign technologies. If this program results in a loss of jobs, Ehrlich opines, "The work week could be cut to thirty-five or thirty hours."

This kind of thinking made a free market economist like Simon cringe. He felt that Ehrlich was blowing smoke and had been getting away with it much too long. In 1980, fed up with Ehrlich's continued predictions of scarcity, Simon challenged him. He asked Ehrlich to pick any five commodities and hold them for ten years. If the prices rose—proving increased scarcity—Simon would buy the commodities back from Ehrlich at the higher price. If the prices fell, Ehrlich would pay Simon the difference.

Simon knew a mark when he saw one. Ehrlich had, to say the least, no great gift for prediction. "If I were a gambler, I would bet even money that England will not exist in the year 2000," he once told Johnny Carson. For Ehrlich, this was not an unusually imprudent wager. Yet like all chronic gamblers, Ehrlich only remembered the winners. So he and two of his Berkeley colleagues took Simon up on his offer. They picked $200 worth each of chromium, copper, nickel, tin, and tungsten.

"Perhaps it was a mistake," says Ehrlich's Web site of the bet with unintended irony. It certainly was. All five commodities dropped in price almost as much as Ehrlich's reputation. In October of 1990, Ehrlich mailed Simon a check for $570.07. He would have been hard-pressed to choose better. During the decade, thirty-three of thirty-five standard metals dropped in price. So did oil. So did food. Ehrlich, however, was undaunted. Flaunting his indifference to the factually minded, he released *The Population Explosion* in 1991.

In this book, Ehrlich acknowledged that new "tricks of modern agri-culture" had helped produce an "unprecedented upward trend in global grain production." But Ehrlich cautioned his readers not to be fooled. Even "absurdly optimistic" projections were now showing "an ominous food crunch facing the world as soon as 2000."

In a 2004 interview, Ehrlich was asked whether the predictions he made in *The Population Bomb* were "right." A sophist and skilled propa-gandist, Ehrlich fell back as usual on evasion and insult.

"Anne [his wife] and I have always followed U.N. population projec-tions as modified by the Population Reference Bureau," he huffed, "so we never made 'predictions,' even though idiots think we have." The man has never learned. He has never had to. The culture that created him was not about to abandon him.

If Ehrlich is the Aristotle of his own Bizarro World, then his Alexander is Al Gore, his disciple and a man who came within 300 votes of being the most influential pseudo-environmentalist of our time. About Gore's bestseller, *Earth in the Balance,* Simon is merciless. "The book," he writes, "is as ignorant a collection of clichés as anything ever published on the subject."

In his book, *Hoodwinking the Nation,* Simon counters every one of those clichés—vanishing farmland, poisonous DDT, deadly dioxin, lethal Agent Orange—with hard and undeniable data. When confronted with the facts, Gore has chosen to ignore them.

"Though Gore undoubtedly cares sincerely about environmental and resource issues," writes Simon, "his ignorance is willful rather than naïve." And that for Simon, and for this author, is the ultimate distinction between fool and fraud.

4
Sexual Fantasies

"The greatest crimes do not arise from a want of feeling for others but from an over-sensibility for ourselves and an over-indulgence to our own desires."

—EDMUND BURKE

NO GODS, NO MASTERS

Planned Parenthood founder Margaret Sanger was not herself a fraud. Not really. During her heyday, this diminutive spitfire was as sincerely outspoken and outrageous as she could be.

Nor can one doubt her commitment to "birth control," the cause to which she dedicated her career. If she trafficked in bad science, there was a lot of bad science in her day to traffic in. There is no real evidence that she did so deliberately.

Remember, though, that fraud is almost inevitably a collaborative effort. As Nazi Germany moved from talk to action on the eugenics front in the late 1930s, Sanger and her allies began to see that they had a problem at hand, a big one—Sanger's literary record tracked goosestep for unholy goosestep with that of her most notorious contemporary. Given her donor base, that record had to be scrubbed. This was not an axis with which it paid to be identified.

Despite the potential for embarrassment, the cultural establishment

215

dared not turn its back on the already iconic Sanger. She had proved herself essential to the flowering of the sexual revolution, and no organization would prove more critical to its sustenance than Planned Parenthood. To this day, the organization does not disguise Sanger's importance. "Margaret Sanger gained worldwide renown, respect, and admiration for founding the American birth control movement and, later, the Planned Parenthood Federation of America," reads the proud tribute to Sanger on the Planned Parenthood Web site.

What Planned Parenthood has disguised—with the help of the cultural establishment—is the very core of Sanger's philosophy. True, the organization does admit that some of the "popular ideas" she adopted are "out of keeping with our thinking today." But from Planned Parenthood's perspective, Sanger's "visionary accomplishments" so over-whelm those "outmoded" ideas that the latter are scarcely worth talking about. Always helpful, Planned Parenthood provides a guide to help the curious and to put Sanger's views in perspective. As one might expect, however, the Planned Parenthood "fact sheet" is almost pure fiction.

Fortunately, Sanger herself has left a detailed record of how she lived and how she thought. The most unimpeachable source of the former is her autobiography, written in 1938, and of the latter, her landmark book, *The Pivot of Civilization*, written in 1922. Sanger wrote clearly and powerfully. Her books offer as insightful a look as any ever written on the development of the radical community in the United States. As it happens, however, only her critics want you to read them.

Although she would later fudge the date to 1883, Margaret Sanger was born in 1879 in Corning, New York, the sixth of what would prove to be eleven children. Oddly, one atheist Web site insists that Sanger came from a "devoutly Catholic family," all the better, one presumes, to position her as someone who saw the light and abandoned her faith. But the site errs. The dominant figure in Sanger's childhood, her Irish immigrant father, was an outspoken socialist and agnostic who seems to have shamed his daughter out of any Christian affections by the time she was an adolescent.

Michael Higgins saw Christianity as a largely inoffensive pastime for the weak-minded. As a means of reform, he much preferred politics to religion. "In fact," writes Sanger of her father, "he took up socialism because he believed it put Christian philosophy into practice, and to me its ideals still come nearest to carrying out what Christianity was supposed to do."

After an indifferent year as a schoolteacher and a sojourn spent caring for her dying mother, Sanger tried her hand at nursing school. It was there that her fortunes changed. That change had less to do with her exposure to health care than to a certain wealthy architect. Small, lithe, and highly attractive, Margaret Higgins caught the eye of Bill Sanger. The first of many useful men in her life, Sanger wooed her hard, wed her, and opened her eyes to the world.

When first married, Sanger contented herself with the simple delights of bourgeois motherhood. She had three children in rapid succession "and wanted at least four more as quickly as my health would permit." Her health, however, did not oblige. The birth of her third child caused complications that led her to stop at three. It probably didn't matter. She was already losing interest in homemaking, and a new class of prophets was luring her to the world beyond her home.

"A religion without a name was spreading over the country," Sanger enthuses. "The converts were liberals, socialists, anarchists, revolutionists of all shades." Now living in New York in these heady days before World War I, Sanger wanted part of the action. Like her new radical friends, she had thrown over her own personal *ancien regime* and was eager to embrace something new. "Each believed he had a key to the gates of heaven," she writes of her fellow radicals. "Each was trying to convert the others."

Although Sanger joined the Socialist Party, Local Number Five, she did so more out of fashion than faith. Unlike her new comrades, she sensed that many of the prophets in this suddenly godless world were false ones. Uninspired by socialism, she found her own calling quite by chance. One evening, a scheduled lecturer had to cancel, and the organizer asked

Sanger to fill in. Knowing little about politics, she spoke about what she did know: health. And she made a great hit with the women present. This led her to start a series of columns called "What Every Mother Should Know" followed by another, more sexually charged series called "What Every Girl Should Know." And a career was born.

No doubt, her advocacy for women's rights was deeply felt and genuine. After a trip to assess attitudes in Europe—more enlightened than those in America, but of course—Sanger returned to New York and in 1914 launched her own publication. She called it *Woman Rebel*. Never one for subtlety, Sanger adopted the altogether revealing slogan: "No Gods. No Masters." In the first issue, the increasingly radical Sanger argued that women had a duty "to look the world in the eyes; to have an idea; to speak and act in defiance of convention." Sanger did just that. Her attempt to preach the gospel of women's rights led to some inspired battles with the protectors of tradition and more than a few arrest warrants along the way.

During this same formative period, Sanger was falling increasingly under the spell of Havelock Ellis. A British socialist, Ellis had penned a six-volume tome on the virtues of sexual liberation, *Studies in the Psychology of Sex*. Despite huge censorship issues of his own, the books found an eager audience among American radicals, few more eager than Sanger.

In late 1914, Sanger met Ellis, and the meeting left her nearly giddy. "He, beyond any other person, has been able to clarify the question of sex," writes Sanger, "and free it from the smudginess connected with it from the beginning of Christianity, raise it from the dark cellar, set it on a higher plane."

As Sanger saw it, Christianity treated sex as though it were a vice and yet insisted that married couples indulge in it without restriction. This paradox maddened her. Even before she had found her faith, she had found her antichrist in the Christian establishment, particularly Catholicism. The faith was evolving. She thought the French idea of a one or two child family too narrow and the British neo-Malthusianism too materialistic. She yearned for a female self-mastery that was "bigger and freer" than either. At a spirited meeting with a few companions, they hit upon the ideal concept and gave it a name: "birth control."

Curiously, Sanger admits to having no great sense of compassion for the less fortunate, a seeming drawback for their would-be liberator. "I hated the wretchedness and hopelessness of the poor," she writes, "and never experienced that satisfaction in working among them that so many noble women have found."

Sanger saw the poor not as a people to be helped but as a problem to be solved, and birth control offered the perfect solution. If *The Pivot of Civilization* is as loud and clear as a bell about this solution, *The Autobiography of Margaret Sanger* is almost entirely silent. Despite the fact that *The Pivot of Civilization* was Sanger's most influential book, there is but one brief passing mention of it in the autobiography and almost no mention of a core idea that inspired *Pivot*.

It is not hard to understand the silence. The autobiography was published in 1938, the same year that Hitler consumed Austria and half of Czechoslovakia, the same year that Nazi propaganda minister, Joseph Goebbels, made the following declaration:

Our starting point is not the individual, and we do not subscribe to the view that one should feed the hungry, give drink to the thirsty, or clothe the naked. . . . Our objectives are entirely different: we must have a healthy people in order to prevail in the world.

Now consider the following from Sanger's *The Pivot of Civilization*, one that makes Goebbels's proclamation seem, by comparison, a model of restraint.

. . . the most urgent problem today is how to limit and discourage the over-fertility of the mentally and physically defective. Possibly drastic and Spartan methods may be forced upon American society if it continues complacently to encourage the chance and chaotic breeding that has resulted from our stupid, cruel sentimentalism.

Books offer a useful gauge of intent. There is nothing hasty about them, and this book came at the peak of Sanger's celebrity and influence in 1922. Planned Parenthood is forever chastising pro-life advocates for quoting Margaret Sanger out of context, but *Pivot* is all context. At the time of its publication, Sanger was in her early forties and no dilettante. Indeed, she had left her husband and all but abandoned her children to further her cause. She also writes more powerfully, methodically, and logically than almost any of her radical peers.

In her book, Sanger argues that the central challenge in any society is "the control and guidance of the great natural instinct of Sex," a control attainable only through birth control. Sanger posits two primary reasons why this control is necessary. The first, the one that has endured in progressive mythology, is "the liberation of the spirit of woman and through woman of the child." The second, the one that has been cleansed from the record, is "to prevent the sexual and racial chaos into which the world has drifted."

In Sanger's view, these two urges complement each other. "The potential mother," she writes, "can then be shown that maternity need not be slavery but may be the most effective avenue to self-development and self-realization. Upon this basis only may we improve the quality of the race."

A product of her age, Sanger had absorbed the Darwinian ethos and made it her own. "We must temper our emotion and enthusiasm with the impersonal determination of science," she argues, and she uses the available science at every opportunity to reinforce her thesis. Often, this science borders on the darkly humorous.

Sanger has a particular weakness for "modern studies." Those she cites manage to prove just about anything she wants to prove. One study, for

instance, confirms "that the least intelligent and the thoroughly degenerate classes in every community are the most prolific." To bolster this
contention, she cites a Sir James Crichton-Browne who had apparently
proved that "the feeble-minded woman is twice as prolific as the normal
one."

A Dr. Tredgold is even more specific. According to his studies, "degenerate families" average 7.3 children compared to the 4 that normal families have. Worse, only 36 percent of the degenerate offspring—456 out of
a total of 1,269—contribute to society in any positive way, and this relatively cheery evaluation comes from their presumably fawning parents.
Other studies are broader still in their implications and in their black
comedy. In the following, Sanger's rhetoric foreshadows the barrier-
leaping, pseudo-sci-fi scare language of the imagined heterosexual AIDS
epidemic to come:

> There is every indication that feeble-mindedness in its protean
> forms is on the increase, that it has leaped the barriers, and that
> there is truly, as some of the scientific eugenists (sic) have pointed
> out, a feeble-minded peril to future generations—unless the
> feeble-minded are prevented from reproducing their kind. To
> meet this emergency is the immediate and peremptory duty of
> every State and of all communities.

Sanger makes it entirely clear that "feeble-mindedness" is more than a
superficial problem. Even if society could turn these people from a life of
crime or degeneracy to some more docile pursuit, the real issue—"the
intelligence of the community"—is not addressed. Here again, science
sheds light on the problem:

> The advent of the Binet-Simon and similar psychological tests
> indicates that the mental defective who is glib and plausible, bright
> looking and attractive, but with a mental vision of seven, eight, or

nine years, may not merely lower the whole level of intelligence in a school or in a society, but may be encouraged by church and state to increase and multiply until he dominates and gives the prevailing "color"—culturally speaking—to an entire community.

The new science of psychology had shown Sanger the scary breadth of the problem. She cites a study by a Robert M. Yerkes, which claimed that nearly half of all American draftees—47.3 percent to be precise—"had the mentality of twelve-year-old children or less." In other words, says Sanger with her typical subtlety, "They are morons."

Sanger reviews the remedies for dealing with a half-retarded nation and finds them all wanting. She reserves her greatest scorn, of course, for the traditional. The Catholic Church's claim that even deformed children have souls, she argues, has had "the practical effect of making this world a vale of tears." To "open minded" individuals, presumably like herself, such orthodoxy appears "crude and cruel" and a "menace to civilization."

Traditional philanthropy, if anything, is crueler still. "Organized charity," writes Sanger, "itself is the symptom of a malignant social disease." By keeping so many "defectives, delinquents, and dependents" alive and breeding, charity at some point becomes an injustice for the self-supporting citizen and a "positive injury to the future of the race." Salvation Army bell ringers get nothing from Sanger but the evil eye. She writes off their efforts as a "debauch of sentimentalism" and argues that they did more harm than good.

Although Sanger applauds the "new vitality" of "Marxian Socialism," she thinks that socialism rather misses the point. Her analysis of Marx just a few years after the Russian revolution is dead on. Few of her intellectual peers would ever see through the Marxist-Leninist illusion as clearly as Sanger did.

As Sanger smartly argues, the Marxists had to reduce all behavior to "class conflict," whether that behavior fit or not. Consequently, its predictions were almost inevitably wrong. Worse, from her perspective,

Marxism, as taught, relieved the proletariat of all responsibility for just about everything, including "its reckless breeding." As far as Sanger could tell, the Marxist leadership encouraged the masses to perpetuate their misery, and she had little use for its propaganda.

Sanger's most interesting philosophical flirtation was with the eugenics movement. In the years post-Hitler, the very phrase "eugenics" has taken on a nasty taint, and Planned Parenthood is quick to absolve its founding mother of any association with the same.

"Margaret Sanger was not a racist, an anti-Semite, or a eugenicist," declares its Web site definitively. Here, Planned Parenthood fudges big time. Sanger did not believe in eugenics. From her perspective, the eugenics movement did not go far enough. So Sanger went one step further into the realm of "negative eugenics." This is her real Scarlet Letter, one now kept under lock and key.

As Planned Parenthood rather lamely explains, Nazis were eugenicists. They opposed the use of abortion and contraception by "fit" women. Nazis also directed the procreative energy of the fit towards the state. Through education and persuasion, the state would try to inspire the fit to outbreed the unfit. This much is true.

The Margaret Sanger of 1922 dismissed this strategy as a "cradle competition." She thought it lethally weak in the knees. Eugenics advocates had no plan for dealing with that "ever-increasing army of undersized, stunted, and dehumanized slaves." Any plan to outbreed these people would inevitably fail the race and deny fit women mastery over their own biological destiny. Society simply could not leave to "chance and chaotic breeding" the perpetuation of the unfit. Sanger insists on more active measures, measures that might have to be "drastic and Spartan." If Sanger does not yoke the destinies of fit women to the "state" per se, she constantly evokes their responsibility to the race, the society, and the community, even if indirectly.

As Planned Parenthood tirelessly repeats, Sanger was not a racist. This is true in that she does not specifically single out African Americans for elimination. The reason why, however, is that she does not have to. Sanger's audience was prepared to believe that most, if not all, African Americans would fall within that "moron" half of the population to be squeezed out of existence.

In *Pivot*, for instance, Sanger cites in detail the case of a "Negro woman" who had given birth to sixteen children. By Sanger's generous standards, all sixteen of them appeared to be criminal or degenerate. They lived, as if they had much choice, in "a thickly populated Negro district." To no one's surprise, this district was reported to be "the head-quarters for the criminal element of the surrounding State." Given the biases of the day, her audience would assume this woman to be more or less typical of her race, a symptom of the "sexual and racial chaos" that so alarmed Sanger. In *Pivot*, Sanger says nothing to suggest otherwise.

Sanger's American Birth Control League and its allies had enormous influence in their day. Two years after *The Pivot of Civilization* was published, the Immigration Restriction Act was passed into law thanks in large part to the supporting testimony of the Eugenics Records Office. In 1927, in a now notorious case known as *Buck v. Bell*, the U.S. Supreme Court accepted the state of Virginia's ruling that Carrie Buck and her infant daughter were mentally defective and thus deserving of forced sterilization.

"It is better for all the world," wrote famed progressive jurist Oliver Wendell Holmes Jr., "if instead of waiting to execute degenerate offspring for crime, or to let them starve for their imbecility, society can prevent those who are manifestly unfit from continuing their kind." Sanger could not have said it better herself. Joining Holmes in that decision was his equally celebrated progressive colleague, Louis Brandeis, who was himself Jewish. Ironically, if perhaps disingenuously, a German doctor during the Nuremberg trials would cite *Buck v. Bell* as the precedent for Nazi race hygiene and sterilization programs.

By 1938, the year of Sanger's autobiography, some thirty American states had mandatory sterilization laws. The next year, Germany would launch its infamous T-4 program, which targeted physically and mentally handicapped children for death by poisoning and starvation. To be fair, Sanger would not have approved. In *Pivot*, for instance, she argues against the proposition "that the community could or should send to the lethal chamber the defective progeny resulting from irresponsible and unintelligent breeding," but she argues this point so matter-of-factly that she makes such a truly ghastly option seem almost respectable.

In 1946, with the full horrors of the Holocaust revealed, the American Birth Control League quietly changed its name to the Planned Parenthood Federation of America. In a memory purge impressive even by Soviet standards, Planned Parenthood and its friends in the cultural establishment proceeded to cleanse all trace of eugenics, positive or negative, from Sanger's record.

"After World War II, nobody was a eugenicist, and nobody had ever been a eugenicist," writes Michael Crichton in the appendix to *State of Fear*. "Biographers of the celebrated and the powerful did not dwell on the attractions of this philosophy to their subjects, and sometimes did not mention it at all."

By the time Sanger died in 1966, the cultural establishment had transformed her into the Mother Teresa of birth control. "Eugenics" does not appear among the 2,200 glowing words in that ultimate arbitrator of establishment worth, the *New York Times* obituary. Nor do "sterilization," "*Buck v. Bell*," "racial chaos," "mentally defective," "abortion," "Nazi," or anything of the kind.

The Margaret Sanger that the *Times* reader is asked to remember is a "dynamic, titian-haired woman whose Irish ancestry also endowed her with unfailing charm and persuasive wit." The only quibble that the *Times* raises is that her opposition to the Catholic Church led her to oppose the election of President John F. Kennedy.

In fact, so strong was Sanger's opposition to the Church that she had threatened—a threat then novel among the elite—to leave the country if Kennedy were elected. The *Times*, however, offers this tidbit not as a criticism, but as proof of her tenacity. Indeed, Sanger's "years of birth control advocacy appeared to be making an inroad in Rome" enthuses the obituary writer. What is more, a papal commission was about to propose "leaving the matter of specific birth control techniques to the individual Catholic conscience." In short, the wonder-working Sanger was about to save the Catholic Church from its own follies. Two years later, of course, Pope Paul VI issued the encyclical *Humanae Vitae* reaffirming the Church's position in spades.

The Supreme Court's *Roe v. Wade* decision in 1973 should have solidified Sanger's reputation for all time. In legalizing abortion, however, the Court unwittingly launched a countermovement. If Sanger's progressive friends were willing to forget her enthusiasm for negative eugenics, the growing pro-life forces wanted everyone to remember. Indeed, it is they who have kept *The Pivot of Civilization* alive and have caused Planned Parenthood to play defense with Sanger's reputation.

Despite their numbers and their votes, however, pro-lifers have as little impact on the cultural establishment as any millions of well-educated citizens could possibly have. For the most part, the major media ignore their very existence. As testament, there has not been to date a single sympathetic pro-life portrait, real or fictional, in any extended broadcast format.

There are plenty of heroes on the other side. In 1995, the TV movie *Choices of the Heart: The Margaret Sanger Story* debuted, starring Dana Delaney as Margaret Sanger. It focuses on the stirring saga of Sanger's censorship battle with Anthony Comstock of Comstock Law notoriety played with suitable menace by Rod Steiger.

Two years later, *Life* magazine welcomed Sanger into the Life Hall of Heroes. "Her once 'obscene' ideas," enthuses *Life* writer Seth Goddard, "had been embraced worldwide." A year later, *Time* magazine enshrined Sanger as one of the most influential people of "Our Century." To be sure, neither *Time* nor *Life* speaks of Sanger's commitment to forcibly sterilizing half of America, an idea that is still considered "obscene" in most quarters, and especially so in progressive ones.

In one of the more illuminating quirks in America's intellectual history, it was none other than William Jennings Bryan who inspired the young Margaret Sanger to change the world. After seeing him speak, Sanger decided that she too "in an obscure and unformed way, wanted to help grasp Utopia from the skies and plant it on earth." Having rejected the biblical God, however, Sanger had no idea what form that utopia would take. "What to do and where to start," she admits, "I did not know."

Bryan did know. He traced the horrors of World War I and its unsettled aftermath back through the eugenics movement to social Darwinism and on to Darwin himself. Each step in the devolution from the Divine deeply offended his traditional Christian sensibilities. So in 1921, he sacrificed his comfortable retirement and eventually his reputation to reverse the process.

"Bryan decried the entire program as 'brutal,'" writes Edward Larsen of the eugenics movement, "and at Dayton offered it as a reason for not teaching evolution." The Scopes trial took place in 1925, just three years after Sanger's *The Pivot of Civilization* and the same year as the most brutal eugenics text of all time, Hitler's *Mein Kampf*. The very title of the book from which John Scopes taught, *Hunter's Civic Biology*, suggests its commitment to a community-oriented eugenics program.

Today, the same progressive establishment that has whitewashed Sanger's contribution to that "entire program" has, in Bryan's case, whitewashed his entire career save for his effort to stop that program. This leads to some wonderfully ironic moments, none more revealing—or more confusing—than those that come out of Hollywood.

In 1960, for instance, Stanley Kramer produced the movie version of *Inherit The Wind*. In the key scene, actor Spencer Tracy, playing the Clarence Darrow character, triumphantly scolds the William Jennings Bryan character for daring to resist Darwin and America's eugenics movement as embodied in *Hunter's Civic Biology*. In 1961, Stanley Kramer produced the movie *Judgment at Nuremberg*. In this movie, Spencer Tracy plays an American judge who, in a key scene, triumphantly scolds his German counterparts for *not* resisting Germany's eugenics movement.

In *Judgment at Nuremberg's* most moving scene, a dim-witted German man played by Montgomery Clift horrifies the judge and the American audience with his tale of forced sterilization. What, one wonders, must Margaret Sanger and friends have been thinking when they saw this scene? Whatever they thought, they didn't apologize. When you control the culture, you don't have to. You simply erase.

FANTASY ISLAND

In San Francisco in 1926, as she prepared to sail away to Samoa, twenty-four-year-old Margaret Mead wrote a farewell letter to her husband, Luther Cressman. When Cressman got the letter back in New York and read it, the cold calculation of it all unnerved him. How had his sweetheart slipped away from him so?

Less than three years earlier, the newly ordained minister had married the petite, quirkily pretty Mead in an Episcopal Church near her childhood home in suburban Philadelphia. According to Cressman, they were both virgins. After the honeymoon, the couple returned to New York City where they pursued their respective studies at Columbia University.

This was an exciting time to be young and a New Yorker. Cressman described the city as a "vortex of new ideas derived from discoveries in science, reaction to and reflection on the lessons of the war, and an awareness that a new phase of life for the Western world had come on stage with the Russian revolution."

Also in the air that fevered decade was the first great whiff of sexual awakening. Margaret Sanger, of course, played her own role in this atmospheric shift as did the inevitable Havelock Ellis, Sigmund Freud, and bright young authors like F. Scott Fitzgerald. In fact, it was Fitzgerald's *Tales of the Jazz Age*, published a year before Mead's marriage, that had given the era its name.

For direct inspiration, Mead looked to another literary prophet of the coming sexual revolution, the "free woman of her age," Edna St. Vincent Millay. Millay's 1920 poetry collection, *A Few Figs from Thistles,* had given Mead much to chew on. The "First Fig" struck close to home:

> My candle burns at both ends;
> It will not last the night;
> But ah, my foes, and oh, my friends—
> It gives a lovely light

Inspired by Millay and the spirit of the times, the Samoa-bound Mead decided it was finally time for a little candle-burning of her own. In concluding her fateful letter to Cressman, she had written, "I'll not leave you unless I find someone I love more."

Unless what? One can understand Cressman's shock at reading this anticipatory fare thee well. Mead had progressed from "Till death do us part" to "Dear John" in a New York minute. And as Cressman would learn the hard way, Mead was still progressing.

For all the aptness of the First Fig, It was Millay's Second Fig that Mead took as her motto. This one proved eerily prophetic:

> Safe upon the solid rock the ugly houses stand:
> Come and see my shining palace built upon the sand!

As the impressionable Mead saw it, the solid rock of traditional America produced some ugly houses indeed, certainly on the inside. Although she would expand the scope of her wrath as her celebrity grew, Mead focused her youthful indignation on the bourgeois American household—this "tiny, ingrown, biological family"—not unlike the Pennsylvania home in which she herself had come of age:

In our ideal picture of the freedom of the individual and the dignity of human relations it is not pleasant to realize that we have developed a form of family organization which cripples the emotional life, and warps and confuses the growth of many individuals' power to consciously live their own lives.

Her professor father and homemaker mother could not have been thrilled with this assessment of family life from Mead's classic *Coming of Age in Samoa* published when Mead was just twenty-six. According to Mead, these families instilled in their children a self-perpetuating set of "Puritan self-accusations" that crimped their libidos and left them burdened by "guilt" and "maladjustment."

Mead was likely not the only twenty-something running around New York with this much emotional baggage. In fact, her life reads like a flapper-era pilot for *Sex in the City*. It's just that she was the one woman uniquely positioned to transform this baggage into social science. The man who made this possible was Franz Boas, her mentor at Barnard and later Columbia and the godfather of modern anthropology. In the fall of 1922, Mead took a course from Boas and his teaching assistant, Ruth Benedict, and her life was never the same.

Today, the cultural establishment applauds Boas for his resistance to the scientific racism so prevalent in his day. At the time, however, such resistance seemed more a matter of academic positioning than principle. No one suffered much for being on either side of that barricade. What drove his resistance was his rejection of the material determinism of the neo-Darwinians. Hardly a traditionalist, Boas replaced it with an equally rigid cultural determinism. In fact, he believed "social conditioning" to be responsible for the complete molding of every human expression of the individual.

If not molded completely by Boas, Mead heeded his words as though they had come from a burning bush. When she accepted a grant to travel to Samoa and study "the problem of which phenomena of adolescence are culturally and which physiologically determined," she already knew the answer. The junket was largely an exercise in proving herself and Boas correct.

Had Mead merely visited Samoa and observed the culture and then finessed the data to fit her thesis, she would have been guilty of garden-variety bad science and little worse. Unknown to Boas, however, Mead had another mission. She needed to make sense of her own confused, omnivorous sexual appetite. At the time, the adventurous Mead had less interest in Luther Cressman than she did in Ruth Benedict with whom she would soon enter "an intimate Sapphic relationship." In full flight from Puritan America, Mead was prepared to employ her humble social science skills to imagine a "shining palace" of sexual fulfillment and stake it precariously in the shifting Samoan sand.

Predictably, the Samoa that Mead discovered and wrote about was everything for which she and Boas could have hoped. "All of her interest is expended on clandestine sex adventures," writes Mead of the adolescent Samoan girl. In fact, these girls often embarked on several such adventures each night. And why not? "The concept of celibacy is absolutely meaningless to them."

Given "the scarcity of taboos," homosexuality was common and masturbation was universal. Illegitimate children were welcome. Prostitution was harmless. And divorce was simple and informal. This casual familiarity with sex, argues Mead, has led to a culture in which "there are no neurotic pictures, no frigidity, no impotence, except for the temporary result of severe illness, and the capacity for intercourse only once in a night is counted as senility."

Better still, Samoan-style openness dissolved the proprietary tensions—"monogamy, exclusiveness, jealousy, and undeviating fidelity"—so problematic in a possessive American culture. "The Samoans laugh at stories of romantic love," writes Mead, "scoff at fidelity to a long absent wife or mistress, believe explicitly that one love will quickly cure another."

Best of all, Mead discovered that the difference between Samoans and

Americans had nothing to do with biology and everything to do with culture, just as Boas predicted. "What accounts for the presence of storm and stress in American adolescents?" asks Mead. The answer was simple enough: "the social environment."

If a "general casualness" characterized Samoan society, Americans faced an "implacable" God and a "half dozen standards of morality," all of them repressive. As a result, sex was "a natural, pleasurable thing" for Samoans, but for Americans it was just the opposite. American girls found themselves crippled by neuroses, frigidity, and Electra complexes as they watched in horror "the huge toll of barren, unmarried women who move in unsatisfied procession across the American and English stage." This young rebel had fled that stage long ago and was determined to avoid an encore.

After only five months of fieldwork among the welcoming Samoans, Mead headed home in a westward direction. On shipboard, she happened to find someone she did "love more" than the hapless Cressman, a young New Zealander named Reo Fortune. Soon enough, she would dump Cressman and marry Fortune. In time, she and Fortune met a famed British anthropologist in New Guinea named Gregory Bateson, the son of the man who exposed the midwife toad fraud. As the *New York Times* discreetly notes, "There was a personal crisis among the three as a result of which there was a divorce." Mead would ultimately marry Bateson and divorce him too, but here we get ahead of ourselves.

Back in New York, working as an assistant curator at the American Museum of Natural History, Mead began to bang out a report on "The Adolescent Girl in Samoa." Boas looked at it quickly and liked what he saw. It seemed to confirm everything he had been preaching. Not overly technical and a wee bit salacious, the book appealed to William Morrow and Company, which published it in 1928 as *Coming of Age in Samoa.*

With Boas's imprimatur on the dust jacket, and that of his friends, like the equally famed anthropologist Bronislaw Malinowski, the book easily swayed the social science community. Ruth Benedict, also on the way to renown, gushed over her sometime lover's book in the pages of the *New Republic,* rightly identifying *Coming of Age* as a blueprint for a neurosis-free sexual utopia. When British sex guru Havelock Ellis mailed in his cheery blurb, the publisher thought it important enough to encode it in a bright red band around the already alluring dust jacket.

Coming of Age seduced the broader cultural establishment as well. The *New York Times* described the book as "warmly human yet never sentimental, frank with the clean, clear frankness of the scientist, unbiased in its judgment, richly readable in its style." The *Times* reviewer gushed in summary, "It is a remarkable contribution to our knowledge of humanity." At the time of Mead's death fifty years later, *Coming of Age in Samoa* was still selling 100,000 copies a year and was widely considered, as the 1973 edition safely asserts, a "scientific classic."

What the *New York Times* did not realize in 1978 nor in 1928, what Mead's millions of fans did not know, what not even Franz Boas knew, is that they had all bought into the greatest scientific hoax since the Piltdown Man. One prime reason they did not know is because they did not want to know. For a variety of reasons, none of them having to do with good science, they obviously liked what Mead had to say.

Derek Freeman did too. So entranced was the young New Zealand anthropologist by Mead's work that in 1939 he took a position as a school teacher in Samoa to follow in her golden footsteps. By that time the Mead myth was so powerful that Freeman found himself ignoring or dismissing any evidence that contradicted her findings.

Only after Freeman had been in Samoa some years and become fluent in the language did he cease denying the warp between the reality he saw and the illusion Mead had spun. "It had become apparent to me, after prolonged inquiry," Freeman writes, "that Mead's depiction of Samoa was gravely defective in numerous ways and that her account of the sexual mores of the Samoans was in outright error."

Upon returning to New Zealand, and later in London where he studied, Freeman shared his misgivings with his professors, but no one took him seriously. In London, he explored the Samoan archives, and they only confirmed his suspicions. Fieldwork took Freeman to Borneo and diverted him for a number of years, but in 1964 he had the occasion to meet Mead and share his concerns. Mead was clearly taken aback but was gracious about it. After all, she was Margaret Mead, and he was not.

In 1965, Freeman returned to Samoa for an extended stay, including a visit to the specific island where Mead had done her research. Only forty years after the fact, he found many individuals who were as able and willing to discuss life in the 1920s as today's baby boomers are life in the 1960s. From their nicely detailed accounts, he came to the conclusion that Mead's take on Samoan sexual practices was "comprehensively in error." At this stage, however, Freeman remained "totally mystified about how an error of such magnitude could possibly have been made."

In fact, as was transparent to anyone who had spent time in the Samoa of the 1920s, the islands were anything but a sexual paradise, at least in the bohemian New York sense of the word. As Freeman observed, every attempt was made to safeguard the virginity of all Samoan girls, even those from common families. There was much at stake. At marriage, the bride had to undergo a formal virginity test, and it was not multiple choice. The results mattered. There was nothing casual about it. The groom-to-be staked his pride and honor on the outcome.

The almost complete Christian overlay on Samoan culture only reinforced the traditional premium on chastity. As Freeman notes, Mead's early correspondence back to Boas strongly suggests her awareness that "Samoa in the 1920s, in contrast to some other parts of Polynesia, had a society in which the virginity of nubile females was of preeminent and vital concern." How could she not know this? While in Samoa, the always-exploitative Mead happily accepted the perks due the ceremonial virgin she shamelessly pretended to be.

Still, Freeman wondered how Mead could have gone so far astray. In 1969, after more research, he sent her a letter on a specific, indisputable point:

There is ample evidence that rape behavior occurred in the 1920s, just as it occurs today. For this, and a range of comparable reasons, I am not in agreement with your depiction of sexual behavior in Samoa as "a light and pleasant dance" and as one of the "smoothest" adjustments "in the world." Indeed, I am greatly puzzled as to what evidence could have led you to this erroneous conclusion.

Mead did not respond. In 1972, she authorized a new edition of the book, specifically rejecting any revision of any kind. Freeman took this as his invitation to correct the record as Mead obviously had no intention of doing the same. After taking care of some commitments, he took up the task seriously in 1978. At the time he attempted to communicate again with Mead, unaware that she was fatally ill. She died later that same year, happily before the 1983 publication by Harvard University Press of *Margaret Mead and Samoa: The Making and Unmaking of an Anthropological Myth.*

In this and in his 1999 book, *The Fateful Hoaxing of Margaret Mead,* Freeman explores just how Mead had gotten it all so wrong. As he relates, Mead had dithered around Samoa aimlessly for months before starting her fieldwork. Hopelessly behind schedule, she frittered away much of this remaining time on an unrelated project. Finally, while traveling around the islands with two teenage girls, she had the opportunity to question them privately about their sex lives and those of their friends.

Mead kept prodding the girls. She did not want to hear about traditional taboos or Christian restraints. She wanted to hear about frolicking on the beach. The girls had no idea what Mead was up to. They didn't know she was an anthropologist or what one even was. But what they did know and enjoy was the "recreational lying" common among Samoan girls. Eager to please, they proceeded to spin the kind of yarns that Mead wanted to hear. Pinching each other all the way, they filled Mead's head with wild tales of nocturnal liaisons under the palm trees.

"She must have taken it seriously," one of the girls would say of Mead on videotape years later, "but I was only joking. As you know, Samoan girls are terrific liars when it comes to joking. But Margaret accepted our trumped up stories as though they were true." If challenged by Mead, the girls would not have hesitated to tell the truth, but Mead never questioned their stories. The girls, now mature women, swore on the Bible to the truth of what they told Freeman and his colleagues.

Generously, Freeman suggests that Mead had been the innocent victim of a hoax and may well have gone to her grave unsuspecting. But even if true, there is no denying her contributory negligence. In the data tables that lend *Coming of Age in Samoa* the illusion of science, Mead lists fourteen of the twenty-five post-pubescent girls in her study as having had "no heterosexual experience." These numbers in themselves would seem to challenge the ubiquity of teen sex, but even these numbers are suspect.

When Freeman questioned Mead as to whether the other eleven had had full sexual intromission, Mead responded yes. He then questioned how it was that none of these girls had ever become pregnant despite the fact that eight of the eleven were at least three years into puberty, and none used any form of contraception. Mead's notes from the time serve up an impressively daft answer. In the nearly fictional Samoa Mead had concocted, promiscuity appeared to ensure against pregnancy.

An equally culpable party in this hoax was Boas who barely supervised Mead's hasty, ill-informed efforts and then approved her thesis largely because it reinforced his own biases. He obviously did not check her data. And although Freeman does not explore this issue, anyone familiar with academia knows how foolishly indulgent aging mentors can be towards certain nubile acolytes.

Like so many naïve souls who pursue science for the right reasons, Freeman had no idea of the buzzsaw that awaits truth tellers. He was walking blithely right into it, what one colleague rightly described as "the greatest controversy in the history of anthropology." He had not guessed just how many of his colleagues had built their own "shining palaces" in Mead's Samoan sand. For more than fifty years, the anthropology community had held Mead's work up as "one of its glories and a solid proof of Boasian culturalism." Now here was an upstart from New Zealand threatening to undo it all.

Following publication, Freeman's professional colleagues launched an unrelenting attack against him, often *ad hominem,* that climaxed at that year's meeting of the American Anthropological Association. The Association held one specific session, a crowded one, dedicated to Freeman's assessment of Margaret Mead. Freeman, in all too traditional academic fashion, was not invited.

What happened to Freeman at that session has happened many times to those independent thinkers who dare question an existing scientific or cultural paradigm, even one as flimsy as Mead's—especially one that flimsy. There was hell to pay.

The session began formally enough, but when the general discussion began, "It degenerated into a delirium of vilification." One eyewitness described it as "a sort of grotesque feeding frenzy." Afterwards, at the Association's business meeting that evening, one of Freeman's peers introduced a formal notion trashing his work as "poorly written, unscientific, irresponsible, and misleading." The motion was promptly seconded, put to a vote, and passed by a show of hands. That none of those present knew Samoa or Mead's work nearly as well as Freeman— an excellent writer and researcher, by the way— mattered little. He had blasphemed "the Mother-Goddess of American Anthropology" and offended those in her thrall.

Since that time, as the recorded and sworn testimony of the two Samoan women has been made public, Freeman has received a large measure of vindication within the anthropological community, but a much smaller measure within the larger cultural establishment.

A random review of the first five online encyclopedias to appear in a Google search give a good indication of Mead's current stature in the larger culture. Three of the five—The *Columbia Encyclopedia,* Sixth Edition, *Encyclopedia.com,* and *Allrefer.com* make no mention at all of any controversy that might dim her luster. In their firmament, Mead's star still shines bright.

Britannica concise admits that "her theories" caused later anthropologists "to question both the accuracy of her observations and the soundness of her conclusions." But in the very next sentence, the reader learns that Mead became "a prominent voice" on issues like women's rights and nuclear proliferation, and that her great fame owed as much to this as "to the quality of her scientific work." End of discussion.

Only *Wikipedia, the free encyclopedia,* goes into detail. The belligerent sophistry of its defense—lifted from popular science writer Steven Pinker's book, *The Blank Slate*—shows just how difficult it is to bring down even a wounded icon.

After an initial flurry of discussion, most anthropologists concluded that the absolute truth would probably never be known. Many, however, find Freeman's critique highly questionable. First, these critics have speculated that he waited until Mead died before publishing his critique so that she would not be able to respond. Second, they pointed out that Mead's original informants were now old women, grandmothers, and had converted to Christianity. They further pointed out that Samoan culture had changed considerably in the decades following Mead's original research, that after intense missionary activity many Samoans had come to adopt the same puritanical sexual standards as the Americans who were once so shocked by Mead's book. . . . Many anthropologists also accuse Freeman of having the same ethnocentric sexual puritanism as the people Boas and Mead once shocked.

The fact that Samoa had been Christianized for a century by the time Mead arrived, or that Freeman first visited Samoa within fifteen years of Mead's visit and stayed many years longer, or that these Christian women swore an oath to the truthfulness of their account matters not all to Pinker and the cultural establishment he represents. What matters is that Mead's take on traditional American sexual customs be allowed to stand as gospel. Only a chauvinist and a prig like Freeman would dare subvert it.

THE HUMAN ANIMAL

In her "Personal Odyssey," Judith Reisman traces the roots of her career to her extended family gatherings—a lively mix of politics and music—at her Aunt Laura's welcoming home in South Orange, New Jersey. Curiously, Reisman makes no mention that her aunt lived in the same small Newark suburb as a family whose celebrated first son, Alfred, would shape the course of Reisman's public life. In time, she would write two exposés about the ambitious sexologist, including her first published work, *Kinsey, Sex, and Fraud,* and almost single-handedly unravel his reputation among those willing to listen.

Alfred Charles Kinsey was born in Hoboken in 1894. He moved to the amiably suburban South Orange ten years later, a little more than thirty years before Reisman was born. Superficially, at least, Kinsey enjoyed a highly successful childhood. He was an accomplished amateur pianist, an Eagle Scout, a Sunday school teacher, a seemingly devout Methodist, and the valedictorian of his high school class—the same school Paul Ehrlich would later attend. Tall, blond, and good-looking, Kinsey might have been neck-deep in self-worth were it not for an overbearing father determined to deny him his due.

The authoritative source on Kinsey's life, early and late, is an epic, dispassionate biography by respected historian James H. Jones. Published in 1997, after more than twenty years of research, *Alfred C. Kinsey: A Public/Private Life* threw the doors open on Kinsey's highly unusual life and career and exposed it to some welcome light. Unless specified otherwise, the account that follows comes from Jones's comprehensive book.

Even as a lad, Kinsey was not quite what he seemed to be. A perfectionist, he could be hard on himself, both figuratively and literally. Despite his efforts at self-discipline, Kinsey could not control his urge to masturbate. Perhaps as a way to punish himself, he masturbated with objects—ouch!—inserted in his penis, graduating from straws to the handle of a hairbrush. This practice, notes Jones, must have caused the boy "exquisite pain." Reisman believes that Kinsey was sexually abused as a boy, but hers is more a deduction from behavior than from any recorded evidence.

In 1912, to please his engineer father, Kinsey enrolled in the Stevens Institute in Hoboken. After two years of training as an engineer, Kinsey mustered the considerable nerve to defy his father, quit Stevens, and enroll in Bowdoin College in Maine as a biology major, the first love of this budding naturalist. Indeed, his high school yearbook had projected him, in a worthy bit of prophecy, to become "a second Darwin."

For all his biological training, Kinsey had no hands-on experience in the real world art of reproductive behavior. Having come of age in a strict Methodist household, Kinsey dated no one in high school or in college. In fact, he married the first person he ever dated, a woman he met at a biology department picnic while a graduate student at Harvard. Although congenial in most ways, Alfred and Clara Kinsey both came to the marriage inexperienced and, on Kinsey's part, uncertain. They would not consummate the marriage for several awkward months.

The recent dramatizations of Kinsey's life portray his and Clara's ignorance as typical of the period. They make this case to show the later Kinsey as a necessary and useful sexual liberator. A little context, however, proves useful here. During the same time period the Kinseys were fumbling, their fellow Ivy-leaguer and contemporary, F. Scott Fitzgerald, was writing *The Beautiful and the Damned* and tending to his just married and pregnant wife, Zelda. The 1920s roared without any help at all from Mr. Kinsey.

At Harvard, Kinsey lost something less inevitable than his virginity, and that was his faith in God. Like so many of his progressive allies,

Kinsey came to see Christianity as oppressive and the source of much of the evil in the modern world. Nature would become his god, biological laws his ten commandments. "As his belief in God waned," affirms Jones, "science rapidly became the integrating principle of his life."

Kinsey imagined his own godless heaven on earth, one where people would be "freed from religiously prescribed notions of right and wrong." Here, writes Jones, "People would be at liberty to act upon their sexual needs, without fear or guilt, provided, of course, their behavior did not harm others." As shall be seen, Kinsey's idea of "harm" and Judith Reisman's idea of the same would diverge dramatically.

In 1920, Alfred and Clara Kinsey "migrated" to Bloomington, Indiana. In this charming university town, he and Clara would live for the rest of his life and raise their four children, one of whom died at an early age. At IU, he taught evolutionary biology with a specialty in entomology, the study of insects. To supplement his humble professor's salary, he turned to the writing of high school textbooks, publishing his first one, *An Introduction to Biology*, in 1926, the year after the Scopes trial.

In the text, Kinsey took an unapologetically pro-evolution stance. Although indifferent to the concerns of mid-America, he was not oblivious to them. To keep parents at bay, he pioneered the kind of bait-and-switch pseudo-science that dominates high school texts to this day. The formula was simple: merely define evolution as "the scientific word for change" and ridicule those who challenged evolution as denying the small changes obvious to anyone who had bred anything in a still largely rural America. In the accompanying teacher's manual, he counseled teachers on how to handle those parents who saw through or around the deception.

A champion of biological purity, Kinsey sang from the same dark hymnal as Margaret Sanger. Throwing a little zoology in the mix, he endorsed the immigration restriction laws passed in the early 1920s in a vain hope to preserve northern Europeans as a "true species." In time, he would come to share Sanger's fondness for negative eugenics as well, approving as he did the sterilization or isolation of "hereditary defectives." In fact, so indifferent was Kinsey to the less fit of his fellow citizens that he closed his ears to the siren song of socialism. Given his contributions to the sexual revolution, however, Kinsey's fellow progressives would forgive him this deviation.

More so than Sanger or certainly Mead, Kinsey spoke the language of biology. In his breakthrough book, *Sexual Behavior in the Human Male,* Kinsey is forever referring to the "human animal," man as "primate," and "mammalian" behavior. Said Mead, in an aptly tart rebuke, "The book suggests no way of choosing between a woman and a sheep." Although Kinsey would quibble with Darwinian mechanics, his career represents a sterling example of applied Darwinian science.

At Indiana, Kinsey switched his field of application from gall wasps, about which almost no one cared, to human sexual behavior, about which almost everyone did. The switch was gradual and understandable. To address his own many sexual concerns, he had been quietly studying the field since the early 1920s. In 1935, he gave his first public talk, an angry one, on the subject of sex. Although the audience was small, the implications for the future were large. He laid the blame for the sexual dysfunction then presumably rampant in America "at the door of the Christian Church." As Kinsey saw it, Christianity channeled the essential animal nature of man into "cultural perversions" like celibacy and asceticism, perversions that ate away at the American family. He would argue later that sexual maladjustment was the single greatest cause of divorce.

As Jones notes, "Kinsey's 1935 lecture to the faculty discussion group showed how badly he wanted to use science, the greatest weapon he commanded, to attack the conventional morality that had caused him so much pain." Although Margaret Mead would mock Kinsey's biological determinism, she and he were scripting the same sexual morality play with identical victims and villains. All that differed was the science that each concocted to affect the outcome.

Two years later, his second book on gall wasps, *The Origin of Higher Categories in Cynips,* failed to excite much attention. Given the title alone, never mind the subject matter, Kinsey should not have been surprised, but he was disappointed, and he started pouring more of his energy into the study of sexology.

In 1938, Kinsey organized a course on marriage at IU and went professional with his sexual interests for the first time. From the beginning, he had planned to use the course as an opening to sex research. His students were to serve as test subjects, human gall wasps to be classified and categorized. It was here that he began to develop the exhaustive and incredibly personal questionnaires around which he would build his science.

As with the textbooks he authored, Kinsey could not conspicuously advance his own agenda. "He had to appear disinterested," writes Jones, "his pronouncements value free." Kinsey, however, knew how to mold young minds. He would marshal his evidence so precisely and present it so matter-of-factly that students were drawn to one inevitable conclusion: his own.

His discussions of the sexual act itself were mind-numbingly mechanical. This style not only lent his teaching the illusion of science, but it also broke down the "pruderies" that traditionally restrained sexual behavior. Appropriately, the course concluded with a discussion of procreation, more specifically the various ways to avoid it. "In short," says Jones, "Kinsey was preaching a new sexual morality with respect for diversity at its center and himself as its prophet."

Had Kinsey progressed no further in his career or in his techniques, he would not deserve attention in this book. The phrase "academic bias," after all, has become something of a redundancy. Many professors, perhaps most, see no reason to hide their prejudices, let alone restrain them. But Kinsey did go further, much further, not just in his celebrity, but in his deceit, a deceit that would soon cross all ethical barriers and assault all accepted standards of common decency.

At this point, a digression to the first person might be in order. In researching this book, I became aware that two major biographies of

Kinsey had been published in a two-year span, one sympathetic, one allegedly not. I ordered them both, forgetting which was which. Jones's book arrived first. Upon reading it, I presumed it to be the sympathetic account. A respected academic, Jones does not even mention Judith Reisman, nor does he identify with the "conservatives" who "vilified" Kinsey. Instead, he implicitly endorses much of what Kinsey has accomplished. "Kinsey pleaded for an end to hypocrisy," writes Jones approvingly, "and for a new ethic of tolerance."

For many in the cultural establishment, however, Jones's endorsement was too tepid and his tone too judgmental. By 1997, in fact, the left had so committed itself to Kinsey's "anarchic" brand of sexual liberation that even its most progressive journals were prepared to defend this Hoosier Republican and to attack Jones for not doing the same.

"Beware the facts," writes Martin Duberman in his review of Jones's book in the *Nation*, "they can lead you away from the truth." In progressive circles, especially in the age of AIDS, facts had become a distraction. Sure, Jones may have reported them accurately, but that doesn't cut it for Duberman.

"Where another biographer might have emphasized Kinsey's remarkable capacity for open-minded exploration," complains Duberman, "Jones persists in negatively labeling unconventional sexual behavior as 'skating near the edge,' as 'compulsive' and 'addictive' risk-taking." Although Jones praises Kinsey as a master researcher and a "debunker of conventional morality," this praise doesn't appease Duberman any more than does Jones's accuracy. From Duberman's perspective, praise is a mere feint, a way for Jones to camouflage his own cryptic moralizing and possibly—low blow here—to sublimate his own "perversions."

A comparably progressive attitude inspired British author Jonathan Gathorne-Hardy to complete his research and pen an alternative Kinsey autobiography two years after the release of Jones's book. What "dismayed" Gathorne-Hardy about Jones was his style, one that he describes—in the lowest of all possible blows— as "the Kenneth Starr school of biography." Again, Gathorne-Hardy does not challenge Jones's facts so much as the interpretation of those facts.

In one self-parodying example out of many, Gathorne-Hardy defends Kinsey against the charge that he was a masochist. "Now it is perfectly true," he admits, "that during the late 1940s it emerged that Kinsey practiced a form of masturbation which did involve urethral insertions." As Gathorne-Hardy knows, but doesn't say, this practice also involved Kinsey's tying a rope around his scrotum and yanking hard on it while he stuck objects up his penis. Gathorne-Hardy knows this because Kinsey filmed the whole eye-popping process. This spectacle might be proof enough of Kinsey's masochism for most people, certainly for most men, but it wasn't for Gathorne-Hardy.

This practice evolved over time, Gathorne-Hardy argues. Besides, Kinsey might very well have undertaken it in the "pursuit of pleasure." If Kinsey were pursuing pleasure in an evolving fashion, he could thus hardly be the lifelong "masochist" Jones describes. Won over by his own bold sophistry, Gathorne-Hardy chastises Jones for suggesting that a filmed exercise of scrotum-yanking and penis-stuffing could possibly hint at any "inner demons."

By any court's "reasonable man" standards, James H. Jones's balanced account of Kinsey remains the definitive one. According to that account, the psychic feedback Kinsey drew from his marriage course inspired him to pursue his sex research virtually full time. He was particularly fond of face-to-face interviews. In June 1939, after teaching his last class of the semester, Kinsey left Bloomington on a novel kind of field trip. This one took him to the gay underworld of Chicago, and it was a trip he would repeat frequently over time. "He liked what he saw," writes Jones.

The gay men that Kinsey interviewed and counseled took to him as a father figure and sought his advice. In one letter from the period, he advised a young man to butch up his personal style as effeminacy irritated Kinsey. He reassured the man, however, that his homosexuality did not make him a deviant. "It is my conviction that the homosexual is biologically as normal as the heterosexual," he wrote. "There is absolutely no evidence of inheritance being involved."

Kinsey argued instead that sexual identity depended to a large degree on early sexual interaction. A pleasurable experience of one sort or another led the individual to seek another of the same kind. "Whether one builds a heterosexual pattern or homosexual pattern depends, therefore, very largely upon the satisfactory or unsatisfactory nature of his first experiences," he concluded. Kinsey may well have been speaking from his own early experience. As he would later admit, he was doing more than advising in Chicago. He was indulging.

Meanwhile Kinsey was adding these new Chicago sexual histories to the ones he had taken in Bloomington and mixing them all in one indiscriminate bouillabaisse—"clear evidence," notes Jones, "of how the targeting of homosexuals would skew his sample in the years ahead."

At about this time, Kinsey was courting an insecure and financially strapped Indiana University student. To keep Clyde Martin close, Kinsey hired him to work in his garden and later on his research team. Not inclined to homosexuality, Martin eventually relented to Kinsey's come-on, but as compensation, he asked if he could also sample the fruits of Kinsey's forty-two-year-old wife Clara, a proposition both the Kinseys assented to eagerly.

From the beginning, Kinsey would insist that all of his researchers pass what Reisman aptly calls Kinsey's "sexual deviance and obedience test," a test that spouses had to pass as well. With only one known exception, new staff members and their spouses were obliged to participate in indiscriminate sex among the research family, occasionally in group, occasionally on film. At least one wife would complain of the "sickening pressure" to join in. "I felt," she said, "like my husband's career depended on it."

To the outside world, though, Kinsey seemed all science. Indiana University's discreetly homosexual president, Herman Wells, strongly supported his work. The National Research Council sponsored his research, and the Rockefeller Foundation funded it. In 1942, Kinsey set up his Institute for Sex Research on the IU campus, and he and his aides began their statistical study of sexual conduct in earnest.

By 1947, Kinsey was ready to publish the massive data he had accumulated. No fool to political realities, President Wells asked him not to release the planned book during the sixty-one days that the Indiana legislature was in session. A state legislature that had still not yet accepted daylight savings time was unlikely to smile on Kinsey's state-sponsored sexual awakening.

Kinsey had no trouble finding a publisher. As scientific as the material appeared, it was steamy enough to be a bestseller, and everyone sensed it. If there was a hitch, it was that Kinsey's editor at W. B. Saunders Company, Lloyd Potter, insisted that the statistical method and data be "bulletproof." Potter worried that the samples were not sufficiently random or well distributed to project to the nation as a whole. Kinsey knew they weren't but indulged Potter and the Rockefeller Foundation by adding disclaimers that, as they all knew, the reading public would never notice.

Harper's certainly didn't. In a pre-release story, the magazine assured its readers that the 12,000 American men interviewed by Kinsey represented "a scientific cross section of the American population." *Harper's* also caught the drift of Kinsey's mission, astutely noting, "Age old ideas about sex embedded in our legal and moral codes are revealed as myths and delusions under the searchlight of this important investigation."

Kinsey was nothing if not a master of public relations. *Sexual Behavior in the Human Male* hit the market with more gusto than any book since *Gone with the Wind*. On January 4, 1948, the day before its release, the *New York Times* gave the book its imprimatur with a lengthy and laudatory review. Other publications quickly fell in line with the magisterial *Times*. Journalists rushed to applaud Kinsey and anoint him the successor to Charles Darwin, just as his high school yearbook had predicted. In the first two months of 1948 alone, the publisher sold 200,000 copies of the 800-page hardback.

The public picked up on the cultural buzz. Although nearly as skewed as Kinsey's data, a Gallup poll some months after the book's release showed that 78 percent of those who knew of the book approved of it. Among those approving was an Illinois University student who consumed Kinsey the way Haeckel had consumed Darwin. "I wrote an editorial about it," remembers Hugh Hefner, "and commented that I thought it was the most important booklet of the year."

Hefner and others saw right through the countless tables and stacks of data to the heart of Kinsey's thesis. Like Mead, Kinsey argued that different societies had different sexual practices, and some followed human nature much more closely than others. America's sexual codes, alas, were among the least natural. Scientists did not create them based on real biological data. Instead, priests and shamans had contrived them long ago out of little more than "ignorance and superstition." Bottom line: these codes had to go. "Society tries to restrict all sexual activities to monogamous relations," Kinsey notes disapprovingly. "And moral codes put a taint on many sorts of sexual gratification."

Hefner got the message. As a graduate student at Northwestern, he did an extensive report applying Kinsey's findings to U.S. laws. "I said that the laws were inappropriate and should be changed," says Hefner. "I had these dreams." In 1953, Hefner converted those dreams into big dollars when he launched *Playboy* magazine. "The sexual revolution began with the *Kinsey Report*," he observes. "I've said many times that Kinsey was the researcher and I was the pamphleteer."

The same year that Hefner launched *Playboy,* Kinsey published the companion piece to the first volume, *The Sexual History of the Human Female.* For a variety of reasons, this book generated less heat than the original. By this time, too, the ever more compulsive Kinsey was burning his own candle at both ends, more extreme sex on the one hand and more excessive work on the other. "His conclusions were both attacked and defended," wrote the Associated Press upon his death in 1956. "The attackers proved more vigorous."

Still, Kinsey had liberated America's sexual genie from its bottle, and there was no putting it back. Said the AP in all its authority, "His conclusions gave statistical evidence for what many clinicians—and indeed many laymen—had guessed might be the sexual conduct of the American people today." And just what was that conduct? According to Kinsey, more than 90 percent of American males had masturbated. Some 70 percent had patronized prostitutes. A shocking 37 percent had indulged in homosexual sex to the point of orgasm. Nearly half of all married men had had extramarital intercourse. At least one out of every six farm boys had had sex with an animal. And the female numbers were only slightly less unnerving. Kinsey's statistics, observes Jones, "showed that sexual morality in the United States was in a shambles."

Judith Reisman, born Gelernter, turned eighteen the year Kinsey published his female volume and Hefner launched *Playboy*. She married soon afterward. Her daughter was born the year Kinsey died. For the next decade, Reisman lived a charmed life raising her family and advancing her own music career as a producer and performer of children's songs, a talent that attracted the attention of the producers of *Captain Kangaroo*, a perennially popular children's show.

Judith Reisman

This idyll came to a halt in 1966 when a local teenager raped her then ten-year-old daughter. In seeking answers, Reisman kept hearing that her daughter may have somehow invited the attack. Children, she was told, are known to be sexual from birth. "I did not know it then," says Reisman, "but as a young mother, I had entered the world according to Kinsey."

When her Captain Kangaroo slots began to wither, Reisman returned to graduate school and proceeded to pursue a Ph.D. in communications from Case Western University in Cleveland. At one point in her studies, a fellow student presented a project on pornography. Upon reviewing it, Reisman began to question its effects on children, particularly her own daughters. She soon learned, however, that her colleagues did not necessarily share her concerns. At an academic conference in Wales, she witnessed a level of tolerance towards pornography and other forms of sexual expression that surprised her. This tolerance extended even to pedophilia.

Curious, Reisman traced the academy's acceptance of this seeming deviance to Kinsey. Now teaching at Haifa University in Israel, Reisman proceeded to review his book on male sexuality in earnest. What she read stunned her. Kinsey appeared to have used infants in his sexual experiments. She reviewed the book more carefully still, "straining to see if there was something I missed, something I may have misunderstood."

Tables 30 through 34 in Kinsey's book documented a series of sexual experiments on children. In table 30, Kinsey charted the age of first erotic arousal. In table 31, he charted the earliest age of attempted orgasm in male children starting, incredibly, with two-month-olds. In that the data began with two-month olds, some adult had to have induced this behavior. In table 32, Kinsey charted the average time it took for these children to reach "climax." In table 33, he charted the time that elapsed between these presumed orgasms. In table 34, he charted the number of "orgasms" children from five months to fourteen years were able to achieve over time. It was clearly Kinsey who had popularized the idea that children were sexual from birth. For Reisman, remembering her daughter's rape, this hit home.

Alarmed, Reisman searched the reams of literature on Kinsey to find the scholarly response to these studies and came to an even more astonishing revelation: "Nowhere was there any criticism of these tables and graphs." Nearly thirty-five years had passed since the book's publication. Literally thousands of international scientists and other cultural observers had reviewed it. And no one—not one person of note—had chosen to comment publicly on Kinsey's arguably illegal, and inarguably unscientific and unethical, sexual exploitation of hundreds of male children.

Reisman wrote to Kinsey's coauthor, Dr. Paul Gebhard, who had succeeded Kinsey as head of the institute. Gebhard responded that the data on the children in Kinsey's tables were obtained from parents, schoolteachers, and homosexuals who liked young boys. According to the non-plussed Gebhard, some of the homosexual men had used "manual and oral techniques" to help them stimulate the orgasm that they would then catalog.

In June 1981, Reisman exposed Kinsey's child data at the Fifth World Congress of Sexology, held that year in Jerusalem. She was confident that these international educators would share her outrage, but she had obviously misplaced her confidence. "I realized clearly," recalls Reisman, "that the entire field of sex research relied on Kinsey's human sexuality model for authority and I was there to tell his disciples Kinsey was a fraud." If there was any outrage, it was directed at Reisman for revealing that the emperor wore no clothes—a practice, in fact, that the exhibitionist Kinsey did not shy from.

If by 1997 Reisman's message had penetrated deeply into the Christian and conservative subculture, it had hit a veritable major media firewall. The cultural establishment did not want to know about Kinsey's fraud and wasn't about to listen. Besides, to a large degree, Reisman could only raise questions. She did not have the resources to answer them.

Jones did, and the answers to Reisman's questions were not pretty. He had gained access to some of the tightly controlled information on the one "researcher" who had proved most useful to Kinsey's studies. The researcher, in fact, was a serial child rapist. Everyone following Kinsey knew at least vaguely of his existence. Kinsey insider Wardell Pomeroy had identified him as "Mr. X" in an early biography of Kinsey and portrayed him discreetly and sympathetically. For the 1998 British documentary, *Secret History: Kinsey's Paedophiles,* award-winning director Tim Tate tracked down this helpful sexual psychopath and confirmed his name as Rex King. A government surveyor from New Mexico, King had kept exquisitely chronicled and often illustrated notes on the 600 preadolescent males and 200 preadolescent females that he had sexually violated.

When Kinsey heard of the man's exploits from another sex researcher, he courted King with ardor. "I congratulate you on the research spirit which has led you to collect data over these many years," he wrote to the man, hoping he would cooperate. The courtship paid off. King agreed to meet. Kinsey and Pomeroy promptly drove out to evaluate King's claims. To prove his capabilities—a scene charmingly recreated in the recent Kinsey movie—King showed the astonished pair of researchers that he could ejaculate from a non-standing start in less than ten seconds.

Impressed, Kinsey specified the kinds of data he was looking for, especially the timed data that showed up in tables 32-34, and King happily obliged. "This is one of the most valuable things we have ever gotten," wrote a grateful Kinsey after receiving some prized information. "I want to thank you for the time you put into it and for your willingness to cooperate." Clara Kinsey neatly typed up this new evidence of King's continued sexual assaults and blithely bound it in notebooks.

In the *Human Male* book, Kinsey describes in detail the nature of youthful "orgasm" that King has so dutifully recorded:

> [The orgasm] involves still more violent convulsions of the whole body; heavy breathing, groaning, sobbing, or more violent cries, sometimes with an abundance of tears (especially among younger children), the orgasm or ejaculation often extended . . . culminating in extreme trembling, collapse, loss of color, and sometimes fainting of subject.

Kinsey may have thought these to be expressions of "definite pleasure," but to Reisman they were unequivocal evidence of child abuse. Aware of the implications of her charges, the Kinsey Institute and its principals were anything but straightforward on the question of how the information in tables 30-34 was acquired. They have argued alternately that trained observers with stopwatches recorded the preadolescent data, including parents and teachers, and on other occasions that it was a sole individual who was sharing past histories. In the *Human Male,* Kinsey does not shed much light on the question of agency. Kinsey's close colleague, C. A. Tripp, further muddied the waters in a 1991 televised interview by the supportive Phil Donahue:

> [Reisman is] talking about data that came from pedophiles, that he [Kinsey] would listen only to pedophiles who were very careful, used stopwatches, knew how to record their thing, did careful surveys. . . . [T]hey were trained observers.

According to Jones, the bulk of the "research" was likely executed by King. "Betraying a huge moral blind spot," writes Jones, "Kinsey took the records of King's criminal acts and transformed them into scientific data." Kinsey likely based at least three of the five relevant tables on the word of this one extremely sick character. This was an individual capable of sexually abusing children less than a year old, dressing up their frenzied responses as orgasms, timing them, and counting them for periods up to twenty-four hours.

In *Secret History: Kinsey's Paedophiles,* Tate documents the assistance Kinsey received from literally scores of contributing pedophiles, including a former Gestapo officer, Dr. Fritz von Balluseck. Balluseck's correspondence with Kinsey was uncovered when he was arrested in Germany for the sex-related murder of a little girl in 1956 and convicted of the abuse of hundreds of small children. Reisman argues that the evidence is absolute that Kinsey trained King and possibly others in his preferred research methodology and sent them back out to enlist new young "partners."

Kinsey calmly notes that in some cases, "Observations were continued over periods of months or years, until the individuals were old enough to make it certain that true orgasm was involved." Here, remember, when Kinsey speaks of "individuals," he is referring to children who were sexually abused, even tortured, over a period of years. His encouragement and bloodless accounting of this extended abuse defies all ethical standards. "Science would have been better served," says Jones in something of an understatement, "had Kinsey not allowed his lust for data to obscure his judgment."

By the mid-1940s, Kinsey's plunge into the sexual abyss had eroded his judgment on many issues, pedophilia high among them. Kinsey's collaborator, Paul Gebhard, shared some of his own concerns with Jones in a 1984 interview:

> Once in a while we'd run across an occasional incest thing or an occasional adult-child contact that seemed to work out favorably, and [Kinsey] would always tell us about this and let us know that pedophilia wasn't as black as it was painted, that it could be, under proper circumstances, beneficial or something like that—which would be heresy nowadays. Well, it was heresy then!

There was little or no follow-up on the fate of these children. Gebhard argued that it would be too expensive, but Reisman wasn't buying. "There is still no answer to the question, Where are the children of Table 34?"

Kinsey's corrupt science has had an extraordinary impact on the culture, and nowhere greater than in the advance of the homosexual movement. In the *Human Male,* Kinsey stresses the need to be careful when reviewing data on homosexuality. "The data should cover every segment of the total population," he argues convincingly. "There is no other aspect of human sexual behavior where it is more fundamental that the sample be secured without any selection of cases which would bias the result." He then fully ignored his own advice.

Kinsey went wrong in just about every possible way, and he likely did so knowingly. Before the publication of the report, he had consulted with one of America's preeminent psychologists, Abraham Maslow, who had warned him that volunteers in sexual studies skewed toward the unconventional. In fact, Maslow himself had given up on sexual surveys since the dishonesty factor in the responses proved unacceptably high. To test this hypothesis, he and Kinsey conducted a small test among Maslow's Brooklyn College students. Wrote Maslow to a friend afterwards:

> As I expected, the volunteer error was proven and the whole basis for Kinsey's statistics was proven to be shaky. But then he refused to publish it and refused even to mention it in his books, or to mention anything else that I had written. All my work was excluded from his bibliography.

The problems with Kinsey's samples were many and consequential. "Despite the huge number of histories he had compiled," writes Jones, "his sample was far from random and therefore far from representative—too many of his histories came from prisoners, too many from college students, and too many from subjects he knew in advance to be gay." The begrudging Gathorne-Hardy backs up Jones on this point. "Jones is, of course, correct here," he notes, adding that Kinsey also collected "far too many sex offender histories and far too many juvenile sex histories." Knowing the sensibilities of the cultural establishment, even Jones downplayed the quiet horrors concealed in these "too many juvenile sex histories."

In addition to these obvious variables, Kinsey relied much too heavily on men who were single, widowed, or divorced, who didn't go to church

and who were college educated, as well as on "several hundred male prostitutes." "[T]he data are probably fair approximations," Kinsey cautions
disingenuously, "but only approximations of the fact." Approximations
they were, but as to "fair," they weren't even close.

The results, of course, were predictably astonishing. "A considerable
portion of the population," writes Kinsey, "perhaps the major portion of
the male population, has at least some homosexual experience between
adolescence and old age." According to Kinsey, at least 37 percent of the
male population had had at least one homosexual experience to the point
of orgasm. Among older teens, nearly one male in three have homosexual
relations. Half of the males who remain single until thirty-five have had
overt homosexual experiences. And 10 percent of white males are "more
or less exclusively homosexual" for at least three years between the ages of
sixteen and fifty-five.

The one number that outlived Kinsey is the *10 percent*. Although
Kinsey was reluctant to deem anyone a "homosexual," homosexual
activists have seized on this number and made it gospel through repeti-
tion. Harry Hay, founder of the Mattachine Society, was among those
who understood the political power of that figure. With 10 percent of the
male population behind him, Hay was not protecting a handful of sexual
adventurers. He was leading a minority group, indeed a voting bloc. The
fact that the number is roughly three to six times higher than what any
other researcher has come up with has proved irrelevant. To quote Lenin
once more, "A lie told often enough becomes the truth."

In the year 2004, Oscar-winning writer-director Bill Condon and star
Liam Neeson teamed up to make *Kinsey*, a filmed biography of the famed
sexologist. Not surprisingly, Condon used Jonathan Gathorne-Hardy's
sympathetic biography as his source material. Thanks to the work of
Judith Reisman and others, however, Condon could not make the film in
a vacuum. Too much of the world knew how Kinsey had lived and what
kind of science he had performed. In its preview, even the *New York
Times* acknowledges his masochism and his use of pedophiles to perform

research. Still, that did not deter the filmmakers from portraying Kinsey as a "Promethean figure, liberating Americans from ignorance, superstition, and hypocrisy."

"He saw a gap in our human knowledge that he wanted to fill," Neeson told the *Times*. "He was driven to investigate it. I admire that extraordinary work ethic."Kinsey's work ethic, however, does not begin to explain why he merits an heroic film portrait. Condon gets much closer to the mark.

"[Kinsey] was an early feminist, though some feminists later took issue with him," Condon told the *New York Daily News*. "He was an influence on the gay movement, and there's a direct line from his work to the sexual revolution of the '60s. I'm not sure if we'd have gotten to where we are now without him." Most mainstream reviewers took a comparable stand. "The world we live in would be unimaginable without Kinsey or someone very much like him," confirms Kenneth Turan of the *L.A. Times* in a fairly typical review.

Condon and Turan are right. Kinsey inspired critical forward movement in three of the major currents of contemporary progressivism—feminism, sexual liberation, and gay rights. Without him, the world we live in now would, in fact, be "unimaginable." To protect this world, the cultural establishment feels compelled to circle the wagons around its icons, none more valuable or as increasingly vulnerable as Kinsey. And so in addition to the 2004 theatrical release, both the A&E Channel and *The American Experience* have recently produced supportive documentaries, an unusual surge of interest given that there are no anniversary dates to celebrate. Even more telling, all major American networks have shied away from the British documentary, *Secret History: Kinsey's Paedophiles*, despite its enthusiastic reception in Britain.

In 1998, when *Secret History* aired in Britain, John Bancroft, then the Kinsey Institute director, told supporters in San Francisco that he went so far as to "pray" that Americans would never get to see the film. So far, with a little help from his friends, he has gotten his way.

STRAIGHT BUT NOT NARROW

Under normal circumstances, progressive currents flow in parallel streams in some kind of rough symmetry. What pushes one forward usually pushes another or at least does not impede it. Occasionally, however, the streams converge in distinctly unsympathetic ways as they did, for instance, at the O.J. Simpson trial. There feminism and minority rights splashed up against each other, and feminism, having less moral force, yielded.

In the late 1980s, the sexual revolution and the gay rights movement converged. By this time, gay rights had greater momentum and considerably more moral force. Within the progressive community, nothing was about to halt its forward movement, not the fading imperatives of the sexual revolution and certainly not the truth.

Starting with the adoption of Kinsey's 10 percent solution, gay activists and their progressive allies built a culture on a foundation of falsehoods. Although it is not within the mission of this book to document them all, it might prove illuminating to document one, the great heterosexual AIDS scare of the late 1980s. Unlike most "facts" about homosexuality and AIDS, this one could be tested and has been.

What makes the scare more relevant is that it swept up the two people, above all, who should have known better, Kinsey's presumptive heirs, William Masters and Virginia Johnson. Together with their colleague Robert Kolodny, they wrote a classic of wrongheaded science called *Crisis: Heterosexual Behavior in the Age of Aids.*

If the book did not launch the heterosexual AIDS scare, it surely breathed the wind of legitimacy into its sails. "*Crisis* was the high-water mark in AIDS cynicism not because it was the most outrageous book on the subject," writes critic Michael Fumento, "but because Masters, Johnson, and Kolodny had the best reputation of any of the alarmist authors." How they came to sacrifice that reputation deserves retelling.

In the way of background, William Masters started following Kinsey's work even before the publication of *Human Male*. A medical doctor,

Masters chose to specialize in obstetrics and gynecology because it would better prepare him to study human sexuality. In 1947, he joined the faculty at Washington University in St. Louis and blazed a successful career as a researcher in the field of hormonal therapy for women. In 1954, with the university's blessing, he began his research into the physiology of sex. He saw his work as a logical continuation of what Kinsey started, a move from sociology—or, more realistically, zoology—to hard science. Where Kinsey focused on case studies and secondhand data, Masters would focus on the measurement of live human sex in a lab setting.

Early in his research, Masters hired sociology student Virginia Johnson to help interview and screen volunteers. Her role both in Masters's lab and in his life would expand greatly in the years ahead. Ever the patient observer, Masters spent eleven years on this initial study, monitoring and measuring 382 women and 312 men as they performed a wide variety of sexual functions. In the beginning, he used prostitutes as surrogates, but this proved controversial. And besides, he found enough willing amateurs, ages eighteen to eighty-nine, to eliminate the need for professionals. To lend his work the feel of real science, Masters used all the techno-tricks of his trade —electroencephalographs, electrocardiographs, color cinematography, even miniature cameras built in to the laboratory equivalent of a dildo.

In 1966, Little, Brown and Co. published Masters and Johnson's first book, *Human Sexual Response*. Like Kinsey, the pair weighted their prose with technical jargon, but this patina of science could barely conceal the red-hot sexual revelations underneath. As with Kinsey's *Human Male*, the book shot quickly up the bestseller list. In no time, the phrase "Masters and Johnson" passed into common parlance and provided the punchline for a thousand jokes.

Masters and Johnson followed up four years later with *Human Sexual Inadequacy*. In this second book, in full progressive spirit, they traced sexual inadequacy within marriage to its primary source, "the influence of channel-visioned religious orthodoxy." As if to prove that he himself was not so channeled, Masters dumped his first wife almost immediately after the book's publication and married Johnson. It was the fourth marriage for Johnson, who, at forty-four, was ten years younger than Masters. Writing in 1976, intellectual historian Paul Robinson argued that these two books did "more to advance the cause of women's sexual rights than anything written in the last quarter century."

In 1975, the pair published *The Pleasure Bond: A New Look at Sexuality and Commitment.* In this book, their first written in everyday prose, the authors made the case for total commitment to one's partner as the foundation for an enduring marriage and a successful sexual partnership. Ignoring their own advice, they would divorce some years later and go their separate ways.

In the late 1970s, just before the AIDS crisis descended on America, Masters and Johnson wandered a bit naïvely into the already politicized realm of homosexual research. In the early part of that decade, the most sexually wide open before or since, gay insurgents had stormed the citadel of the American Psychiatric Association (APA) to advance their cause. They had picked an easy target. Embarrassed to find themselves on the unfashionable side of the cultural barricades, the APA worthies were prepared to surrender without a fight.

"Psychiatry is the enemy incarnate," charged an outside agitator at the 1971 APA gathering. "Psychiatry has waged a relentless war of extermination against us. You may take this as a declaration of war against you." The goal of these activists was to force the APA into removing homosexuality from the list of psychiatric disorders. What they lacked in new evidence—there being none—the activists compensated for in multicultural rhetoric and angry guerilla theater. Relying on Kinsey's data and little else, the insurgents managed to mau-mau the psychiatrists into submission in less than two years.

In 1979, Masters and Johnson released their first book on homosexuality, *Homosexuality in Perspective.* Following in the Kinsey tradition, they argued that in most cases homosexuality was not an illness or a genetic disorder, but rather, like heterosexuality, a form of "learned behavior." Projecting from Kinsey's data, they claimed that there were some twenty to twenty-one million homosexuals in the United States, and that they too deserved the same therapeutic attention as heterosexuals. In interviews, Masters smugly chastised his less enlightened fellow citizens for "homophobia," a word few Americans had ever heard before.

To most readers, the Masters and Johnson take on homosexuality seemed appropriately progressive. But not to all. High and dry in their Midwest lab, the pair missed a subtle shift in the prevailing currents. They continued to preach that what could be learned could also be unlearned. In the book, they report how they successfully reeducated two-thirds of the sixty-seven homosexual men and women who had come to them wanting to change. In 1979, the claimed success rate generated more public controversy than the attempt at conversion, but in hardcore progressive circles, the very attempt at conversion rankled.

Two years later, in 1981, Dr. Jeffrey Satinover was called into his New York City medical center to do a neurological assessment on a patient. Satinover had never seen anything like this. A complex of deforming symptoms had ravaged the once good-looking young man. The most obvious of these symptoms was the angry, cancerous purple of Kaposi's sarcoma, a condition so rare at the time as to be memorable. The man, imprisoned in a nightmare jungle of tubes and IV drippings, would not last the week. He was among the first in America to die of what was then known as GRID, "Gay-Related Immune Disorder." For Satinover, the memory would last a lifetime. It would change his career, indeed his worldview, in ways that he could not have anticipated.

In August of that same year, The Kinsey Institute released the results of a study that gave gay activists the ammunition they were looking for. After interviewing 979 homosexuals and 477 heterosexuals on a grant from the National Institute of Health, institute researchers claimed that homosexuality was not a learned condition but was present from birth and likely biological in origin. That this new claim reversed the findings of the institute's founder seemed not to trouble the researchers. They knew which way the wind was blowing.

"We found homosexuality is deep-seated and not something that one chooses to be or not to be," senior author Dr. Alan Bell, a Kinsey Institute researcher, told the *Washington Post*. "One cannot legislate against a state over which a person has no control." In the Kinsey tradition of politicizing science, Bell argued that these new findings could and should lead to serious changes in law and even in church doctrine. And as to those like Masters and Johnson who tried to reverse a homosexual's condition, they should cease and desist. Such efforts merely set their patients "swimming against their developmental history."

This is exactly what gay activists wanted to hear. As leaders in the progressive vanguard, they were in a position to dictate biology as well as psychology. According to the new party line, homosexuality was now genetic and irreversible. If gays were to claim the same civil rights as, say, African Americans, it had to be both. Their condition could be no more ambiguous than the color of a black man's skin. The very idea, as one activist put it, that "queers could be changed to breeders," was now apostasy. A public figure could destroy his or her career for daring to suggest as much.

More conveniently still, the Kinsey Institute had chosen not to release the results of a 1970 study that would have undermined the activists' power. This new study revised downwards the number of active homosexuals to 3.3 percent of the male population and of exclusively homosexual to 1.4 percent. With the lower figures suppressed, Kinsey's original 10 percent figure was allowed to stand. Thanks to this politically inspired math and some dubious biology, the gay political bloc acquired a moral and numerical clout nearly that of African Americans. As Fumento notes, "The importance of the forty-year-old statistical assumption to the cause of the acceptance of homosexuality in our society simply cannot be overstated."

Feeling their power, gay activists turned their attention to GRID and scored an early and indicative success by getting the name changed to the open-ended AIDS, "Auto Immune Deficiency Syndrome." "They worked to insure that GRID would not be perceived," Satinover observes, "as in any way related directly to their sexual way of life." As Satinover became more and more aware of how "gay activism distorts the truth," and as he watched young people die for want of it, he himself became an activist. His activism, however, came at a price. It put this Harvard-Yale-MIT trained Jewish psychiatrist on the opposite side of the barricades from all but a few of his peers and the mass of the cultural establishment.

Michael Fumento willed himself on to the same side of those barricades. Coming of age in 1970s, the son of a Marxist English professor on the radicalized University of Illinois campaign, Fumento did not even know what a conservative was. When he asked his father, he was told, "A liberal wants progress. A conservative wants things to stay the same." Fumento just wanted the truth, and he did not see much of it on the

Michael Fumento

Champaigne campus, especially in regards to the Vietnam War. Almost in the way of protest, he joined the U.S. Army after graduating from high school. His father was not pleased.

After getting his college degree in the service, Fumento started law school at the University of Illinois in the early 1980s. Although far removed from the AIDS front lines, he could see what Satinover was seeing in New York. AIDS had become unmoored from reality. After graduating in 1985, Fumento began to accumulate the data he saw every-where around him. "It wasn't hidden data," Fumento remembers. "It was in fact much more readily available to the doom-saying politicians, activists, and reporters than it was to me."

By the middle of the 1980s, gay activists and their allies had all but succeeded in de-linking AIDS and homosexuality. This was no easy trick. They began by fingering other groups as the possible source of the initial outbreak, including Haitians, Africans, prostitutes, and intravenous drug users.

Gabriel Rotello was among those gay activists. The fear of dying and of losing his community to death had turned the New York-based Rotello from rock musician to rebel with a cause. Fear, however, also clouded his vision.

"I believed, as most of my activist colleagues believed, that AIDS was an accident. That we were its heroes as well as its innocent victims." If gay male behavior had played some role in the generation of the disease in America, Rotello did not want to know about it, and he certainly did not want straight America to know about it either. "In all these respects," he laments, "I not only followed the party line, I helped write it."

Gay activists may have succeeded in shifting the blame, but their strategy did not do much to generate sympathy or funding. The groups fingered were, if anything, even more out of the American mainstream than gays. To create the mass hysteria that was to follow, gay activists needed a broader strategy and the friends to execute it. They did not have to look far.

Always in search of new moral heights, of still more novel ways to elevate themselves above their more grounded fellow citizens, progressives quickly adopted homosexual rights as a pet cause. The more morally vain among them took to expressing their solidarity in buttons or bumper stickers with double-edged declarations like "straight but not narrow." Together with their gay allies, progressives made AIDS the first fashionable disease since "consumption" a century earlier.

Fumento does not see a conspiracy in the mania that was to follow. Most who participated did so out of ignorance or fashion. But a few among them—educators, public health officials, science writers—knew what they were doing. They consciously worked to eliminate phrases like "high-risk group" and replace them with phrases like "high-risk behavior" and to erase phrases like "gay plague" and "gay disease" altogether. They added powerful new slogans as well: "It's not who you are but what you do" or "AIDS: the equal opportunity destroyer." More insidiously, they finessed the numbers to democratize the disease's reach.

Rotello calls the phenomenon the "degaying of AIDS." Unfortunately, gays themselves came to believe the propaganda that the activists, gay and straight, were spreading. "If AIDS was not a 'gay disease,'" notes Rotello, "why should gay men examine the ecological reasons their community was so devastated? Clearly it was just an accident of history, a fluke, a momentary incursion of an otherwise universal pandemic."

Heterosexuals came to believe the degaying propaganda as well. It was spreading much faster than the disease and infecting people who should have known better. In early 1987, the beloved and usually believable Oprah Winfrey began her show as follows:

Hello everybody. AIDS has both sexes running scared. Research studies now project that one in five—listen to me, hard to believe—one in five heterosexuals could be dead from AIDS at the end of the next three years. That's by 1990. One in five. It is no longer just a gay disease. Believe me.

Oprah's audience had no reason to disbelieve. In 1987, the scare was everywhere. Virtually all media sources were repeating the same rough message. "Now No One Is Safe from Aids," proclaimed the cover of *Life*. "The disease of them is suddenly the disease of *us*," added *US News & World Report*. The popular magazine covers affirmed just who that *us* was—white, middle class, heterosexual mid-Americans. Even the more sober and credible media fed the flames. "AIDS has infiltrated the hetero-sexual population," the *Washington Post* cautioned its readers in November 1987, "and a meteoric rise in reported cases of HIV infection is expected because of false assumptions that AIDS is a homosexual disease."

It was in this fevered environment that Masters and Johnson composed *Crisis: Heterosexual Behavior in the Age of Aids.* Under attack by gay activists for their now scorned belief in conversion therapy, awash in the mania that was sweeping America, the chastened therapists rushed their book to market with a message that could not have been starker. "AIDS is breaking out," declared the authors in all their turgid authority. "The AIDS virus is now running rampant in the heterosexual community."

Unfortunately for them, Masters and Johnson and their partner Kolodny had gotten to the market just a bit too late. By mid-1988, when the book was published, the cultural establishment had begun to sober up. The calamity was not unfolding quite as predicted. Through 1989, when Fumento was writing, middle-class white heterosexual Americans still accounted for less than half of one percent of AIDS cases, and the percentage wasn't changing. In New York City, the AIDS capital of the United States, only seven males out of eighteen thousand diagnosed cases had contacted AIDS through heterosexual intercourse, and those seven could have been lying. As Fumento observes, even at the height of the scare, a mid-American, middle-class heterosexual non-drug user had a greater chance of drowning in a bathtub than of catching AIDS.

Masters and Johnson had made a terrible tactical blunder. Until this point, like Kinsey before them, they had been generating "scientific" data that could not really be proved or disproved. In their first two books, as historian Robinson observes, the writing style was so "vague or clumsy" that it protected the vagueness and clumsiness of the ideas being expressed.

In the book *Crisis,* however, the language was relatively clear and straightforward. Worse, Masters and Johnson had followed the Kinsey formula, relying on recall data from volunteers. But in this instance, the numbers mattered. If a farm boy lied about whether he had sex with a sheep or a girl, no one died as a result of his dishonesty. If an HIV victim lied about whether he had sex with a man or a woman, resources could be dramatically misappropriated, and people could and would die.

In this hothouse environment, the results from the Masters and Johnson sample had to square with the real world numbers now being diligently recorded around the nation. In fact, their numbers came nowhere close. Their sexually active heterosexual sample of four hundred American adults produced results of 7 percent HIV infection among women and 5 percent among men, figures that would have been laughably high were this not such a deadly business.

"Only a fool would publish something like that," said one senior scientist at the NIH. "There is no data to support it at all." Even AIDS alarmists like Alexander Langmuir were alarmed. Said he, "This is the most venal, damaging thing that has happened in AIDS in five years." *Newsweek* magazine, which had contracted to excerpt the book, caught hell from the other newsweeklies, the very ones that had been peddling the same snake oil a year earlier. Had Masters and Johnson slipped this witches brew into the public conscious at the height of the scare, they might have added to the mania. Instead, they served it up to a cultural establishment in early hangover mode.

Still, once unleashed, manias are not easily reined in. Too many people had an interest in keeping this one alive. Some traditional moralists helped push the propaganda because it had the potential to undo much of the sexual revolution. Birth control activists did the same because it created a huge new interest in and demand for condoms. For gays, the denial ran deeper still. The degaying of AIDS allowed them, as Rotello puts it, to avoid a "sober evaluation of the ways the sexual culture of the seventies produced the AIDS epidemic."

So deep was the denial that when Fumento's *The Myth of Heterosexual AIDS* was published in 1990, gay critics attacked the book as "part of an antigay conspiracy." Rotello continues, "The idea that Fumento was penetrating a homophobic hoax became so entrenched in gay and AIDS prevention circles that it has been difficult to acknowledge that his epidemiological predictions have come true." When Rotello's own brave and smart book, *Sexual Ecology: Aids and the Destiny of Gay Men* was published in 1997, he too would feel the sting of progressive backlash.

Confronted by so much disease, death, and dishonesty—all of it avoidable and unnecessary—Dr. Jeffrey Satinover turned philosophical. He asked himself how this could have happened and why. The answer at which he arrived is not likely to be found in any popular text on sex ed or public health.

In his own defiant book, *Homosexuality and the Politics of Truth*, Satinover traces the roots of the sexual revolution to the very denial of God. For nearly four thousand years, Jews and later Christians found in the glory of an ethical, just, monotheistic God an agreed upon morality and a higher, more transcendent purpose than the satisfying of one's own entirely natural instincts. The discipline this tradition imposed on man's nature allowed him to thrive and to accomplish wonders that the nature-worshipping, polytheistic pagan world never could.

"The entire debate about homosexuality," writes Satinover, "is inextricably rooted in the Judeo-Christian concept of sin." Satinover argues that the rejection of sin in this tradition is not a rejection of the unnatural but the rejection of a slavish, compulsive addiction to what is natural and pleasurable. In essence, the sinner violates the first commandment, "I am the Lord thy God and thou shall not have strange Gods before me." That "strange god" is man's nature, tooth and claw.

Rotello does not talk about God, but he does talk about slavery to one's nature. Be warned, the following paragraph about the homosexual revolution of the 1970s and beyond is not for the faint of heart.

Multipartner anal sex was encouraged, celebrated, considered a central component of liberation. Core group behavior in baths and sex clubs was deemed by many the quintessence of freedom. Versatility was declared a political imperative. Analingus was pronounced the champagne of gay sex, a palpable gesture of revolution. STDs were to be worn like badges of honor, antibiotics to be taken with pride.

Taken together, these practices formed what Rotello calls "a sexual ecology of almost incalculably catastrophic dimensions." As Rotello regrets, "Degaying had the opposite effect that many activists hoped." The resulting panic actually caused federal and local governments to shift resources away from the people who were most at risk to people who were not at risk at all.

This, and more, is what Kinsey and his fellow adventurers wrought. These sexual revolutionaries—like the Marxists, the radical naturalists, and, to a lesser degree, the multiculturalists—have left a legacy of death and disease as unnecessary as it is undeniable. They have paved their way to this earthly hell on a semblance of good intentions and on a reality of deceit. An honest reassessment at this point would fatally undermine the identities they have crafted and the culture they have built. So they keep on keeping on.

As progressives, really, they don't have much choice.

Afterword

On March 10, 2005, the BBC released a highly disturbing story. Citing a study by an Oxford team, the BBC reported 500 million active cases worldwide of plasmodium falciparum malaria, the deadliest form of the disease, twice as many as the World Health Organization had suspected.

To be sure, the BBC did not mention DDT, which has the power to check malaria like no other tonic. Nor did the BBC cite the almost singular role of Rachel Carson in DDT's demise, she of the Calliope voice and the Cassandra vision. No, in progressive circles, even as the disease spreads, DDT is not to be talked about.

In less enlightened circles, however, the talk is intense and often angry. As stated before, Harvard-trained M.D. and best-selling author Michael Crichton describes the needless banning of DDT as "arguably the greatest tragedy of the twentieth century." This, alas, is a highly competitive designation. The radical naturalism that Carson championed has encouraged other disasters as well—communism and fascism among them.

Enabled or ignored by the Anglo-American cultural establishment, communism claimed some 100 million lives in the century past. Despite the body count, that establishment's most recent take on the subject was *The Motorcycle Diaries,* a cinematic celebration of the life of Che Guevara produced by Robert Redford.

Through its natural offspring, AIDS and STDs, the sexual revolution has claimed millions of lives as well and damaged countless millions more. The establishment responded in 2004 with *Kinsey,* a celebration of the life of the one man most responsible for this carnage, Alfred Kinsey.

When their own dreams fail, as those dreams inevitably do, progressives are more likely to either ignore or romanticize the past than to reevaluate it. An alternate strategy is to revert to the mindless nihilism of multiculturalism, as seen now in Chomsky, Churchill, and Moore. Within days of September 11, for instance, each had responded with ugly taunts mocking those who died and the nation that nurtured their presumed evil. In the days since, they have formed an unholy alliance with our enemies, encouraging them in their thuggish behavior and fascist ambitions.

The cultural establishment has largely followed the nihilist lead. In the first four years after September 11, the only Hollywood movie that actually showed the true enemy did so with puppets—Matt Stone and Trey Parker's *Team America.* One need only contrast Hollywood's response to Pearl Harbor to understand how deeply the culture has been undermined.

As our cultural bonds weaken, and the body count mounts, one is compelled to ask two questions: How could these tragedies have happened and why do we let them continue? Here is what history suggests:

- Progressives do not set out to do evil. They set out to do good.
- They do their good in a world in which God is irrelevant, and "everything is permitted."

- With God out of the picture, they are free to do good by their own lights, better than it has ever been done before.
- The "good" they devise quickly calcifies into orthodoxy.
- Lesser mortals who fail to heed the new dogma risk reeducation.
- Reeducation can be brutal. An "over-sensibility for ourselves and an over-indulgence to our own desires," said Burke shrewdly, leads to the "greatest crimes."
- Once committed to those desires, progressives don't look back. The dead, the damaged, and the aborted are ignored or quickly forgotten.
- Unwilling to undo or even question, they respond to disaster with sad and superficial correctives like mosquito nets or condoms or more "education."
- Unbound by God, progressives are thus also unbound by any traditions that claim divine inspiration.
- To the degree that those traditions threaten their progress, progressives are hostile to those traditions, specifically Judeo-Christianity and its twin towers of resolve, America and Israel.

In the worldwide culture war, our progressive friends honor no conventions. Unchecked by God or tradition, largely unedited by their peers in the academy or the media, they fall back promiscuously on the one weapon that their opponents are loath to use: fraud.

As weapons go, however, it is no match for the truth. At the end of the day, one prays, it is the latter that goes marching on.

Endnotes

1. POSTER BOYS

In the early morning hours . . . Unless specified otherwise, the facts of this case come from Buzz Bissinger, "The Famous and the Dead," *Vanity Fair*, August 1999. To the degree possible, I have used references from ideologically neutral or even sympathetic sources like this one.

In the book, *Executing Justice* . . . Daniel Williams, *Executing Justice* (New York: St. Martin's Press, 2001), pp. 299–300.

National Public Radio served up . . . Williams, pp 300–301.

The noise soon reached . . . Williams, p. 228.

In December 1997 . . . "International People's Tribunal: The Case of Mumia Abu–Jamal," *Revolutionary Worker* #937, 21 December 1997.

Despite Mumia's seeming innocence . . . Williams, p. 301.

The Title . . . Williams, *Afterword*.

Journalist Christopher Hitchens . . . Christopher Hitchens, "Unfairenheit 9/11: The Lies of Michael Moore," *Slate*, 21 June 2004.

Unfortunately for Churchill . . . Kevin Flynn, "Prof's Genealogy Is Sketchy; He Offers Little Clarification," *Rocky Mountain News*, 5 February 2005.

Writer David Horowitz . . . David Horowitz, *Radical Son* (New York: The Free Press, 1997), p. 59.

Contrasted with the ancient civilization . . . H.G. Wells, Margaret Sanger, *The Pivot of Civilization*, published online by World Wide School Library. Given its online nature, all references will be by chapter.

The heaven of the traditional theology . . . Sanger, *The Pivot of Civilization*, Chapter Seven.

Obviously, not all progressives . . . Whittaker Chambers, *Witness* (Washington: Regnery Gateway, 1980), p. 11.

Despite Williams's eager endorsement . . . Williams, Afterword.

Although a shameless trafficker . . . Michael Moore, *Dude, Where's My Country?* (New York: Warner Books, 2003), p. 189.

Without fully understanding the consequences . . . Staff, "Personal Foul—Michael Moore and Mumia as a 'Political Football,'" *The Black World Today*, 24 November 2003.

Caught in an unexpected truth . . . Larissa MacFarquhar, "The Populist," *New Yorker*, 16 February 2004.

Thus from the beginning . . . Williams cites an *Enquirer* headline from 9 December 1981, p. 84.

"In the ends–justifies–the–means" . . . Jayson Blair, *Burning Down My Masters' House* (Beverly Hills: New Millennium Press), p. 1.

"A low point" . . . Blair, p. 53.

2. THE SOUNDS OF SILENCE

The Innocents' Clubs

Martin Amis calls it . . . Martin Amis, *Koba the Dread: Laughter and the Twenty Million* (New York: Hyperion, 2002), p. 5.

"The world was offered a choice" . . . Amis, p. 8.

In "Why Lucky Jim Turned Right" . . . Amis, p. 273.

"The dictatorship of the proletariat was a lie" . . . Amis, p. 258.

"Marxism's greatest success" . . . Robert Conquest, *Reflections on a Ravaged Century* (New York: W.W. Norton & Company), p. 46.

"He was not interested in finding the truth" . . . Paul Johnson, *Intellectuals* (New York: Perennial Library, Harper & Row, 1990), p. 54

"Religion is only the illusory sun" . . . From Marx's "Contribution to the Critique of Hegel's *Philosophy of Right*," quoted in Johnson, p. 58.

In the mid–1880s two Cambridge scholars . . . Johnson, p. 67.

"From start to finish" . . . Johnson, p. 69.

Munzenberg pioneered two new lines . . . Stephen Koch, *Double Lives* (New York: Enigma Books, 2004), p. 15. The Munzenberg story, unless otherwise specified, is taken from Koch's book.

Always the cynic . . . Koch, p. 20.

A Couple of Wops in a Jam

On May 5, 1920 . . . Unless specified otherwise, the facts of the arrest come from Robert H. Montgomery, *Sacco–Vanzetti: The Murder and the Myth* (Boston: Western Islands, 1968), pp. 1–9.

A socialist newsman . . . Koch, p. 42. Unless specified otherwise, the politics of the Sacco–Vanzetti defense strategy are as told by Koch, pp. 41–48.

"The so–called radicalism" . . . As related in Montgomery, p. 156.

He focused his American efforts . . . Koch, p. 40.

"It was Munzenberg's idea" . . . Koch, p. 41.

"All right we are two nations" . . . John Dos Passos, *U.S.A. III: The Big Money* (Boston: Houghton Mifflin, 1960), pp. 413–414.

"The only thing we considered" . . . Montgomery, p. 156.

Liberal historian Arthur Schelsinger Jr. provides . . . As quoted in Montgomery, p. 10.

Budging but barely . . . Ibid.

In his retelling . . . Felix Frankfurter, *The Case of Sacco and Vanzetti* (New York: Little, Brown, and Company, 1976), p. 7.

"The extensive carrying of guns" . . . Frankfurter, p. 39.

"Lawlessness and hysteria" . . . Frankfurter, p. 43.

"New proof" . . . What follows is a summarized account of this "new proof" from Frankfurter, pp. 92–102.

On the night of the execution . . . Koch, pp. 45–48.

In her memoir, *The Never–Ending Wrong* . . . As excerpted in Koch, p. 45.

"The whole point" . . . Koch, p. 45.

The indefatigable Robert Montgomery . . . The following account is summarized from Montgomery, pp. 29–36.

"Beyond all reasonable doubt" . . . Koch, p. 43.

The Famine Is Mostly Bunk

The most thrilling month . . . The following account is summarized from S.J. Taylor, *Stalin's Apologist* (New York: Oxford University Press, 1990), pp. 4–5.

"Felt as pleased as punch" . . . Walter Duranty, *I Write as I Please* (New York: Simon and Schuster, 1935), p. 279.

"Greatest living statesman" . . . Duranty, p. 341.

"To socialize, virtually overnight" . . . Duranty, p. 283.

"The influence of his false reporting" . . . Conquest, p. 23.

"Recent research" . . . Unless otherwise specified, the following summary of the forced collectivization and the Great Famine comes from Stephane Courtois, et al., *The Black Book of Communism* (Cambridge: Harvard University Press, 1999), pp. 146–168.

"There were no tools" . . . Courtois, et al., p. 154.

"The Soviet state is powerful" . . . Courtois, et al., p. 163.

"We Bolsheviks cannot afford" . . . Courtois, et al., p. 164.

"These are not abuses" . . . Courtois, et al., p. 166.

"Curt vigor" . . . Duranty, p. 285.

"These people deliberately tried" . . . Courtois, et al., pp. 166–167.

"A heroic chapter" . . . Duranty, p. 340.

"According to Mr. Duranty" . . . Conquest, p. 143.

For the sake of context . . . Duranty's biography is summarized from Taylor's account of the same.

The Paris workings . . . Taylor, p. 36–37.

"The war in France" . . . Duranty, p. 7.

"I sat and wondered" . . . Duranty, pp. 304–305.

Conquest believes . . . Conquest, p. 123.

"Russians may be hungry" . . . Quoted in Taylor, p. 185.

In that same year . . . Taylor, p. 196.

"One of the most monstrous crimes" . . . Quoted in Taylor, p. 206.

"Would greatly enhance" . . . Quoted in Taylor, p. 203.

"The 'famine' is mostly bunk" . . . Quoted in Taylor, p. 210.

The Committee cited . . . Taylor, p. 182.

The Nation, the quintessential progressive journal . . . cited in Conquest, p. 123.

"One of the great foreign correspondents" . . . Taylor, p. 4.

Jayson Blair first encountered . . . Blair, p. 85.

"Millions of people were deliberately starved" . . . Ward Churchill, *A Little Matter of Genocide* (San Francisco: City Lights Books, 1997), p. 33.

Scoundrel Time

On the night of . . . Unless specified otherwise, biographical details of Hellman's lfe come from Joan Mellen, *Hellman and Hammett* (New York: Harper Perennial, 1997).

"Let it be recorded" . . . As quoted on inside page of Lillian Hellman, *Scoundrel Time* (Boston: Back Bay Books, 2000).

"With candor, calm, and a weariness" . . . Ibid.

"Villainous liar" . . . Hellman, *Scoundrel Time*, p. 83.

"The most important single power–broker" . . . Johnson, *Intellectuals*, p. 301.

"The only one I can think of" . . . Carol Gelderman, *Mary McCarthy: A Life* (London: Sidgwick & Jackson, 1989), p. 332.

"It's not just two old ladies" . . . As quoted in Gelderman, p. 333.

"Communists must always consider" . . . As quoted in Kenneth Lloyd Billingsley, *Hollywood Party* (Roseville, CA: Prima Publishing, 2000), p. 20.

"It was true" . . . Hellman, *Scoundrel Time*, p. 47.

"I joined the Communist Party" . . . As quoted in Mellen, p. 300.

"Hammett, obsessed by lying women" . . . Mellen, p. 37.

By 1930, Hammett had a good head start . . . Mellen, p. 194.

"Had shaken many of us into radicalism" . . . Lillian Hellman, *Pentimento* (New York: New American Library, 1973), p. 100.

"Columbus discovered America" . . . As quoted in Koch, p. 91.

Later estimates . . . Billingsley, p. 250.

In 1935, Katz traveled to Tinseltown . . . Koch, pp. 91–92.

"Virtually written" . . . Mellen, p. 92.

"Hellman's senior mentor" . . . Koch, p. 93.

"That Hellman and Hammett were already Party faithful" . . . Mellen, p. 109.

"Politically a strategic tactic and morally a fraud" . . . Koch, p. 160.

"Party membership swelled" . . . Koch, p. 161.

"All over town" . . . As quoted in Billingsley, p. 67.

To this point . . . McCarthy's political evolution is summarized from Gelderman's account of the same, pp. 52–77.

Hellman supported the verdict . . . Mellen, p. 112.

"I did not even know" . . . Lillian Hellman, *An Unfinished Woman* (New York: Bantam, 1970), p. 68.

The *Black Book of Communism* . . . Courtois, et al., p. 190.

Those singled out for execution . . . Courtois, et al., pp. 198–200.

"Lillian Hellman didn't notice" . . . Mellen, p. 121.

"I had up to the late 1940s" . . . Hellman, *Scoundrel Time*, p. 40.

"So believe that you have" . . . Hellman, *Pentimento*, p. 113.

In *An Unfinished Woman* . . . Hellman, *An Unfinished Woman*, p. 69.

"I'm not sure I knew" . . . As quoted in Gelderman, p. 333.

"It must be said" . . . Koch, p. 92.

"I trust absolutely" . . . Hellman, *Pentimento*, p. 92.

When *Pentimento* came out . . . Johnson, *Intellectuals*, p. 303.

In 1984, Boston University professor . . . The following account is summarized from Samuel McCracken, "Julia and Other Fictions by Lillian Hellman," *Commentary*, June, 1984.

On August 14, Hellman and Hammett . . . Billingsley, p. 72.

They discarded their belligerent anti–fascism . . . Mellen, p. 161.

Hellman herself helped create . . . Mellen, p. 166.

"I don't believe in that fine, lovable little Republic" . . . As quoted in Mellen, p. 162.

After the pact was signed . . . Bruce Cook, *Dalton Trumbo* (New York: Charles Scribner's Sons, 1977), pp. 142–43.

"It was literally no change" . . . Cook, p. 148.

"The Motherland has been invaded" . . . As quoted in Billingsley, p. 84.

The pair both signed . . . Mellen, p. 169.

"Every screen writer worth his salt" . . . As quoted in Billingsley, p. 90.

As Billingsley relates . . . p. 90.

Five minutes of Party line . . . Koch, p. 91.

With the war in Europe all but over . . . As summarized from Billingsley, including Trumbo quote, pp. 116–118.

Screenwriter Albert Maltz . . . As summarized from Billingsley, 136–145.

"Did he say that?" . . . As told to Cook, p. 167.

"The left wing, by its insistence" . . . As quoted in Billingsley, p. 141.

When Bogart found out otherwise . . . As quoted in Billingsley, p. 196.

"There has never been a single line" . . . As quoted in Billingsley, p. 198.

When Hammett turned to Hellman . . . Mellen, p. 287.

"Most deplorably dishonest" . . . Mellen, p. 141.

After two years of running . . . Koch, p. 341. There is a good deal of mystery as to who did the hanging.

The power of that myth . . . As summarized from Billingsley's insightful take on the anniversary, pp. 1–10.

I Got My Job through the New York Times

"I discovered" . . . Herbert Matthews, *A World in Revolution* (New York: Charles Scribner's Sons, 1971), p. 5.

"The right person at the right moment" . . . Georgie Anne Geyer, *Guerilla Prince: The*

Untold Story of Fidel Castro (Kansas City: Andrews McMeel Publishing, 2001), p. 163.

"Taking him, as one would" . . . Matthews, p. 441. The three critical articles that Matthews wrote for the *New York Times* for its February 24, 25, 26, 1957 editions are condensed in the Appendix of *A World in Revolution.*

"Matthews thought he was in a jungle" . . . Geyer, p. 163.

"I agree that we oversimplified" . . . Matthews, p. 12.

By way of background . . . Overview of Spanish Civil War as condensed from Courtois, et al., pp. 333–334.

No sooner had Fischer arrived . . . Phillip Knightley, *The First Casualty* (New York: Harcourt Brace Jovanovich, 1975), pp. 193–194.

"Too weak. Too objective" . . . As quoted in Knightley, p. 195.

"In the end" . . . Knightley, p. 196.

"Abysmally bad" . . . Knightley, p. 213.

"The directors of the Popular Front" . . . Koch, p. 308.

"To purge all political opponents" . . . Courtois, et al., pp. 338–339.

Best estimates . . . Courtois, et al., p. 343.

"Total failure to report" . . . Knightley, p. 213.

Dos Passos could not help but notice . . . As summarized from Koch, pp. 310–320.

"This was not a round up of criminals" . . . George Orwell, *Homage to Catalonia* (New York: Harcourt Brace Jovanovich, 1952), p. 211.

No American publisher . . . Knightley, p. 216.

"Rabid Red partisan" . . . As quoted in Matthews, p. 30.

"Affected his judgment" . . . Knightley, p. 215.

"Disorder in the country" . . . This and the following quotes from Matthews, pp. 16–17.

"Of a world turned into a police state" . . . Matthews, p. 11.

At the end of the day . . . Matthews, p. 18.

As to Juan Negrrin . . . Courtois, et al., p. 341.

"I still say" . . . Matthews, p. 18.

"Old–fashioned liberal" . . . Matthews, p. 323.

"Extreme leftist" . . . As quoted in Matthews, p. 335.

"A revolutionary movement that calls itself socialistic" . . . This and following quotes from Matthews, pp. 439–445.

"My ideological training" . . . This and following information about Guevara from Courtois, et al., pp. 651–654.

Matthews missed all of this . . . Matthews, p. 296.

"He has strong ideas of liberty" . . . Matthews, p. 442.

"There is no question" . . . This and following quote from Geyer, p. 181.

The *Black Book* narrates . . . Courtois, et al., pp. 649–656.

"Solid virtues and ideals" . . . Matthews, p. 295.

Matthews acknowledges . . . Herbert Matthews, *Cuba* (New York: The MacMillan Company, 1964), p. 105.

Castro has, after all . . . Matthews, *Cuba*, p. 111.

"One of the most extraordinary men" . . . Matthews, *Cuba*, p. 104.

"I was now in the same category" . . . Blair, pp. 53–54.

To no one's surprise . . . Matthews, *World*, p. 338.

Ye Shall Be as Gods

"She was the most miraculous thing" . . . Whittaker Chambers, *Witness* (Washington: Regnery Gateway, 1980), p. 16.

As Chambers would come to see . . . Chambers, pp. 9–10.

"Moral strength" . . . Chambers, p. 11.

"So far as I know" . . . As excerpted in John Chabot Smith, *Alger Hiss: The True Story* (New York: Holt, Rinehart, and Winston), p. 170.

"That sense of moral superiority" . . . Chambers, p. 11.

In January 1980 . . . Mellen, p. 443.

At Johns Hopkins . . . Smith, p. 52.

In turn, Frankfurter recommended Hiss . . . Smith, p. 58.

Hiss had met . . . G. Edward White, *Alger Hiss's Looking Glass War* (Oxford: Oxford University Press, 2004), p. 11.

"Holy moment" . . . Smith, p. 3.

There, he fell in . . . White, p. 29. The synopsis of Hiss's communist involvement comes from White, a relatively neutral source.

By his own lights . . . Smith, p. 161.

"Only in communism" . . . Chambers, p. 195.

Despite a chilly reception . . . Chambers, p. 71.

"In the two weeks preceding" . . . Dalton Trumbo to Elsie McKeogh, *Additional Dialogue: Letters of Dalton Trumbo, 1942–1962* (New York: M. Evans and Company, Inc., 1970), p. 37.

Trumbo would later deny . . . To Murray Kempton, *Additional Dialogue*, p. 392.

"Short, squat, solitary" . . . Chambers, p. 5.

Biographer Smith . . . Smith, p. 177.

That next morning . . . Smith, p. 180.

"Will you ask him to say something" . . . This account, including the excerpted testimony, comes from Chambers, pp. 605–608.

"The comedy had gone far enough" . . . As quoted in White, p. 58.

Sobell assured Hiss . . . Smith, p. 430.

"I should be profoundly interested" . . . As quoted in Smith, p. 45.

"True wisdom" . . . Chambers, p. 19.

Lacking any new evidence . . . White, p. 133.

"As a work of scholarship" . . . White, p. 131.

"The unholy trinity" . . . This and related quotes from White, p. 209.

One exchange . . . As excerpted in White, p. 150.

Smith acknowledges . . . Smith, p. 295.

"Some kind of a nut" . . . Smith, p. 293.

Smith repeats the old canards . . . Smith, pp. 210–213.

To protect his job . . . Smith, p. 202.

"Psychiatric case" . . . Smith, p. 268.

Absurd as it seems . . . Polling data, as summarized in White, pp. 167–169.

In March 1976 . . . As recounted in White, pp. 179–180.

Some reviewers . . . White, p. 182.

He accused Weinstein . . . Victor Navasky, "The Case Not Proved against Alger Hiss," *Nation*, 8 April 1978.

As Chambers told the FBI . . . Allen Weinstein, *Perjury: The Hiss–Chambers Case* (New York: Random House, 1997), p. 104.

Despite its documentary nature . . . White, pp. 101–102.

Volkogonov reviewed the KGB files . . . White, pp. 213–214.

The major media exploded . . . Through to the Tony Hiss quote, White, p. 216.

The embarrassed Volkogonov . . . White, p. 218.

The files, however incomplete, were stunning . . . White, pp. 224–225.

On the very day . . . Jennings, as quoted in White, p. 231.

"Doctored physical evidence" . . . Churchill, *Genocide*, notes, p. 370.

No Usable Political Meaning

"He was immensely pro–Soviet" . . . As quoted in Chambers, p. 14.

"Soul in agony" . . . And the longer quote that follows, Chambers, p. 15.

"No party claims him" . . . Noam Chomsky, *The Chomsky Reader*, ed. By James Peck (New York: Pantheon Books, 1987), p. viii.

"Leading terrorist state" . . . As quoted in Noam Chomsky, *9–11* (New York: Seven Stories Press, 2001), p. 40.

"In a certain sense" . . . Chomsky's own account of his childhood from Chomsky, *The Chomsky Reader*, pp. 13–14.

By this time in his life . . . Chomsky, *The Chomsky Reader*, p. 7.

Both of Horowitz's parents . . . David Horowitz, *Radical Son* (New York: The Free Press, 1997), p. 63.

There, he joined up . . . For an account of his Berkeley days, Horowitz, pp. 102–113.

The cover headline. . . Philip Nobile, *Intellectual Skywriting* (New York: Charterhouse, 1974), p. 33.

"Journalist's journalist" . . . As quoted in Jonah Goldberg, "Why Can Gadflies Only Flit Left?" *American Enterprise*, January 2000.

"The conscience of investigative journalism" . . . Ibid.

"America's premier independent journalist" . . . Bill Moyers, "Bill Moyers," *yes!* (online), Spring 2005.

"There's no disputing" . . . Nobile, p. 167.

The book served up . . . Nobile, p. 164.

"The great leap leftward" . . . Nobile, p. 39.

"We can hardly avoid" . . . Chomsky, "The Responsibility of the Intellectuals," reprinted in *The Chomsky Reader*, p. 60.

"The facts are known" . . . Chomsky, *The Chomsky Reader*, p. 61.

Until mid–1964 . . . Chomsky, *The Chomsky Reader*, p. 77.

"The Indochinese Communist Party" . . . This condensed history of Vietnam comes from Courtois, et al., pp. 565–76.

In May 1959 . . . Courtois, et al., p. 571.

"It is the responsibility of intellectuals" . . . Chomsky, *The Chomsky Reader*, p. 78.

In the post–war period . . . David Horowitz, *Unholy Alliance* (Washington, Regnery, 2004), p. 81.

"Intellectual crookedness" . . . As quoted in Nobile, p. 170.

"If we've lost Cronkite" . . . For a useful account of this exchange, "Covering the War," *Online NewsHour*, PBS, 20 April 2000.

In 1972, for instance . . . B.G. Burkett and Glenna Whitley, *Stolen Valor* (Dallas: Verity Press, 1998), pp. 118–119.

It was a heavily promoted . . . Summarized from Burkett and Whitley, pp. 87–108.

Wallace Terry . . . Summarized from Burkett and Whitley, pp. 452–463.

In *Conduct Unbecoming* . . . Summarized from Burkett and Whitley, pp. 443–451.

Critics hailed Fred Wilcox's 1983 book . . . Summarized from Burkett and Whitley, pp. 536–538.

Perhaps the most influential . . . Summarized from Burkett and Whitley, pp. 395–398.

Oliver Stone's fellow dabbler . . . Including information on John Kerry, summarized from Burkett and Whitley, pp. 130–138.

In January 1973 . . . Horowitz, *Radical Son*, p. 202.

Horowitz heard his own silent scream . . . Horowitz, *Radical Son*, pp. 244–250.

"There was only silence" . . . Horowitz, *Radical Son*, p. 258.

"I began to ask myself" . . . Horowitz, *Radical Son*, p. 271.

"These are not intellectual lapses" . . . Horowitz, *Unholy Alliance*, p. 95.

"The most radical social transformation" . . .Coutois, et al., p. 577.

These "New People" . . . As summarized in Courtois, et al., pp. 583–85.

"Traitors collaborating with the CIA" . . . Courtois, et al., p. 587.

Realistic estimates . . . Coutois, et al., pp. 624–625.

Although Chomsky would turn . . . Noam Chomsky and Edward S. Herman, "Distortions at Fourth Hand," *Nation*, June 1977.

"*Washington has become*" . . . Noam Chomsky and Edward S. Herman, *The Political Economy of Human Rights, Vol. 1* (Boston: South End Press, 1979), p. 16.

As to Cambodia . . . Noam Chomsky and Edward S. Herman, *The Political Economy of Human Rights, Vol. II* (Boston: South End Press, 1979), pp. vii–viii.

In *The Anti–Chomsky Reader* . . . Stephen J. Morris, "Whitewashing Dictatorship in Communist Vietnam and Cambodia," in *The Anti–Chomsky Reader*, ed. by Peter Collier and David Horowitz (San Francisco: Encounter Books, 2004), p. 21.

British historian Paul Johnson . . . Johnson, *Intellectuals*, p. 341.

"Quite a sensational testimonial" . . . Chomsky and Herman, *Nation*, June 1977.

"The incident had no usable political meaning" . . . Horowitz, *Radical Son*, p. 258.

3. COLORS OF THE WIND

"The white race" . . . Susan Sontag, "What's Happening to America" symposium, *Partisan Review*, Winter 1967.

"It's not African Americans" . . . Michael Moore, *Stupid White Men* (New York: ReganBooks, 2001), p. 59.

Ward Churchill has elevated . . . Churchill, *Genocide*, p. 81.

You think you own . . . Alan Menken and Stephen Schwartz, "Colors of the Wind," 1995.

"White is a state of mind" . . . As quoted in Scott Smallwood, "Aloha, Ward Churchill," *The Chronicle of Higher Education*," 4 March 2005.

Black writer and social critic . . . Shelby Steele, *A Dream Deferred: The Second Betrayal of Freedom in Black America* (New York: Harper Collins, 1998), p. 163.

"A bunch of crazy Miamians" . . . Moore, *Stupid White Men*, p. 164.

An Almost Useful Hoax

"This article addresses" . . . Ute Sartorius Kraidy, "Sunny Days on Sesame Street? Multiculturalism and Resistance Postmodernism," *Journal of Communication Inquiry*, Vol. 26, No. 1, 2002.

It has thus become . . . Alan Sokal, "Transgressing the Boundaries: Toward a Transformational Hermeneutics of Quantum Physics," *Social Text*, 46/47 (Spring/Summer), 1996.

The editors of *Social Text* . . . Andrew Ross, "Response to Sokal in THES–6.6.96," *Times Higher Education Supplement*, 17–22 June 1996.

"It was hard to imagine" . . . Alan Sokal and Jean Bricmont, *Fashionable Nonsense: Postmodern Intellectuals' Abuse of Science* (New York: Picador USA, 1998), p. 2.

Sokal's goal in the article . . . Sokal and Bricmont, p. 6.

"Unabashed Old Leftist" . . . Sokal and Bricmont, p. 269.

What bothered him about postmodernism . . .. Sokal and Bricmont, p. 201.

Sokal finds this all paradoxical . . . Sokal and Bricmont, pp. 201–202.

If you throw out hard science . . . Sokal and Bricmont, p. 274.

A month after the horrors . . . Alan Sokal, Frederick C. Crews, "An Urgent Matter," letter, *New York Review of Books*, 18 October 2001.

"Kill unknown numbers" . . . Chomsky, *9/11*, p. 55.

"Cruel and vengeful superpower" . . . Chomsky, *9/11*, p. 29.

Not Out of Africa

"The aim of the book" . . . George G. M. James, *Stolen Legacy* (Newport News: United Brothers Communications Systems, 1989), p. 7.

"The Greeks" . . . James, p. 154.

The erroneous opinion . . . James, p. 7.

Like James, Garvey looked to Egypt . . . Mary Lefkowitz, *Not Out of Africa* (New York: A New Republic Book, 1997), p. 132.

The reviewer for the *Journal of Negro Education* . . . William Leo Hansberry, *Journal of Negro Education*, 1955, excerpted in the profile of James on the *Africa Within* Web site.

"The most influential Afrocentrist text" . . . Lefkowitz, p. 124.

"Not seem to possess the natural ability" . . . James, p. 3.

It was for this reason . . .. James, p. 132.

To secure western dominance . . . James, pp. 133–134.

When resistance surfaced . . . Lefkowitz, pp. 2–4.

"Universities are here" . . . Lefkowitz interview with author, 19 January 2005.

"The Egypt of the myth" . . . Lefkowitz, p. 124.

As to more specific charges . . . Lefkowitz, p. 137.

At his own trial . . . Lefkowitz, pp. 144–145.

"James introduced a new school" . . . Lefkowitz, p. 153.

"It does not matter" . . . Lefkowitz, p. 163.

Stolen Legacy

"Can help alleviate" . . . Alex Haley, *Roots* (New York: Dell Publishing, 1976), p. 729.

Slaves were "respected people" . . . Haley, p. 65

Only the "greed and treason" . . . Haley, p. 136.

"Give me liberty" . . . Haley, p. 298.

"But if he foun' Injuns" . . . Haley, p. 291.

"Ain't gon' be no peace" . . . Haley, p. 303.

Approaching seventy when *Roots* debuted . . . The account of the Courlander suit derives largely from Lee Lescaze and Saundra Saperstein, "Bethesda Author Settles 'Roots' Suit for $500,000," *Washington Post*, 15 December 1978.

"The uniqueness of *Roots* . . . Philip Nobile, "Death of a Black Dream," *Sunday Times* (London), 21 February 1993.

"A hoax, a literary painted mouse" . . . Philip Nobile, "Uncovering Roots," *Village Voice*, 23 February 1993.

"We expected ineptitude" . . . As quoted in Nobile, *Sunday Times*.

Alex Haley himself died . . . Philip Nobile, interview with author, 14 January 2005.

"Elegant and complex" . . . Nobile, *Village Voice*.

That thought did not occur . . . Ibid.

"It was sort of like Piltdown Man" . . . Philip Nobile, interview with author, 14 January 2005.

"A sob hit me somewhere" . . . Haley, p. 722.

"Back home to the Portuguese" . . . As recorded by Haley and reported in Nobile, *Village Voice*.

"There was no Kunta Kinte" . . . Nobile, interview with author, 14 January 2005.

Black critic Stanley Crouch . . . Stanley Crouch, "The Roots of Huckster Haley's Great Fraud," *Jewish World Review*, 18 January 2002.

Nobile suggests a third reason . . . Nobile, *Sunday Times*.

"One of the great literary hoaxes" . . . Nobile, interview with author, 14 January 2005.

"Nobody wanted to touch it" . . . Ibid.

"Can anyone tell me" . . . Abiola Sinclair, "Alex Haley Posthumously Beheaded in Village Voice," *Amsterdam News*, 27 February 1993.

"Two weeks ago" . . . Esther B. Fein, "Booknotes," *New York Times*, 3 March 1993.

In an amusing open letter . . . Philip Nobile, "Alex Haley's Advice to Ambrose and Goodwin," *History News Network*, 29 January 2002.

News from Indian Country

"There is nothing in this message" . . . Paul DeMain, "Leonard Peltier, Now What Do We Do?" *News from Indian Country*, February 2002.

"The Peltier case" . . . Peter Matthiessen, *In the Spirit of Crazy Horse* (New York: The Viking Press, 1980), p. 478.

To a remarkable degree" . . . Scott Anderson, "The Martyrdom of Leonard Peltier," *Outside Magazine*, July 1995.

With the exception of its climax . . . The biographical data draws from both Anderson and Matthiessen. Conflicts will be noted.

"They're getting out of the vehicle" . . . The account of the shooting is from Anderson, *Outside Magazine*, July 1995.

"At first I resisted the police–state implications" . . . Matthiessen, p. xxiv.

"Multicultural spiritual sensibility" . . . Ken Lopez, "Collecting Peter Matthiessen," *Ken Lopez–Bookseller*, Lopez.com.

"You Christians" . . . As quoted in Matthiessen, p. 284.

Matthiessen crudely stereotypes . . . Matthiessen, p. 327.

"All the Indians" . . . Matthiessen, p. 562.

June '75 Pine Ridge Reservation . . . "Leonard Peltier," words and music by Steve Van Zandt, from *Revolution*, 1989.

As Matthiessen tells it . . . The Mr. X story is told in Peter Matthiessen, "Who Really Killed the FBI Men?" *Nation*, 13 May 1991.

In August of 1990 . . . Anderson, *Outside Magazine*, July 1995.

"I did not choose to take their lives" . . . As quoted in Anderson, July 1995.

When Matthiessen asked . . . Matthiessen, p. 261.

"Well, there is no Mr. X" . . . E.K. Caldwell, "Relinquishing a Legacy of Hatred; Embracing Respect for All Life: Conversations with Dino Butler," *News from Indian Country*, 30 April 1995.

In a January 1992 *Esquire* article . . . As reported in Anderson, *Outside Magazine*, July 1995.

The fury and detail of it . . . Peter Matthiessen, "Mean Spirit," *Outside Magazine*, October 1995.

In the book . . . Mathiessen, p. 58.

"Eastern liberal press"s . . . As quoted in Anderson, *Outside Magazine*, July 1995.

Out of Place

"Mr. Said was born in Jerusalem" . . . Janny Scott, "A Palestinian Confronts Time," *New York Times*, 19 September 1998.

"*Orientalism* is written" . . . Edward Said, *Orientalism* (New York: Vintage Books, 1994), p. 337.

"Orientalism is more particularly" . . . Said, p. 6.

"The life of an Arab Palestinian" . . . Said, p. 27.

Said emerged . . . Tony Judt, "The Rootless Cosmopolitan," *Nation*, 19 July 2004.

Upon his death . . . Richard Bernstein, "Edward Said, Leading Advocate of Palestinians, Dies at 67," *New York Times*, 25 September 2003.

"A symbolic gesture of joy" . . . As quoted in Brian Whitaker, "Scholar Edward Said Dies," *Guardian*, 26 September 2003.

So central was the house . . . As reported in Justus Reid Weiner, "'My Beautiful Old House' and Other Fabrications by Edward Said," *Commentary*, September 1999.

"Virtually everything I learned" . . . Weiner, *Commentary*.

"I was born, in November 1935" . . . As quoted in Weiner, *Commentary*.

After their forced departure . . . Ibid.

Although its headline . . . Janny Scott, "Israeli Says Palestinian Thinker Has Falsified His

Early Life," *New York Times*, 26 August 1999.

"Most of 1947" . . . Edward Said, *Out of Place* (New York: Vintage Books, 2000), p. 107.

But he does provide detail . . . Said, *Out of Place*, p. 108.

Its obituary closes . . . Whitaker, 26 September 2003.

Edward Said was born . . . Bernstein, *New York Times*, 25 September 2003.

Little Eichmanns

"His screeds usually attract" . . . "There they go again," *Wall Street Journal*, 28 January 2005.

One of those screeds . . . Ward Churchill, "Some People Push Back: On the Justice of Roosting Chickens," first published online, *Dark Night Press*, 11 September 2001.

Churchill describes himself . . . Churchill, *Genocide*, p. 11.

Perhaps more telling . . . Ward Churchill, *From a Native Son: Selected Essays on Indeginism 1985–1995* (Cambridge, MA: South End Press).

To answer that question . . . Kevin Flynn, "Prof's genealogy is sketchy; he offers little clarification," *Rocky Mountain News*, 5 February 2005.

The primary thesis . . . Churchill, *Genocide*, p. 1.

A strong secondary thesis . . . Churchill, *Genocide*, pp. 34–35.

In *A Little Matter* Churchill . . . Churchill, *Genocide*, pp. 169–170.

Churchill claims that in June 1837 . . . Churchill, *Genocide*, pp. 155.

As Thomas points out . . . Thomas Brown, "Assessing Ward Churchill's Version of the 1837 Smallpox Epidemic," originally posted on Lamar University's Web site, as updated 13 February 2005.

According to the best estimates . . . Churchill acknowledges the "federally established–and–maintained" Smithsonian count but dismisses it as a "fiction," *Genocide*, p. 131.

"Some aboard the steamer" . . . As quoted in Brown.

"If Churchill has sources" . . . As quoted in David Kelly, "Colorado Professor Faces Claims of Academic Fraud," *Los Angeles Times*, 12 February 2005.

"I consider it hate speech" . . . As quoted in Charlie Brennan, "Churchill a Lightning Rod," *Rocky Mountain News*, 28 January 2005.

The Public Burning

The Chronicle of Higher Education accurately . . . Robin Wilson, "Anthropologist Challenges Veracity of Multicultural Icon," *The Chronicle of Higher Education*, 15 January 1999.

"This has become *the* book" . . . As quoted in Wilson," *The Chronicle of Higher Education*, 15 January 1999.

Conservative critic Dinesh D'Souza . . . The following is recounted in Dinesh D'Souza, "I Rigoberta Menchu . . . Not," *Weekly Standard*, 28 December 1998.

She received fourteen honorary doctorates . . . David Stoll, *Rigoberta Menchu and the Story of All Poor Guatemalans* (Boulder, CO: Westview Press), p. 167.

Menchu describes in heartbreaking detail . . . As summarized from Rigoberta Menchu, *I, Rigoberta Menchu: An Indian Woman in Guatemala* (New York: Verso, 1993), pp. 102–161.

In the book's most dramatic scene . . . Menchu, pp. 177–179.

The following year . . . Menchu, pp. 184–187.
Soon after . . . Menchu, pp. 185–190.
"My job was to organize people . . . Menchu, p. 156.
"The world I live in . . . Menchu, p. 246.
"I had no reason to doubt" . . . Stoll, p. 8.
"The army burned prisoners" . . . Stoll, p. 1.
"At this point" . . . Stoll, p. 10.
Stoll's "peers" . . . Stoll, p. 11.
"The reactions corroborate" . . . Stoll, p. 242.
"I must say" . . . Menchu, p. 1.
"Spanish she spoke easily" . . . As quoted in Stoll, p. 160.
Nor did anyone . . . Stoll, p. 159.
"My father fought" . . . Menchu, p. 103.
The reality . . . Stoll, p. 105.
He even worked . . . Stoll, p. 107.
What he discovers . . . Stoll, p. 112.
"Thieves, criminals, and liars" . . . Menchu, p. 106.
One explanation Stoll heard . . . Stoll, pp. 112–113.
"Blame that they had focused" . . . Stoll, p. 133.
After leaving the EGP . . . As quoted in Stoll, p. 138.
"Protected revolutionary sympathizers" . . . Stoll, p. 246.
"Rigoberta's story of oppression" . . . Stoll, p. 245.
"To his and the paper's credit" . . . Larry Rohter, "Tarnished Laureate," *New York Times*,
     15 December 1978.
"They say it doesn't matter" . . . Wilson, *The Chronicle of Higher Education*, 15 January
     1999.
"All autobiographies embellish" . . . As quoted in Rohter, *New York Times*, 15 December
     1978.
"If anyone thinks" . . . As quoted in Julia Preston, "Guatemala Laureate Defends 'My
     Truth,'" *New York Times*, 21 January 1999.
"You can understand" . . . Ibid.
"The biggest hoax" . . . Marcello Truzzi, as quoted in Richard DeMille, *The Don Juan
     Papers* (Santa Barbara: Ross–Erikson Publishers, 1980).
"Our people have taken Catholicism" . . . Menchu, p. 9.
"Tell the world" . . . As quoted in Knightley, p. 195.
"If someone will give me his body" . . . As quoted in Preston, *New York Times*, 21
     January 1999.

Disarming America

For historians . . . Peter Charles Hoffer, *Past Imperfect* (New York: Public Affairs, 2004),
     p. 15.
We will find . . . Michael Bellesiles, "The Origins of Gun Culture in the United States,
     1760–1865," *Journal of American History*, Volume 83, Issue 2 (September 1996).
"If the probate data" . . . As quoted in Hoffer, p. 155.
"I could add a few more quotes" . . . As quoted in Hoffer, p. 156.

In reality . . . Cramer interview with author, 14 December 2004.

"Bellesiles did not refute" . . . Hoffer, p. 156.

"Major publishing event" . . . Hoffer, p. 161.

Although guns are . . . Gary Wills, "Spiking the Gun Myth," *New York Times*, 10 September 2000.

"I could flip his book open" . . . Cramer interview, 14 December 2004.

"It took me twelve hours" . . . Ibid.

"I have changed my mind" . . . As quoted in Hoffer, p. 156.

Further, "every citizen" . . . As printed in the 2000 Knopf edition of *Arming America* and cited in Cramer's presentation at Columbia University, 18 April 2001, and on Cramer's blog, ClaytonCramer.com. The quote appears to have been edited out of Michael Bellesiles, *Arming America* (Brooklyn: Soft Skull Press, 2003), on relevant pages 231–232, the source with which author is working.

That every citizen so enrolled . . . As cited at Cramer Columbia presentation, 18 April 2001 and on Cramer blog.

What troubled Cramer . . . Travel documents as cited at Cramer Columbia presentation, 18 April 2001, and on Cramer blog.

"Hundreds of shockingly gross falsifications" . . . Cramer interview, 14 December 2004.

In January 2002 . . . account of Bellesiles' demise in Hoffer, pp. 165–167.

"I make no apology" . . . Hoffer, p. 157.

The bias in this chapter . . . Michael Bellesiles, *Arming America* (Brooklyn: Soft Skull Press, 2003), on relevant pp. 111–141.

"Militia companies throughout New England" . . . Bellesiles, p. 117.

"At length they came" . . . Mary Rowlandson, "The Narrative of the Captivity and the Restoration of Mrs. Mary Rowlandson," 1682, found complete on line at StudyGuide.org.

"But as Mary Rowlandson's famous account" . . . Bellesiles, p. 118.

"Politically motivated effort" . . . Jon Weiner, *Historians in Trouble* (New York: The New Press, 2005), p. 83.

"I would not bother" . . . Cramer interview, 14 December 2004.

"A Brief History" . . . From *Bowling for Columbine*, 2002, written and directed by Michael Moore, a joint production of United Artists, Alliance Atlantis, and Dog Eat Dog Films.

"The very definition" . . . Richard Schickel, "The Alternate Reality of Hot Documentaries," *Time*, 14 July 2003.

"Riddled with errors" . . . "Dishonest White Man," *New Republic*, 7 April 2003.

British socialist and critic . . . As quoted in Clive Davis, "Not So Stupid White Men Fight Back," *The Times* (London), 18 June 2003.

"The point is not . . . David T. Hardy and Jason Clarke, *Michael Moore Is a Big Fat Stupid White Man* (New York: ReganBooks, 2004), p. 65.

What the viewer does not learn . . . Hardy and Clarke, pp. 67–80.

In 2002 . . . Statistics come from the United States Department of Justice: www.ojp.usdoj.gov/bjs/homicide/race.htm.

"Slippery logic, tendentious grandstanding" . . . A.O.Scott, "Seeking a Smoking Gun in U.S. Violence," *New York Times*, 11 October 2002.

"To describe this film" . . . Christopher Hitchens, "Unfairenheit 9/11: The Lies of Michael Moore," *Slate*, 21 June 2004.

Borrowed Dreams
"Not a single instance" . . . As cited in Theodore Pappas, *Plagiarism and the Culture War* (Tampa: Hallberg Publishing Corporation, 1998), pp. 68–69.
By way of background . . . Pappas, p. 127.
Still, despite these drawbacks . . . Pappas, p. 69.
Although King never made them . . . Pappas, p. 4.
In 1984, King's widow . . . Pappas, pp. 85–86.
"On a scale so vast" . . .. Eugene Genovese, Introduction, Pappas, p .2.
"It is not merely that" . . . Pappas, p. 71. Examples follow on pp. 72–80.
He plagiarized his Nobel Prize lecture . . . Pappas, p. 133.
In October 1989 . . . Pappas, p. 92.
In December 1989 . . . As cited in Pappas, p. 67.
"I suspect that we pursue" . . . As quoted in Pappas, p. 98.
The various researchers . . . Pappas, pp. 98–99.
"The King plagiarism story" . . . Pappas, p. 82.
In November 1990 . . . Pappas, p. 98.
Committee member John Cartwright . . . As quoted in Pappas, p. 138.
"They lied" . . . Genovese, in Pappas, p. 11.
In a 1993 article . . . As cited in Pappas, p. 55.
"Grunting savage" . . . Pappas, p. 55.
"I recommend against publishing" . . . As quoted in Pappas, p. 174.
"In decades past" . . . Genovese in Pappas, p. 6.

4. DARWIN'S HEIRS

"A royal pain" . . . . As quoted in Casey Luskin (and elsewhere), "Icons Still Standing," posted on University of California San Diego Web site, updated 14 March 2002.
"There is no obvious reason" . . . Charles Darwin, *On the Origin of Species* (London: Penguin Books, 1968), p. 441.
"The purpose of" . . . Louis Menand, *The Metaphysical Club* (New York: Farrar, Straus, and Giroux, 2001), p. 121.
"For Darwin, any evolution" . . . Richard Dawkins, *The Blind Watchmaker* (New York: W.W. Norton & Co., 1996), p. 249.
"Highly speculative" . . . Menand, p. 140.

A Textbook Case of Fraud
Among the earliest . . . Biographical information from Benjamin Wiker, *Moral Darwinism* (Downers Grove, IL: InterVarsity Press, 2002), pp. 257–266.
"The modern science of evolution" . . . As quoted in Wiker, p. 258.
Indeed, one review . . . Kevin Padian and Alan Gishlick "The Talented Mr. Wells," *Quarterly Review of Biology*, March 2002.
"I spent a year" . . . Joanathan Wells, interview with author, 31 December 2004, also the source of the biographical information to follow.

Two years later . . . Phillip E. Johnson, *Darwin on Trial* (Downers Grove, IL: InterVarsity Press, 1991).

For the record . . . The information on Haeckel's science is condensed from Jonathan Wells, *Icons of Evolution* (Washington: Regnery Publishing, 2000), pp. 81–109.

"All the important evidence" . . . As quoted in Wells, p. 88.

"These famous images" . . . As quoted in Wells, p. 91.

Stephen Jay Gould . . . Wells, p. 92.

"The whole theory of recapitulation" . . . Stephen Jay Gould, *Ever Since Darwin* (New York, W.W. Norton & Company, 1977), p. 219.

Nazis in the Woodshed

The unhappy fact . . . Daniel Gasman, *The Scientific Origins of National Socialism* (London: McDonald & Co., 1971). The following account derives from a 14,000 word online edition accessed through www.helsinki.fi/~pjojala/Gasman.htm.

The First Cricket Bat

In 1861, just two years . . . Wells, p. 112.

As a result, adds Darwin . . . As cited in Wells, p. 111.

For decades . . . Wells, p. 115.

Among the hunters was Charles Dawson . . . The Piltdown story has been told in many places. The chief sources for this account are Wells, 217–219, Edward J. Larson, *Summer for the Gods* (Cambridge: Harvard University Press, 1997), pp. 11–13, 29–32. Marcel C. LaFollette, *Stealing into Print: Fraud, Plagiarism, and Misconduct in Scientific Publishing* (Berkeley: University of California Press, 1992), pp. 44–45, William Broad and Nicholas Wade, *Betrayers of The Truth* (New York: Simon and Shuster, 1982), pp. 118–121, and *Nature* article cited below.

"Darwin's Theory proved True" . . . As quoted in Larson, p. 14.

A 1996 *Nature* article . . . Henry Gee, "Box of Bones 'Clinches' Identity of Piltdown Palaeontology Hoaxer," *Nature* 381, 23 May 1996.

Slippery Partners

As Koestler relates . . . Arthur Koestler, *The Case of the Midwife Toad* (New York: Random House, 1971), pp. 59 and following.

Lamarck had proposed two related concepts . . . Well explained in Dawkins, pp. 287–289.

In his most hotly . . . Koestler, p. 43.

Mendel argued correctly . . . Dawkins, p. 113.

In the beginning . . . Anonymous, published as "Peas on Earth," *Horticultural Science* 7: 5 (1972), quoted in Broad and Wade, p. 33.

"It is rare to find" . . . Koestler, p. 56.

"The popular media" . . . Koestler, p. 91.

"I think [William Bateson] always knew" . . . As quoted in Koestler, p. 51.

Kammerer paid the price . . . Koestler, p. 93.

"Indeed, the real mystery" . . . Broad and Wade, p. 121.

Inherit the Spin

But when a play . . . Jerome Lawrence and Robert E. Lee, *Inherit the Wind* (New York: Bantam Books, 1960), Foreword.

"[Inherit the Wind] may not have been accurate history" . . . Larson, p. 241.

"The town, I confess" . . . As quoted in Larson, p. 93.

What happened in this town . . . Nicely captured in Larson, pp. 83–93.

"Something has happened" . . . As quoted in Larson, p. 91.

"Everything about this case" . . . Larson, p. 92.

"The Reverend Jeremiah Brown" . . . Lawrence and Lee, p. 9.

"Let him feel the terror" . . . Lawrence and Lee, p. 59.

The populist Bryan . . . Larson, pp. 38–39.

But he also believed . . . Larson, p. 198.

"The writers transformed Bryan" . . . Larson, p. 241.

"I hold that the right to think" . . . Lawrence and Lee, p. 64.

"An idea" . . . Lawrence and Lee, p. 83.

"You smart–aleck!" . . . Lawrence and Lee, p. 112.

"He half–smiles" . . . Lawrence and Lee, p. 115.

"How can you be so sure" . . . Lawrence and Lee, p. 77.

"Where does man get" . . . Larson, p. 72.

"Basically atheistic" . . . Gould, p. 33.

"Darwin made it possible" . . . Dawkins, p. 6.

"Darrow, of course" . . . Larson, p. 156.

"Highest type of all" . . . As quoted in Larson, p. 24.

"If such people" . . . . As quoted in Larson, p. 27.

For the record . . . Larson, pp. 200–201.

"Do you think" . . . Lawrence and Lee, p. 96.

"The mighty Evolution Law" . . . Lawrence and Lee, p. 103.

"Millions of people" . . . Lawrence and Lee, p. 109.

"The collapse of rural idealism" . . . As quoted in Larson, p. 235.

That collaboration was entirely evident" . . . Phillip Johnson, "Inherit The Wind in Reverse," *Weekly Wedge Update*, Access Research Network, 23 April 2001.

The Piltdown Bird

In November 1999, *National Geographic Magazine* . . . As reported in Wells, p. 124.

Storrs Olson of the Smithsonian . . . Wells, p. 125.

"One icon (the Miller–Urey experiment" . . . Wells, pp. 229–230.

The Age of Poisons

If there is any one man . . . A good recounting of Edwards's life is offered by Jerry Goldsmith and others on the occasion of Edwards's death, posted on BlogOfDeath.com, 7 October 2004.

At the time of the book's release . . . J. Gordon Edwards, "The Lies of Rachel Carson," first published in *21st Century*, Summer 1992, available online, 21stCenturyScienceTech.com.

"I noticed many statements . . . Ibid.

"As I neared" . . . Ibid.

"She was carefully omitting everything" . . . Ibid.

"The most important chronicle" . . . Back cover, Rachel Carson, *Silent Spring* (Greenwich, CT: Fawcett Publications, 1972).

There is no God . . . Carson, p. 17.

There is no mistaking . . . Carson, p. 261.

The title of the book . . . Carson, pp. 13–14.

"Ours is the "age of poisons" . . . Carson, p. 157.

Had Gordon Edwards . . . J. Gordon Edwards, "Mosquitos, DDT, and Human Health," *21st Century*, Fall 2002.

"To Albert Schweitzer" . . . As cited by Edwards in "Lies."

"Deceptions, false statements, horrible innuendoes" . . . Ibid.

"Exposing fraud and deception" . . . LaFollette, p. 137.

When Carson alludes . . . Edwards, "Lies."

In September 1971 . . . As cited by Edwards in "Mosquitos."

In the one year . . . Ibid.

"It was not until 1942" . . . "Rachel Carson Dies of Cancer; 'Silent Spring' Author Was 56," *New York Times*, 15 April 1964.

Only a valiant effort . . . Amir Attaran, et al., "Balancing Risks on the Backs of the Poor," *Nature Medicine*, July 2000.

"Arguably the greatest tragedy" . . . Michael Crichton, *State of Fear* (New York: Harper Collins, 2004), p. 487.

"Social program masquerading" . . . Crichton, p. 578.

Edwards describes the Carson philosophy . . . Edwards, "Lies."

The Bet

"Finding out that there was so much DDT" . . . Interview with editors, "Paul in a Day's Work," *Grist Magazine* (online), 9 August 2004.

"Environmental hero" . . . Ibid.

"In the first nine weeks" . . . Ibid.

"My belief" . . . "Darwin's Ghost," a filmed panel discussion, available online at *Uncommon Knowledge*, 1 June 2001.

One of the crueler ironies . . . *Grist* interview.

"Cancerlike disease" . . . Paul and Anne Ehrlich, "Why Isn't Everyone as Scared as We Are," posted at Acme.Highpoint.edu.

"The battle to feed" . . . Paul Ehrlich, *The Population Bomb* (New York: Ballantine Books, 1968), p. 36.

"An urge to reproduce" . . . Ehrlich, *The Population Bomb*, p. 29.

Ehrlich lays out three . . . Ehrlich, *The Population Bomb*, pp. 77–80.

In 1969, Ehrlich added . . . Mike Toth, "Paul Ehrlich Gets Stanford Reviewed," *Stanford Review*, 10 March 1998.

For all the parallels . . . A good source for Simon's bio, Nicholas Eberstadt, "Revisiting Life of Scholar Who Shaped How We Think about Global Bounty," *Washington Times*, 30 June 2002.

Ehrlich would dismiss Simon . . . Paul Ehrlich and Anne Ehrlich, *The Population*

Explosion (London, Hutchinson, 1990), p. 20.

Length of life and health . . . Julian Simon, *The Ultimate Resource 2* (Princeton: Princeton University Press, 1996), p. 9.

"The record of food production" . . . Simon, p. 86.

"The best overall index" . . . Simon, p. 6.

"The ultimate resource" . . . Simon, p. 589.

"If we also consider" . . . Simon, p. 4.

"increasingly efficient use" . . . Ehrlich, *Explosion*, p. 52.

But he is not at all enthused . . . Ehrlich, *Explosion*, p. 37.

"The straw that broke" . . . Ehrlich, *Bomb*, p. 32.

"Our population consists" . . . Ehrlich, *Bomb*, p. 66.

"Grossly overpopulated" . . . Ehrlich, *Explosion*, pp. 129–132.

Ehrlich admits grudgingly . . . Ehrlich, *Explosion*, pp. 63–64.

Ehrlich presents a straightforward . . . Ehrlich, *Explosion*, pp. 180–184.

"I would bet" . . . As cited in Stephen Moore, "Julian Simon Remembered: It's a Wonderful Life," CATO Online *Policy Report*, March/April 1998.

All five commodities dropped . . . Ibid.

"Tricks of modern agriculture" . . . Ehrlich, *Explosion*, p. 69.

"An ominous food crunch" . . . Ehrlich, *Explosion*, p. 102.

"Anne [his wife] and I" . . . *Grist* interview.

Simon is merciless . . . Paul Simon, *Hoodwinking the Nation* (London: Transaction Publishers, 1999), pp. 87–90.

5. SEXUAL FANTASIES

No Gods, No Masters

"Margaret Sanger gained" . . . And following quotes from "Margaret Sanger," Planned Parenthood Federation of America Inc. Web site,www.PlannedParenthood.org.

Although she would later . . . Biographical details from Margaret Sanger, *The Autobiography of Margaret Sanger* (Mineola, NY: Dover Publications, 2004).

"Devoutly Catholic family" . . . "Margaret Sanger," About Agnosticism/Atheism, Atheism.About.com.

"In fact," writes Sanger of her father . . . Sanger, *Autobiography*, p. 23.

"And wanted at least four more" . . . Sanger, *Autobiography*, p. 65.

"A religion without a name" . . . Sanger, *Autobiography*, p. 69.

"Each believed he had a key" . . . . Sanger, *Autobiography*, p. 73.

This led her to start . . . Sanger, *Autobiography*, p. 77.

Never one for subtlety . . . Sanger, *Autobiography*, p. 109–110.

"He, beyond any other person" . . . Sanger, *Autobiography*, p. 135.

At a spirited meeting . . . Sanger, *Autobiography*, pp. 107–108.

"I hated the wretchedness" . . . Sanger, *Autobiography*, p. 87.

Our starting point . . . As quoted in Edward Rothstein, "The Tainted Science of Nazi Atrocities," *New York Times*, 8 January 2005.

"The most urgent problem today" . . . Margaret Sanger, *The Pivot of Civilization*, published online by World Wide School Library, Chapter I. Given its online nature, all references will be by chapter.

"The control and guidance" . . . Sanger, *Pivot*, I.

"The liberation of the spirit" . . . Ibid.

"The potential mother" . . . Ibid.

"We must temper our emotion" . . . Ibid.

"That the least intelligent" . . .Sanger, *Pivot*, IV.

"The feeble–minded woman" . . . Ibid.

According to his studies . . . Ibid.

"There is every indication" . . . Ibid.

"The advent of the Binet–Simon" . . . Ibid.

She cites a study . . . Ibid.

"The practical effect" . . . Sanger, *Pivot*, IX.

"Organized charity" . . . Sanger, *Pivot*, V.

Although Sanger applauds . . . Sanger, *Pivot*, VII.

"Margaret Sanger was not a racist" . . . "Margaret Sanger," Planned Parenthood, Web site.

The Margaret Sanger of 1922 . . . Sanger, *Pivot*, I.

The case of a "Negro woman" . . . Sanger, *Pivot*, IV.

"It is better" . . . *BUCK v. BELL*, 274 U.S. 200 (1927), available online at www.law.du.edu.

In *Pivot*, for instance. . . Sanger, *Pivot*, IV.

"After World War II" . . . Crichton, *State of Fear*, p. 577.

"Eugenics" does not appear . . . "Margaret Sanger Is Dead at 86; Led Campaign for Birth Control," *New York Times*, 7 September 1966.

In 1995, the TV movie . . . Paul Shapiro, director; Matt Dorff, writer, *Choices of the Heart: The Margaret Sanger Story*, 1995.

Two years later . . . Seth Goddard, "Margaret Sanger, Family Planner," *Life*, 29 August 1997.

In an obscure and unformed way . . . Sanger, *Autobiography*, p. 39.

"Bryan decried the entire program" . . . Larson, p. 40.

Fantasy Island

In San Francisco in 1926 . . . Derek Freeman, *The Fateful Hoaxing of Margaret Mead* (Boulder, CO: Westview Press, 1999), p. 66.

Cressman described the city . . . Freeman, p. 39.

For direct inspiration . . . As cited in Freeman, p. 157.

Inspired by Millay . . . As cited in Freeman, p. 66.

It was Millay's Second Fig . . . As cited in Freeman, p. 198.

"Tiny, ingrown, biological family" . . . Margaret Mead, *Coming of Age in Samoa* (New York: American Museum of Natural History, Special Members Edition, 1973), p. 118.

"In our ideal picture" . . . Mead, p. 119.

"Puritan self–accusations" . . . Mead, p. 135.

Left them burdened by "guilt" . . . Mead, p. 124.

"When she accepted a grant" . . . Freeman, p. 54.

"An intimate Sapphic relationship" . . . Freeman, p. 38.

"All of her interest" . . . Mead, p. 19.

"The concept of celibacy" . . . Mead, p. 35.

"The scarcity of taboos" . . . Mead, 45.

"This casual familiarity" . . . Mead, p. 84.

"The Samoans laugh" . . . Mead, p. 58.

"What accounts for" . . . Mead, p. 110.

If a "general casualness" . . . Mead, p. 112.

American girls . . . Mead, p. 117.

"There was a personal crisis" . . . Alden Whitman, "Margaret Mead Is Dead of Cancer at 76," *New York Times*, 16 November 1978. It was from Whitman, who himself had pled the Fifth before a congressional committee on the question of his own communist affiliations, that John Chabot Smith had picked up his pro–Hiss project.

With Boas's imprimatur . . . Freeman, p. 194.

The *New York Times* describes the book . . . As cited in Freeman, p. 193.

"It had become apparent to me" . . . Freeman, p. 204.

But in 1964 . . . Freeman, pp. 205–206.

"Comprehensively in error" . . . Freeman, p. 206.

As Freeman observed . . . Freeman, p. 94.

"Samoa in the 1920s" . . . Freeman, p. 111.

"There is ample evidence" . . . As quoted in Freeman, p. 206.

After taking care . . . Mead, pp. 205–206.

Eager to please . . . Mead, pp. 140–141.

"She must have" . . . Freeman, p. 3.

In the data tables . . . Mead, pp. 160–161.

In the nearly fictional Samoa . . . Freeman, p. 177.

"The greatest controversy" . . . And following information about critical reaction, Freeman, pp. 208–209.

"After an initial flurry" . . . "Coming of Age in Samoa," *Wikipedia, The Free Encyclopedia*, www.wikipedia.org/wiki/Margaret_Mead.

The Human Animal

In her "Personal Odyssey" . . . Judith Reisman, "A Personal Odyssey to the Truth," 1996, available at www.special–guests.com/reisman4.html.

Alfred Charles Kinsey was born . . . Early biographical information condensed from James H. Jones, *Alfred C. Kinsey: A Public/Private Life* (New York, W.W. Norton & Co., 1997), pp. 3–102.

"As his belief in God waned" . . . Jones, p. 154.

"Freed from religiously prescribed notions" . . . Jones, p. 336.

At IU, he taught evolutionary biology . . . Jones, pp. 188–189.

A champion of biological purity . . . Jones, pp. 194–195.

In his breakthrough book . . . Alfred Kinsey, Wardell Pomeroy, Clyde Martin, *Sexual Behavior In The Human Male* (Philadelphia: W. B. Saunders Company, 1948): "human animal," p. 8; "primate," p. 182; "mammalian," p. 173.

In 1935 he gave . . . Jones, pp. 306–307.

"Kinsey's 1935 lecture" . . . Jones, p. 309.

"He had to appear disinterested" . . . Jones, p. 329.

"In short" . . . Jones, p. 336.

"Kinsey pleaded" . . . Jones, p. 772.

"Beware the facts" . . . Martin Duberman, "Kinsey's Urethra," *Nation*, 3 November 1997.

What "dismayed" Gathorne–Hardy . . . Jonathan Gathorne–Hardy, *Sex the Measure of All Things: A Life of Alfred Kinsey* (Bloomington: University of Indiana Press, 1998), p. viii.

"Now it is perfectly true" . . . Gathorne–Hardy, p. 291.

"Pursuit of pleasure" . . . Gathorne–Hardy, p. 292.

"He liked what he saw" . . . Jones, p. 379.

"It is my conviction" . . . As quoted in Jones, p. 383.

"Whether one builds" . . . As quoted in Jones, p. 384.

"Clear evidence" . . . Jones, p. 387.

Martin eventually relented . . . Kinsey, p. 393.

"Sexual deviance and obedience test" . . . Reisman, interview with author, 13 December 2004.

At least one wife . . . Jones, p. 607.

To the outside world . . . Jones, p. 414.

No fool to political realities . . . Jones, p. 536.

If there were a hitch . . . Jones, p. 539.

Harper's certainly didn't . . . As cited in Jones, p. 550.

Kinsey was nothing . . . Jones, p. 564–569.

"I wrote an editorial" . . . Hugh Hefner, "How We Got Started," *Fortune Small Business*, September 2003.

America's sexual codes . . . Kinsey, et al., p. 203.

"Society tries to restrict" . . . Kinsey et al., p. 205.

As a graduate student . . . Hefner, *Fortune Small Business*, September 2003.

"His conclusions were both attacked" . . . "Dr. Kinsey is Dead; Sex Researcher, 62," Associated Press, 26 August 1956.

Kinsey's statistics . . . Jones, p. 528.

Judith Reisman, born Gelernter . . . The biographical info that follows comes from Reisman, "Personal Odyssey."

Tables 30 through 34 . . . Found in Kinsey, et al., pp. 175–180.

Alarmed, Reisman . . . Reisman, "Personal Odyssey."

According to the non–plussed Gebhard . . . Ibid.

"I realized clearly" . . . Ibid.

For the 1998 British documentary . . . Tim Tate, producer and director, *Secret History: Kinsey's Paedophiles*, Yorkshire TV, 8 October 1998.

King had kept . . . Jones, p. 507.

"I congratulate you" . . . As quoted in Jones, p. 508.

Back in Indiana . . . Reisman interview, 13 December 2004.

"This is one of" . . . As quoted in Jones, p. 310.

"[The orgasm] involves still more" . . . Kinsey, et al., p. 161.

Kinsey's close colleague . . . As quoted in Judith Reisman, "Kinsey and the Homosexual Revolution," *The Journal of Human Sexuality* (Addison, TX: Lewis and Stanley Publishers, 1996), p. 4.

According to Jones . . . Jones, p. 310.

Reisman argues . . . Reisman interview, 13 December 2004.

"Observations were continued" . . . Kinsey et al., p. 177.

"Science would have been better served" . . . Jones, p. 310.

"Once in a while" . . . As quoted in Jones, p. 512.

"There is still no answer" . . . Reisman interview, 13 December 2004.

"The data should cover" . . . Kinsey, et al., p. 618.

"As I expected" . . . As quoted in Judith Reisman and Edward Eichel, *Kinsey, Sex, and Fraud* (Lafayette, LA: Huntington House, 1990), p. 221.

"Despite the huge number" . . . Jones, p. 522.

"Jones is, of course, correct" . . . Gathorne–Hardy, p. 362.

"[T]he data are probably" . . . Kinsey, et al., p. 153.

"A considerable portion of the population" . . . Kinsey, et al., p. 610.

According to Kinsey . . . Kinsey, et al., p. 651.

Harry Hay . . . Reisman and Eichel, p. 105.

In the year 2004 . . . Bill Condon, writer and director, *Kinsey*, 2004.

In its preview . . . Dinitia Smith, "Liam Neeson as Kinsey Loses His Private Self," *New York Times*, 9 November 2004.

"Promethean figure" . . . "Darkness Ruled: He Shone a Bight Light," A. O. Scott, *New York Times*, 12 November 2004.

"He saw a gap" . . . Smith, 9 November 2004.

"[Kinsey] was an early feminist" . . . Joe Neumaier, "The Kinsey Effect," *New York Daily News*, 7 November 2004.

"The world we live in" . . . Kenneth Turan, "Kinsey," *Los Angeles Times*, 11 November 2004.

In 1998, when *Secret History* aired . . . As quoted in Judith Reisman, "Congress Should Probe and Defund the Kinseyites," *Human Events*, 21 October 2003.

Straight but Not Narrow

"*Crisis* was the high–water mark" . . . Michael Fumento, *The Myth of Heterosexual AIDS* (New York: A New Republic Book, 1990), p. 262.

In the way of background . . . Biographical information from Jane Brody, "30 Years of Pioneering in Sex Therapy," *New York Times*, 29 October 1984, and Paul Robinson, *The Modernization of Sex* (New York: Harper & Row, 1976), pp. 120–190.

"The influence of channel–visioned religious orthodoxy" . . . William Masters and Virginia Johnson, *Human Sexual Inadequacy* (New York: Bantam Books, 1980), p. 247.

Writing in 1976 . . . Robinson, pp. 151–152.

"Psychiatry is the enemy incarnate" . . . As quoted in Jeffrey Satinover, *Homosexuality and the Politics of Truth* (Grand Rapids: Baker Books, 1996), p. 33.

In 1979 Masters and Johnson . . . As reported in Victor Cohn, "Homosexuality a 'Learned Behaviour,' And Not an Illness, Therapists Reports," *Washington Post*, 17 April 1979.

Two years later . . . Satinover, pp. 9–11.

In August of that same year . . . As reported in Victor Cohn, "Homosexuality Tied to Biology, New Study Says," *Washington Post*, 25 August 1981.

"We found homosexuality" . . . Ibid.

According to the new party line . . . Satinover, p. 18.

"Queers could be changed" . . . "Remastering Justice," *Queer Scribbles*, 8 May, 2001.

More conveniently still . . . Fumento, p. 270.

"The importance of" . . . Ibid.

"They worked to insure" . . . Satinover, p. 15.

Michael Fumento willed himself . . . Fumento interview with author, 14 November 2004.

"It wasn't hidden data" . . . Ibid.

By the middle of the 1980s . . . Fumento, p. 202.

"I believed" . . . Gabriel Rotello, *Sexual Ecology: AIDS and the Destiny of Gay Men* (New York: Penguin, 1997), p. 3.

Fumento does not a see . . . Fumento, pp. 147–149.

"If AIDS was not" . . . Rotello, p. 116.

"Hello everybody" . . . As quoted in Fumento, p. 1.

Virtually all media sources . . . As cited in Fumento, p. 129.

Even the more sober . . . As cited in Fumento, p. 6.

"AIDS is breaking out" . . . William Masters, Virginia Johnson, Robert C. Kolodny, *Crisis: Heterosexual Behavior in the Age of Aids* (New York: Grove Press, 1988), p. 7.

Through 1989 . . . Fumento, p. 17.

In their first two books . . . Robinson, p. 123.

Their sexually active heterosexual sample . . . Masters, Johnson, Kolodny, p. 9.

"Only a fool would publish" . . . And following quotes as cited in Fumento, pp. 261–263.

The degaying of AIDS . . . Rotello, p. 89.

So deep was the denial . . . Rotello, pp. 166–167.

For nearly 4,000 years Jews . . . Satinover, pp. 146–147.

Multipartner anal sex . . . Rotello, p. 89.

"A sexual ecology" . . . Ibid.

The resulting panic . . . Rotello, p. 116.

Index

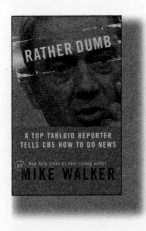

RATHER DUMB
A Top Tabloid Reporter Tells CBS How To Do News
By Mike Walker
1-5955-5018-6

In this blisteringly humorous book, *National Enquirer* gossip columnist Mike Walker rips into the arrogance and presumption of the news media—the elitist, agenda-driven mentality that allows its journalists and editors to ignore basic rules of journalism. With scorching insight and irreverent humor, Walker uses Dan Rather (and the recent Rathergate scandal) as a touchstone to explain how real news is properly gathered and vetted, how it's properly written and reported, and why some journalists and editors think they're above such things.

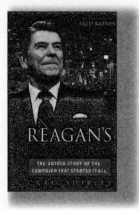

REAGAN'S REVOLUTION
The Untold Story of the Campaign That Started It All
By Craig Shirley
0-7852-6049-8

This is the remarkable story of that historic campaign—one that, as Reagan put it, turned a party of "pale pastels" into a national party of "bold colors." Featuring interviews with a myriad of politicos, journalists, insiders, and observers, Craig Shirley relays intriguing, never-before-told anecdotes about Reagan, his staff, the campaign, the media, and the national parties and shows how Reagan, instead of following the lead of the ever-weakening Republican Party, brought the party to him and almost single-handedly revived it.

TAX REVOLT
The Rebellion Against an Overbearing, Bloated, Arrogant, and Abusive Government
By Phil Valentine
1-5955-5001-1

This book is the powerful rallying cry to all Americans to continue to fight against our ever-increasing taxes. Taking a close look at the heroic incident in Tennessee, when citizens converged on the state capitol to protest and repeatedly beat back attempts to pass a state tax, Valentine weaves an inspiring story of how patriotic citizens have stood up to taxes in the past, how many intrepid constituents continue to fight, and how Americans should resist and even revolt against taxes on a state and national level.

INFILTRATION
How Muslim Spies and Subversives Have Penetrated Washington
By Paul Sperry
1-5955-5003-8

Infiltration explodes the facade of moderation and patriotism that Muslim leaders in America have conveyed in the wake of the 9/11 terrorist attacks. In reality, the Muslim establishment that publicly decries the radical fringe is actually a part of it. The only difference is that they use words and money instead of bombs to accomplish their goals. Now, thanks to Sperry's peerless research, piquant prose, and forthright presentation, their cover is blown as he explains the full scope of the dangerous threat of Islam in America.

BIG FAT LIARS
How Politicians, Corporations, and the Media Use Science and Statistics to Manipulate the Public
By Morris E. Chafetz M.D.
1-5955-5008-9

Morris Chafetz, president of the Health Education Foundation, has spent decades carefully observing trends in science, government, the legal system, and the media, and now he reveals his unexpected findings in this sharp exposé of the many statistical lies—lies about everything from terrorism to the environment to alcohol and tobacco addiction—that manipulate Americans for the sinister motives of government, the media, corporations and metertricious lawyers. Clear-sighted and far-reaching, this book will change how you look and listen to the scads of stats that are thrust on us every day—and will inspire you to reclaim your liberties and, as Chafetz says, "send packing those who think they know more about you than you do."

COMING SOON FROM NELSON CURRENT